WARTIME ORIGINS OF THE EAST-WEST
DILEMMA OVER GERMANY

The historian must not wait until the legend is established. He must seek to shape the historical picture of our times even if he runs the risk of becoming subconsciously involved in the struggle he describes, of reopening wounds that have barely healed, and of raising against him angry protests from more than one side . . .

Gerhard Ritter, THE GERMAN RESISTANCE

WARTIME ORIGINS OF THE EAST-WEST

Dilemma Over Germany

JOHN L. SNELL
Tulane University

THE PHAUSER PRESS
Publishers of Galleon Books

NEW ORLEANS, U.S.A.

For

MARCIA, *who knows there is a dilemma over Germany,*
for

LESLIE ANN, *who will soon find out about it,*
and for

MAX, *whose life may depend upon its solution.*

CONTENTS

~~~~~

ACKNOWLEDGMENTS

This book attempts to show how "Cold War" disputes over Germany were foreshadowed and had their origins in the wartime planning of Washington, Moscow, and London, 1941-1945. It treats a decisive period in German history, one which has been shaped by non-Germans and whose history must be written from non-German sources.

I have been aided by many people in putting this story together. Letters from the following persons helped to clarify many points on which factual uncertainties existed: Mrs. Anna Roosevelt Halsted; former Secretary of War and United States High Commissioner of Germany John J. McCloy; Mr. Ernest A. Gross; and Professors David Harris of Stanford University, Philip E. Mosely of Columbia University, and Harold Zink of Ohio State University. One of the major theses of this book, the "policy of postponement" theme, may not satisfy the grievances which these and other experts have understandably held against top-level leadership, but it is to be hoped that this thesis may help to explain the origins of those grievances. Without giving their approval to the interpretation I have offered, Robert M. Morgenthau, John M. Blum and Arthur Schlesinger, Jr. helped clarify some of the mysterious or confusing elements surrounding the Morgenthau Plan of 1944. I gratefully remember a considerable discussion of matters of common concern with Walter L. Dorn. Maurice Matloff wrote to me at some length about a point I could not otherwise clarify. Research in the Department of State was facilitated and made more accurate by the help which the following persons cheerfully gave: G. Bernard Noble, Chief of the Historical Division, E. Taylor Parks, G. M. Richardson Dougall, William F. Franklin, and Francis L. Loewenheim.

Professor David R. Deener of Tulane University critically read and improved the manuscript. I am indebted to Miss Betty Mailhes and to Mrs. Dorothy Lawton of the Howard Tilton Memorial Library of Tulane University for invaluable help in securing materials for my use through the Inter-Library Loan system. The Tulane University Council on Research provided the grant which made possible intensive research in 1955 for this volume. Mrs. Betty Rankin typed the manuscript. My indispensable ally, Maxine Pybas Snell, prepared the index and helped in many ways that must go untold.

I wish to thank the following publishers who have allowed me to quote material from the publications noted below: Time, Inc., for material from Harry S. Truman's *Memoirs;* Harper and Brothers, publishers of Robert E. Sherwood, *Roosevelt and Hopkins;* Houghton Mifflin Company, publishers of Winston Churchill's six-volume memoir-history of World War II; The Macmillan Company, publishers of Cordell Hull's *Memoirs;* the Princeton University Press, publishers of E. F. Penrose's *Economic Planning for the Peace;* John Wiley and Sons, publishers of Edward J. Rozek's *Allied Wartime Diplomacy;* and Rinehart and Co., Inc., publishers of Carl J. Friedrich and associates, *American Experiences in Military Government in World War II.*

JOHN L. SNELL

New Orleans, Louisiana
April 27, 1959

A PROLOGUE
FOR READERS OF 1984

For many years after 1945, called by nervous contemporaries the period of the "Cold War," American and Soviet leaders talked much of fighting but kept their peace. Both sides knew that victory in an actual conflict would be an uncertain gamble. Wise men in both camps said neither side could win an all-out war.

The one area on earth that many people could imagine to be worth the great risk of war was Germany, or what was left of that once-hegemonic complex of power and culture. The one city in the world over which war seemed likely to erupt was that split metropolis on the Spree where German troops had paraded in 1871, victorious from a war against France to unify the German Empire; where civilian recruits had rallied to hail their Kaiser in 1914 before marching off to a two-front war that couldn't be won; where brown-shirted Nazis had goose-stepped down Unter den Linden under the grim eyes of a half-brilliant, half-mad Führer.

At Berlin the Red Army and the forces of the North Atlantic Treaty Organization met in the Cold War era, barely separated by the remains of the Brandenburg Gate. Most people were too worried to think much about how this situation had arisen. A few elder statesmen remembered. Journalists had half-forgotten and half-garbled the details. It was too early for cautious historians to tell their versions of the origins of the dilemma. Vaguely, the man on the street thought that it had somehow resulted from the last of the earth-bound struggles, usually known as World War II . . . .

Chapter I

THE SPIRIT OF THE TIMES
1939-1945

A NY attempt to understand how the dilemma over Germany
arose after 1945 must start with Nazism and Adolf Hitler's
aggressive foreign policy. These were the forces that wrenched
Germany out of the paths of peaceful recovery after World War I
and set her on the road to ruin. These were the forces that inflamed the minds of millions of Allied people against Germany
during World War II. The hostility that was then common is
now rarely seen in the United States. But it lives on among the
peoples of eastern Europe, obstructing compromises on the contemporary German problem. It is necessary to recall that wartime
spirit of animosity if the postwar German dilemma is to be understood at all.[1]

GREAT BRITAIN

Winston Churchill's countrymen were slow to counteract the
threat of Nazi Germany in the 1930's, but Great Britain was the
first of the "Big Three" powers to declare war against Hitler's

[1] This is no place for a history of Nazism and Germany's foreign
policy. The interested reader may begin to explore these matters by consulting the essays and bibliography in Gordon A. Craig, *From Bismarck to
Adenauer: Aspects of German Statecraft* (Baltimore, 1958); and John L.
Snell ed., *The Nazi Revolution: Germany's Guilt or Germany's Fate?* (Boston,
1959), especially the bibliography. See also the suggestive remarks of Walter
L. Dorn, "The Debate over American Occupation Policy in Germany in
1944-1945," *Political Science Quarterly*, LXXII (1957), 483-485. On the
origins of the war of 1939 and of the German attack against Russia, see
William L. Langer and S. Everett Gleason, *The Challenge to Isolation,
1937-1940* (New York, 1953) and *The Undeclared War, 1940-1941* (New
York, 1953); an opposing interpretation by C. C. Tansill, *Back Door to War,
1933-1941* (Chicago, 1952); and Gerhard L. Weinberg, *Germany and the
Soviet Union, 1939-1941* (Leiden, 1954).

Reich. British wartime opinion reflected this conflicting background. Tempers slowly aroused to anger were highly mobilized by the time the Big Three began in 1941 to discuss their plans for postwar Germany.

"I used to think that the German people weren't altogether to blame for the war," a chastened Briton told a pollster in the spring of 1942. Now, he added, "I have decided that any feelings of pity I might have for them as *people* must be over-ruled by the fact that they are as a *nation,* cruel, aggressive and morally decadent . . . the best German is a dead one." According to a well-known polling service, Mass Observation, 43 per cent of the people of England in the spring of 1942 either hated or had no sympathy for the German people; and by the month of February, 1945, their numbers had increased to 54 per cent or more.[2]

In Britain, even highly rational intellectuals tended to regard the Germans as unique among men. German history, wrote Gilbert Murray, "surpasses all others in its ingenious mixture of all the elements calculated to stimulate self-pity, self-worship and desperate pugnacity." Lord Robert Vansittart, the retired dean of the Foreign Office who did most to alert his countrymen to the unique nature of the German problem, estimated that at least 75 per cent of the German people were "incurably bellicose." Between "Germanity and humanity," Vansittart insisted, there was a "great gulf fixed." Even commentators like Harold Nicolson, who deplored Vansittart's use of "muscle-bound metaphors," shared Vansittart's distrust, if not his hatred, of the Germans. Nicolson, an urbane and perceptive observer of German affairs, insisted that most individual Germans were "decent, orderly and humane," but he avowed that in all of them there was "a little pocket—a vermicular appendix—of bile and rancour which at any moment may become inflamed." Small minorities of Germans who believed in violence and cruelty were able "at stated intervals to infect the mass of their compatriots." Yet, the essential moderation of the British never completely surrendered to emotions as they thought of their enemies beyond the Rhine, although the conflict became a close one during the months of V-1 and V-2 attacks. The equivo-

<hr/>

[2] H. D. Willcock, "Public Opinion: Attitudes to the German People," *The Political Quarterly,* XIX (1948), 160-166.

cal position in which most Britons were left was summed up by an unskilled, middle-aged working woman, who in 1943 told a pollster: "Well, in my opinion they should all be killed. But still, that's rather drastic really. Because, after all, they've got fathers and mothers, haven't they?" [3]

The people of Great Britain were offered a variety of non-official proposals for the treatment of Germany after the war. All of the proposals agreed that peace must be assured against the renewal of aggression by Germany, but they disagreed radically as to how this could be accomplished. Almost all proposed that war criminals should be punished, that Nazism should be eliminated, that at least a brief period of military occupation of Germany should be required, and that Germany should be disarmed.

Beyond this there was little agreement. Those who believed that the German people could be changed placed their hopes upon the removal of Nazi leaders, upon Allied promotion of the democratic forces in Germany, and upon sweeping re-education. Those who believed that the Germans were "incurable," or at best hard to teach, advocated stern repressive measures. Lord Vansittart was not the most extreme of these, contrary to popular opinion; but he was probably the most influential. Vansittart would occupy Germany for as long as a generation. He would make sure that disarmament was permanent. He would control German industry, and even eliminate certain dangerous branches of it, such as the aviation, machine tool, and oil refining industries. He would place the industry-rich Ruhr under permanent Allied control. He would break up the remainder of Prussia into smaller states. On the other hand, Vansittart admitted that the Germans might be re-educated, in time, and he did not propose that all German industry

---

[3] Gilbert Murray, "De-Nazification," *Spectator*, CLXXIII (Sept. 8, 1944), 214-215; Robert Vansittart, *Bones of Contention* (New York, 1945), 46-69 and *passim;* Vansittart's preface to Wladyslaw W. Kulski (W. M. Knight-Patterson, pseud.), *Germany from Defeat to Conquest, 1913-1933* (London, 1945), 5-6; Harold Nicolson, "Marginal Comment," *Spectator*, CLXX (April 23, 1943), 382; *ibid.*, CLXXII (June 30, 1944), 590; Willcock, "Public Opinion," *loc. cit.*, 163; Lord Pakenham, *Born to Believe: An Autobiography* (London, 1953), 166; R. B. McCallum, *Public Opinion and the Last Peace* (London, 1944), vii. Vansittart's memoirs carried only to 1936 due to his death indicate that he did not change his views after 1945 and throw light on the origins of his animus against Germany; see *The Mist Procession: The Autobiography of Lord Vansittart* (London, 1958).

be destroyed. Nor would he destroy the Reich by partitioning Germany into two or more states, as would certain other British spokesmen.[4]

Vansittart's program was harsher than some Englishmen wished to impose on Germany. Arthur Bryant expressed a conviction of the moderates when he cautioned that peace should not be made "so onerous and humiliating that future generations of Germans will court death to destroy it." R. B. McCallum of Oxford offered one of the wiser suggestions when in 1944 he proposed the creation of a Western European union to shape the future of Germany and Central Europe in conjunction with the United States and the U.S.S.R.[5] But tempers ran generally high among the people of Great Britain, and their views of Germany's future showed that Vansittart had spoken for many of them. Polls taken in 1944 by the British Institute of Public Opinion revealed that 66 per cent of those asked were in favor of permanently separating the Ruhr ("containing about 40% of Germany's industries") from Germany; that 70 per cent thought Germans should help rebuild the countries they had destroyed; that 74 per cent believed Britain should try to get reparations from Germany after the war. Others—56 per cent of those who were questioned—would go farther than Vansittart and dismember Germany into a number of small states.[6]

Anti-Nazi Germans who had sought temporary political refuge in England may have strengthened the English moderates. The

---

[4] Harold Nicolson, "Marginal Comment," *Spectator*, CLXX (June 4, 1943), 522; Vansittart, *Bones of Contention*, 46-69; Salvador de Madariaga in *Spectator*, CLXXII (Oct. 27, 1944), 388. See also the review article by Donald F. Lach, "What *They* Would Do about Germany," *Journal of Modern History*, XVII (1945), 227-243. For some of the more moderate British wartime proposals, see: E. H. Carr, *Conditions of Peace* (New York, 1942); Royal Institute of International Affairs, *The Problem of Germany: An Interim Report* . . . (London, 1943); Julius Braunthal, *Need Germany Survive?* (London, 1943); a Penguin Book by five anti-Nazi German refugees: *The Next Germany* (London, 1943); H. N. Brailsford, *Our Settlement with Germany* (London, 1944). Among the harsher proposals, see: Paul Einzig, *Appeasement: Before, during and after the War* (New York, 1941); Robert Vansittart, *The Black Record* (London, 1941); Vansittart, *Lessons of My Life* (New York, 1943); T. H. Minshall, *What to Do with Germany* (London, 1941).

[5] Arthur Bryant in *Illustrated London News*, CCV (Nov. 11, 1944), 534; McCallum, *Public Opinion and the Last Peace*, 190-206.

[6] Hadley Cantril and Mildred Strunk, *Public Opinion, 1935-1946* (Princeton, 1951), 1115, 1153, 1154.

German émigrés themselves were not in full agreement. One prominent German Social Democrat who lived in England during the war years, Curt Geyer, approved and publicized Lord Vansittart's anaylsis of German national character, calling it "the truth about Germany without sentimental gloss." But most of the several hundreds of German socialist émigrés, including Erich Ollenhauer and Hans Vogel, leaders of the Social Democratic Party (S.P.D.) executive-committee-in-exile, repudiated the German Vansittart's. Some of them even suggested that Geyer had been "bought." The leading German socialists refused to admit that Nazism reflected the German national character. Instead, they demanded the "liberation" of the people of Germany along with the liberation of other peoples whom the Nazis had conquered. They opposed the idea of dismembering Germany. They opposed the de-industrialization of Germany. They also argued against any annexation of German territory by neighboring states.[7]

In short, the nationalism of the S.P.D. in the Bonn Republic was foreshadowed by the attitudes of S.P.D. émigré leaders in Britain during World War II. They reminded the British that there was "another Germany" besides the Germany of Hitler. They may have contributed in some degree to the relative moderation of official British policy for postwar Germany.

THE SOVIET UNION

Germans also lived in the U.S.S.R. during World War II, but they failed to moderate the policies of Soviet leaders toward Germany. The most noted of these Germans whose work was given publicity during the war were those *Wehrmacht* officers who, upon being captured by the Red Army, appealed to fellow Germans by radio and leaflets to turn against Hitler. One of the first to do so was a great-grandson of Otto von Bismarck, Lieutenant Heinrich Count von Einsiedel. Another early puppet of the Russians was General Walter von Seydlitz. In August, 1944, even Field-Marshal Friedrich Paulus, who had commanded the German

---

[7] Erich Matthias, *Sozialdemokratie und Nation: Ein Beitrag zur Ideengeschichte der sozialdemokratischer Emigration in der Prager Zeit des Partei Vorstandes 1933-1938* (Stuttgart, 1952), 268-281. See also: Lewis J. Edinger, *German Exile Politics: The Social Democratic Executive Committee in the Nazi Era* (Berkeley etc., 1956), 225-243.

Sixth Army at Stalingrad, appealed over the Soviet radio and in Soviet trench propaganda to his fellow Germans, asking them in vain "to bring about conditions that will make it possible for our people to survive." These men, while trying to serve Germany, served the Soviet cause during the Second World War.[8]

Other Germans, political émigrés in the U.S.S.R. during the war, were to serve the Soviets far better after 1945 than before. Chief among them were Wilhelm Pieck, future president of the East German satellite state, and Walter Ulbricht, future head of East Germany's Politburo under the sponsorship first of Stalin, later of Malenkov, and—a remarkable tribute to his political longevity—then of Khrushchev.

Wilhelm Pieck was about the same age as another German who would win fame after 1945, Konrad Adenauer. Pieck had participated in the German revolution of 1918-1919, and was one of the founders of the German Communist Party (K.P.D.). Ulbricht, who turned fifty during World War II, remained virtually unknown in Germany until 1923, when he helped stage an ill-advised and unsuccessful Communist revolt in his native Saxony. Both Pieck and Ulbricht were unswervingly loyal Stalinists in the K.P.D. during the 1920's. Both were methodical party bureaucrats. Forced to wander abroad by Hitler's rise to power in 1933, both Pieck and Ulbricht were living in the U.S.S.R. when the *Wehrmacht* struck eastward into Soviet territory on June 22, 1941.

While Pieck possessed a certain geniality, Ulbricht won notoriety even among Communists for his icy cold, colorless and humorless personality. As after 1945, Pieck was the more decorative figure, while Ulbricht did the work. During the war Ulbricht's chief service to the Soviet regime was two-fold, to talk German prisoners-of-war into collaborating with the Russians, while, for the Soviet propaganda machine, exaggerating the extent of this collaboration. Within a few days after the German invasion began, Ulbricht was already speaking over the Soviet radio with "an encouraging announcement" for the Russian people: "As early as

---

[8] Heinrich von Einsiedel, *I Joined the Russians* (New Haven, 1953), 30-78; Wolfgang Leonhard, *Child of the Revolution,* C. M. Woodhouse, trans. (London, 1957), 188, 238, 256, 258, 277-278 and *passim.*

22nd June, the first German soldier deserted to the Soviet side!"[9]

The wartime function of Germany's Communist émigrés in the Soviet Union was, thus, to boost Soviet morale against the armies of their native Germany. They held out hope to Germans for a softer peace if they would rise against Hitler, but there is no evidence that they exerted any influence upon Soviet policy for the future of Germany. Their's was to serve, not to lead, as the postwar period would confirm. Like the German refugees from Nazism in England, they reminded their hosts of "another Germany," but the presence inside the U.S.S.R. of Hitler's legions blinded Russians to its virtues.

The wartime attitudes of the Russian people toward Germany is difficult to estimate precisely. At least half a million ex-Soviet citizens actually fought with Hitler's armies during World War II, and much has been made of those civilians who welcomed the Nazi legions in 1941. Though numerous at first, they were quickly disenchanted by Hitler's ruthless policies. Ukrainians, outraged by Hitler's brutal satrap, Erich Koch, fought as bitterly as Great Russians against the German armies in the last year of the war. The degree of support for Germany among Soviet citizens has been exaggerated in the American press since 1945.

The unanimity of the patriotic defense of Russia by her people was also exaggerated in the Soviet press during the war. The attitudes toward Germany that appeared in print in the hard pressed Soviet empire, such as Ilya Ehrenburg's Vansittart-like ideas, must be seen in this light and discounted as officially inspired releases. But even so, the circumstances of the war suggest more than many volumes how the majority of the Russian people must have felt. For the second time in a generation their land was subjected after June 22, 1941, to a three-year invasion by German armies, armies that spurned a welcome even when it was given. By December, 1941, the Germans were in the outskirts of Leningrad, within sight of Moscow, had taken Kiev, and occupied most of Crimea.

[9] Leonhard, *Child of the Revolution*, 121, 146, 150, 161, 163, 238, 288, and *passim;* Ruth Fischer, *Stalin and German Communism: A Study in the Origins of the State Party* (Cambridge, Mass., 1948), 500-510 and *passim;* Ossip K. Flechtheim, *Die kommunistische Partei Deutschlands in der Weimarer Republik* (Offenbach a.M., 1948), *passim.*

One needs to visualize foreign armies outside Boston, threatening Cleveland, holding Memphis, and spearheading their way toward the Texas oil fields in order to imagine how the Russian people felt. After 1942, it would appear, virtually "the whole of Russia" hoped that victory would bring a "day of judgment for Germany." And it is possible that, as was reported in the West, the Russian people shared the concern among Soviet leaders that the United States and Britain might let Germany off too easy after the war. Certainly to politically conscious Russians the future of Germany appeared as "the foremost problem of their national security." [10]

THE UNITED STATES

Views on Germany that were expressed in the United States were as anti-German as those in Great Britain, although Americans were not so close to the war. A book published in 1941 actually argued that all German males should be sterilized. A Harvard anthropologist, Professor Earnest A. Hooten, suggested a variant form of reproductive retribution: the German army should be forced to work in devastated areas after it surrendered, the single soldiers procreating while re-creating; thus the German birth rate would decline, while that of neighboring states would rise, and the aggressiveness of Germany would be counterbalanced as the

---

[10] See the comments by Leonhard, *Child of the Revolution*, 109-239 *passim;* Einsiedel, *I Joined the Russians, passim;* Clarence A. Manning, *Ukraine under the Soviets* (New York, 1953), 167-184; John A. Armstrong, *Ukrainian Nationalism, 1939-1945* (New York, 1955), 101-186, 277-288; Nicholas P. Vakar, *Belorussia: The Making of a Nation, a Case Study* (Cambridge, Mass., 1956), 170-206; Alexander Dallin, *German Rule in Russia, 1941-1945: A Study of Occupation Policies* (London, 1957); George Fischer, *Soviet Opposition to Stalin: A Case Study in World War II* (Cambridge, Mass., 1952); I. Deutscher, *Stalin: A Political Biography* (New York etc., 1949), 538; Anna Louise Strong, "Russia's Post-War Policy," *Nation,* CLIX (Oct. 21, 1944), 460-461; Hajo Holborn, *American Military Government: Its Organization and Policies* (Washington, 1947), 23; John W. Wheeler-Bennett, *The Nemesis of Power: The German Army in Politics, 1918-1945* (New York, 1954), 520-521; and, more generally, Michael Balfour and John Mair, *Four-Power Control in Germany and Austria, 1945-1946* (London, 1956), 40-48. A number of contemporary accounts—most of them colorful—contain incidental comment on Russian attitudes toward Germany. See, e.g., Margaret Bourke-White, *Shooting the Russian War* (New York, 1942); Henry C. Cassidy, *Moscow Dateline, 1941-1943* (Boston, 1943); Walter Graebner, *Round Trip to Russia* (Philadelphia etc., 1943); Alexander Werth, *Moscow War Diary* (New York, 1942).

virulent genes of Germans mixed with those of more passive Europeans! [11]

Public opinion polls taken during the war showed a spreading hostility toward Germany. In July, 1942, some 3000 Americans were asked if they thought most of the German people were supporting Hitler; 51 per cent said yes. On January 27, 1943, 3000 were asked whether the Allies should enter into peace talks with German generals if they should overthrow Hitler and offer to negotiate; 63 per cent said no. In February, 1944, 81 per cent of the persons contacted in another survey stated that they favored the policy of "unconditional surrender" of Germany. Another poll indicated that in June, 1944, 60 per cent of the people of the United States believed Germany would begin planning another war as soon as she was defeated in World War II. To prevent any such possibility, 73 per cent of the persons asked (3000) in a Gallup poll of August 1, 1944, stated that they favored the reduction of Germany to a "3rd rate" nation after the war. One week after Germany's defeat in World War II, 90 per cent of those who answered the question put by the National Opinion Research Center stated that the new peace treaty with Germany should be harsher than the treaty imposed in 1919 at Versailles.[12]

More than in England, European refugees in the United States fanned the flames of wartime hatred. Five Dutch émigrés approvingly revived a sixteenth century ditty, which seemed to verify the belief that Germany suffered from national paranoia:

> When the "Hun" is poor and down,
> He's the humblest man in town;
> But once he climbs and holds the rod,
> He smites his fellow-men and God.

A few émigré Germans spoke out for moderate treatment of a defeated Reich, but were denounced as Pan-German militarists by fellow refugees, like the noted pacifist, Professor Friedrich Wilhelm Foerster. The famous novelist, Emil Ludwig, was among

---

[11] Louis Nizer, *What to Do with Germany* (Chicago etc., 1944), 6; Theodore N. Kaufman, *Germany Must Perish!* (Newark, 1941), as reviewed in Lach, "What *They* Would Do about Germany," *loc. cit.*, 228.

[12] For these and other statistics see: Cantril and Strunk, *Public Opinion, 1935-1946*, 1107, 1115, 1141, 1143, 1144; Herman Edward Bateman, "The Election of 1944 and Foreign Policy," 137-138 (Ph.D. dissertation, Stanford University, 1952).

the most influential of those who helped to increase distrust of Germany. Ludwig would create a special Prussian state east of the Elbe and shorn of East Prussia. He would leave the rest of Germany to the German people, but agreed they should be totally disarmed, occupied and re-educated. Professor Foerster in the presence of President Franklin D. Roosevelt's personal Chief of Staff stated that Germany should be divided into separate states.[13]

This proposal of dismemberment was most influentially advanced in 1943 by Sumner Welles, a personal friend of the President and Under-Secretary of State. Freed of his official duties in the fall of 1943, Welles carried his peace proposals to the American people in a widely read book of 1944. In this he contended that the chief source of evil in Germany was militarism; that the chief source of militarism in Germany was Prussia; within Prussia, the General Staff; and that the General Staff was dangerous only in a unified Germany. Therefore, reasoned Welles, the only way to offset the German menace in the future was to carve up the Reich into three separate states. Welles, like most other wartime writers on the German problem, was prepared to give East Prussia to Poland. Welles would also control German heavy industry after the war, but would guarantee the German people economic opportunities equal to those of other Europeans.[14]

Not so Louis Nizer, active New York speech-maker and author of another widely read book on the German problem. Nizer opposed partition, but would destroy the machine tool, steel, power, and certain other heavy industries of Germany. How, under

---

[13] The paranoia thesis is developed by Richard M. Brickner, *Is Germany Incurable?* (Philadelphia, 1943). The poem is in Lach, "What *They* Would Do about Germany," *loc. cit.*, 230, which also reviews the moderate émigré proposals of: Gerhart H. Seger and Siegfried K. Marck, *Germany: To Be or Not to Be* (New York, 1943); Paul Hagen, *Germany after Hitler* (New York, 1944); Ferdinand A. Hermens, *The Tyrants' War and the Peoples' Peace* (Chicago, 1944), and Werner Richter, *Re-educating Germany* (Chicago, 1945). F. W. Foerster has briefly sketched his World War II activities in his memoirs: *Erlebte Weltgeschichte 1869-1953: Memoiren* (Nuremberg, 1953), 560-562. Emil Ludwig's most important treatise of the war period on the German problem was: *The Germans: Double History of a Nation* (Boston, 1941); see also his shorter books, *How to Treat the Germans* (New York, 1943), and *The Moral Conquest of Germany* (Garden City, 1945); *The Germans* was a Book of the Month Club selection. See also William D. Leahy, *I Was There: The Personal Story of the Chief of Staff to Presidents Roosevelt and Truman . . .* (New York etc., 1950), 242.

[14] *The Time for Decision* (New York etc., 1944), especially 336-361.

these circumstances, Nizer would "prevent the collapse of German economy," he failed to make clear.[15]

Not all American proposals were so drastic. The most thoughtful of the unofficial American wartime plans for the prevention of future German aggression was that by Harold G. Moulton and Louis Marlio. They called for moderate economic controls, international arms inspection and forceful prevention of German rearmament. Their book was too closely reasoned to wield mass influence. And few Americans read Koppel S. Pinson's wartime reminder that, beyond the Nazi facade, there was "another Germany which would like to be different from what it is today." [16]

This theme of "the other Germany" was developed by several scholars, American natives and emigrants from Europe, in American learned periodicals during the war. One of the more perceptive of these writers must be credited with having made the most embarrassing prediction of them all: Sigmund Neumann insisted that the victors must promote the growth of a democratic and healthy society in postwar Germany by wisely selecting German leaders for posts in a new central government; that such men might be found among some large-city mayors; but—this in September, 1944 —that "the few great mayors of pre-1933, such as Adenauer of Cologne, will be too old and too long retired to assume active responsibilities of such importance." Another German émigré scholar, Arnold Brecht, argued against proposals to partition Germany, but recommended that Prussia's hegemony in Germany should be broken. To accomplish this aim, Brecht would consolidate the smaller states of Germany into larger units that could hold their own, and divide Prussia. James K. Pollock added his recommendation that Germany be decentralized to the similar proposals which Brecht advanced. The restraint these scholars showed in wartime

---

[15] Nizer, *What to Do with Germany*, 188-201.

[16] Harold G. Moulton and Louis Marlio, *The Control of Germany and Japan* (Washington, 1944); Koppel S. Pinson, "On the Future of Germany: A Survey of Opinions and Proposals," *Menorah Journal*, XXXII (1944), 126-160. See also the review article by Lach, "What *They* Would Do about Germany," *loc. cit.*, 227-243, which notes the following wartime books on Germany: Louis P. Lochner, *What about Germany?* (New York, 1942); Alexander Gerschenkron, *Bread and Democracy in Germany* (Berkeley, 1943); and Benedetto Croce, *Germany and Europe: A Spiritual Dissension* (New York, 1944), transl. by Vincent Sheean.

was admirable. Unfortunately, their views influenced relatively small numbers of the American people.[17]

With all their faults, the "public opinion" polls of the war years provide the historian with his most precise measurement of attitudes toward Germany. The following questions and answers showed how significant samples of the American people in 1944-1945 foresaw the treatment of postwar Germany: *Should or should not be broken up into smaller states?* Should: 30 to 40 per cent. *Should or should not be occupied for several years?* Should: 73 to 85 per cent. *Should or should not be allowed to rebuild heavy industries after the war?* Should: 30 to 40 per cent. *Should or should not be totally demobilized?* Should: 77 to 85 per cent. *Should or should not be forced to make up for destruction in other countries?* Should: 86 per cent. *Should or should not be allowed to vote in free elections after the war?* Should: 47 per cent. (In 1942 it had been 62 per cent.)[18]

Thus, the majority of the people of Britain, the U.S.S.R., and the United States during World War II seemed to expect that Germany should never again "climb and hold the rod." Some Americans demanded more extreme measures than did Britons, and the Russian people probably wanted to impose even more radical restrictions upon Germany. Frenchmen played little part in shaping Big Three policy toward Germany, but by late 1944 they were even more harsh than the British and Americans in their proposals for Germany's future. A survey of some 2800 Parisians in October, 1944, by the French Institute of Public Opinion put 76 per cent of them on record in favor of the dismemberment of Germany. In the provinces, 76 per cent of those contacted by a French survey of January, 1945, favored the separation of the left bank of the

---

[17] Sigmund Neumann, "Transition to Democracy in Germany," *Political Science Quarterly*, LIX (1944), 341-362; Arnold Brecht, "On Germany's Postwar Settlement," *Social Research*, XI (1944), 428-440; James K. Pollock, "The Role of the Public in a New Germany," *American Political Science Review*, XXXIX (1945), 470, 472. Pollock set forth his ideas at greater length in his booklet, *What Shall Be Done with Germany?* (Carleton College, 1944). For other moderate statements see Shepard Clough, "What about Reparations This Time?," *Political Science Quarterly*, LIX (1944), 220-226; and Glenn E. Hoover, "The Outlook for War Guilt Trials," *Political Science Quarterly*, LIX (1944), 40-48.

[18] Cantril and Strunk, *Public Opinion, 1935-1946*, 268, 1115, 1153, 1154.

Rhine from Germany.[19] In the United States, even so wise and moderate a commentator as Walter Lippmann admonished his 1944 readers: "Our primary war aim must be unalterable: It must be to make it impossible for Germany to hold the balance of power in Europe. . . . " Lippmann further caught the spirit of the times when he warned: "If any important neighbor of Germany turned away from the existing alliance to become the ally of Germany, it would begin the fateful disruption of all control over Germany." The crucial period, Lippmann cautioned, would come in 1970, not in 1960.[20]

The point of all this is not that Roosevelt, Churchill, and Stalin were dominated by "public opinion." In varying degrees they were influenced by it. But the more significant and demonstrable fact is that, in varying degrees, they *shared* the widespread animosity toward Germany. One official who was significantly involved in the planning of United States policy toward Germany has recalled that "anyone who tried to adopt a fairly tolerant attitude toward Germany was suspect." Another American official, critical of the first, at least agrees with him on this point, recalling that: "The first problem with which we had to try to cope was, to put it brutally, an ignorant animus against Germany.[21]

Little men who after 1945 criticized the wartime folly of their leaders often forgot that they themselves had demanded the very policies they found in the hindsight of peacetime to be full of faults.

---

[19] *Ibid.*, 1116.
[20] Walter Lippmann, *U.S. War Aims* (Boston, 1944), 110-117.
[21] Confidential letter from a participant to the author.

Chapter II

THE POLICY OF POSTPONEMENT
1941-1943

CHURCHILL recalled after the war that several official attempts were made in London before 1944 to draft a program for postwar Germany, but that they were scrapped: "They looked so terrible when set forth on paper . . . that their publication would only have stimulated German resistance. They had in fact only to be written out to be withdrawn."[1] Churchill's remarks might well stand as the obituary to the "policy" of 1941-1943. At the top level it was to be a policy of postponing the final determination of policy toward Germany.

FRONTS FOR A POLICY VACUUM

As Churchill's comment suggests, great differences of opinion developed between policy-making personalities and their technical experts. It has been well said that there is "something at once humble and superior about an expert—a trying combination." Each of the Big Three would have agreed with this. The experts wished to plan policy early, and win Big Three formal acceptance of it; the statesmen decided to delay. The Big Three were bound to consider the uninformed emotions of the masses. The experts, on the other hand, strove only to fashion a logical and workable peace. The resulting conflicts hampered the development of policy toward Germany in all three Allied capitals. So did conflicts which arose between the personalities, philosophies, and jurisdictions of members of the British and American cabinets, and almost certainly in

---

[1] Winston S. Churchill, *The Hinge of Fate* (Boston, 1950), 689. This and other brief excerpts from the Churchill volumes are quoted by permission of the publisher, the Houghton Mifflin Company.

the Politburo as well. The "battle of Washington" and its counter-
parts in London and Moscow were seldom reported in the press,
for the sea of troubles of official planning could not be allowed
to drown out the war effort. Instead, it was restrained from the
public by two magnificent dikes, erected by Roosevelt and Churchill and accepted without enthusiasm by Stalin at two vastly different stages of the war. The first was the "Atlantic Charter." The
second was the formula of "unconditional surrender." They were
as different as fear and confidence, the two moods in which they
alternately were built.

The "Atlantic Charter" was a document of high principle, "a
publicity handout" which Roosevelt and Churchill sought to use
as a general blueprint for peace. Roosevelt and Churchill announced
the "Charter" after their secret meeting off Newfoundland in
August, 1941. Its text alone suggests that it was to be used
against Germany, not as a basis for negotiation with her. The
original British draft included no statement which guaranteed the
benefits of the "Charter" to Germany. The final draft assured,
with verbal qualifications, that the two statesmen would try to
provide "all states, great or small, victor or vanquished" with equal
access to the trade and raw materials of the world after the war.
The clause against territorial changes never restricted the thought
or action of the authors of the "Charter" in their consideration of
the peace they would impose upon Germany, and the promise to
respect the right of all people "to choose the form of government
under which they will live" obviously applied to the victims of
Nazi Germany, not to its own citizens. In England, King George
VI privately noted the Charter for what it was: "The joint statement said all the right things," he wrote to Queen Mary, "but how
are we going to carry them out?"[2]

The potential ability of Germans to claim benefits under
the "Atlantic Charter" was canceled out in January, 1943. Then

---

[2] For the text of the British preliminary draft and the final text see
William L. Neumann, *Making the Peace, 1941-1945: The Diplomacy of the
Wartime Conferences* (Washington, 1950), 11. See also Herbert Feis,
*Churchill, Roosevelt, Stalin: The War They Waged and the Peace They
Sought* (Princeton, 1957), 20-22, 27; John W. Wheeler-Bennett, *King
George VI: His Life and Reign* (New York, 1958), 529; Günter Moltmann,
*Amerikas Deutschland Politik im zweiten Weltkrieg: Kriegs-und Friedensziele
1941-1945* (Heidelberg, 1958), 23-39.

Roosevelt publicly announced at Casablanca that the Allies would demand the "unconditional surrender" of the Axis Powers. Actually, Hitler had left them little choice in this, since he had repeatedly proclaimed that Germany faced either total victory or total defeat. "There is to be no capitulation to the powers outside, no revolution by the forces within," he announced on many occasions. Hitler remembered the revolution of 1918. So did Roosevelt and Churchill, who also recalled the Fourteen Points and the way Germany had abused Woodrow Wilson's memory after 1918. Both were determined that there should be no opportunity after World War II for Germans to shout that wartime promises had been broken; there would be no promises this time. As early as June, 1941, both Roosevelt and Churchill had concluded that there should be no negotiated peace with Hitler. The Casablanca announcement merely made this conclusion public.[3]

The best case that can possibly be made against the unconditional surrender policy has been made by many authors. The case in its favor has seldom been presented. Entries on both sides of the ledger must be considered.

Critics have suggested that Roosevelt made the announcement without consulting his advisers. But the President was informally advised before the Casablanca meeting that a special State Department sub-committee on postwar security problems thought this policy preferable to a negotiated peace; and the Joint Chiefs of Staff approved the policy in advance of the Casablanca meeting. Critics have insisted that Roosevelt surprised a hapless Churchill with the slogan when he announced it publicly, leaving the Prime Minister little choice but to say: "Me too." In actuality Churchill knew of Roosevelt's intentions five days in advance and even informed the War Cabinet in London of the proposed move. Critics at the time and later argued that it hampered the work of Allied propagandists because it strengthened the internal unity of the German people; but Churchill insisted that any more specific state-

---

[3] For typical Hitlerian wartime pronouncements see Chester Wilmot, *The Struggle for Europe* (New York, 1952), 95-96. On Roosevelt-Churchill attitudes before January, 1943, see Robert E. Sherwood, *Roosevelt and Hopkins: An Intimate History* (New York, 1948), 126, 410-415 and 445; Wilmot, *The Struggle for Europe*, 78. Roosevelt frequently expressed his desire to avoid Wilson's mistakes; and see Churchill, *Hinge of Fate*, 690.

ment of genuine Allied war aims would unite the Germans far more resolutely than would the controversial formula. Critics have insisted that it stiffened the resistance of German troops and it probably did. But an entire German army surrendered at Stalingrad exactly one week after the announcement was made to the world.

Critics have insisted that the slogan discouraged the rise of opposition against Nazism within Germany, and it probably did. But the critics overlook two facts: (1) there was only an inconsequential Resistance movement in Germany before January, 1943; and (2) the Resistance movement grew during the next year-and-a-half and produced two major attempts to assassinate Hitler in 1943-1944. Still other critics insist that Roosevelt's announcement was either a naive or a traitorous device to please the U.S.S.R. But the controversial formula must have been poor consolation to Russians who knew that they would have to fight on without help on a second front. Stalin privately made known his opposition to the formula soon after it was announced. Pacifists have condemned the formula as a vicious war aim; but other pacifists have seen in it an effort to postpone the task of making peace until the passions of war had cooled.

The most important reason for the formula was that the Allies could discuss specific terms of the future peace settlement only at the risk of disrupting the wartime unity of the three Great Powers. It thus became deliberate American policy in 1942 to adopt no specific policy toward the defeated enemy until after the war. Hull, Roosevelt and the Joint Chiefs of Staff approved this "policy of postponement." It became the basic element of official American tactics in negotiations concerning the future of Germany until 1944, and was strongly reaffirmed at Yalta in February, 1945. The military counterpart and facade for this political strategy was the unconditional surrender formula. As a war measure its superb virtue was that it preserved the unity of the "strange alliance" at a time when Soviet leaders were issuing vague but dark threats to make a separate peace with Hitler. Bickerings over peace terms might well have disrupted the "strange alliance." For the West, the policy held yet another, seldom remembered, advantage: it postponed crucial decisions about the future balance of power in

Europe until after British and American armies were "heavily in France and Germany," as Harry Hopkins noted in March, 1943. As a war measure the formula was useful.[4]

As a statement upon which peace could be based the unconditional surrender slogan was, of course, impossible. Both Roosevelt and Churchill clarified the formula in the months that followed its announcement, after Nazi propagandists claimed that it was intended to destroy Germany. Roosevelt announced in February, 1943, that the Allies meant "no harm to the common

[4] John L. Chase, "Unconditional Surrender Reconsidered," *Political Science Quarterly*, LXX (1955), 258-279; William L. Langer, "Turning Points of the War: Political Problems of a Coalition," *Foreign Affairs*, XXVI (Oct., 1947), 84; Sherwood, *Roosevelt and Hopkins*, 693-697, 715, 782; United States Department of State, *Postwar Foreign Policy Preparation, 1939-1945* (Washington, 1949), 127; Wilmot, *The Struggle for Europe*, 122; Feis, *Churchill, Roosevelt, Stalin*, 108-113; Churchill, *Hinge of Fate*, 684-691; William H. Standley and Arthur A. Ageton, *Admiral Ambassador to Russia* (Chicago, 1955), 201; Sumner Welles, *Seven Decisions That Shaped History* (New York, 1951), 123-125, 134-135; also the intelligent discussion by Moltmann, *Amerikas Deutschland Politik im zweiten Weltkrieg*, 63-77.

There was very little criticism of the policy of unconditional surrender in Congress in 1943; see H. Bradford Westerfield, *Foreign Policy and Party Politics, Pearl Harbor to Korea* (New Haven, 1955), 135, 139; Roland Young, *Congressional Politics in the Second World War* (New York, 1956), 148. For evidence of the contemporary criticism see: Forrest C. Pogue, *The Supreme Command* (Washington, 1954), 95, 339-342; James P. Warburg, *Germany—Bridge or Battleground* (New York, 1946), 260-262; Ernest J. King, *Fleet Admiral King: A Naval Record* (New York, 1952), 425. Among the postwar criticisms see the following: Hans Habe, *Our Love Affair with Germany* (New York, 1953), 1-3; Hanson Baldwin, "Churchill Was Right," *Atlantic Monthly*, CXCIV (July, 1954), 26-28, in which Baldwin ignores some of the evidence in the very volumes of Churchill's memoirs which he reviews in this article; Harold Strauss, *Division and Dismemberment of Germany* (Ambilly, 1952), 55-57; and see the longer criticism by Russell Grenfell, *Unconditional Hatred: German War Guilt and the Future of Europe* (New York, 1953). A brief defense is ably presented by Wheeler-Bennett, *The Nemesis of Power*, 536 and 558-563.

As one example of a "vague but dark" Soviet threat, see Stalin to Roosevelt, March 16, 1943: ". . . I think I must give a most emphatic warning, *in the interest of our common cause*, of the grave danger with which further delay in opening a second front in France is fraught." (My italics.) See also Stalin to Churchill, June 24, 1943: ". . . the point here is not just the disappointment of the Soviet Government, but the preservation of its confidence in its Allies, a confidence which is being subjected to severe stress." From: Ministry of Foreign Affairs of the U.S.S.R., *Correspondence between the Chairman of the Council of Ministers of the U.S.S.R. and the Presidents of the United States and the Prime Ministers of Great Britain during the Great Patriotic War of 1941-1945*, 2 vols. (Moscow, 1957), II, 59, 76. Cf. Arthur Bryant, *The Turn of the Tide: A History of the War Years Based on the Diaries of Field-Marshal Lord Alanbrooke, Chief of the Imperial General Staff* (Garden City, 1957), 433-434.

people of the Axis nations," and on several other occasions he stated that the Allies did not intend "to enslave the German people." Churchill also emphasized that the Allies would not stain their honor "by inhumanity or by mere lust for vengeance." But criticism of "unconditional surrender" persisted, and by December, 1943, Churchill as well as Stalin seemed willing to abandon the slogan in favor of more specific terms. Roosevelt's State Department and General Dwight D. Eisenhower also pressed for a more concrete statement. But the President refused to budge beyond his early clarifications. Thus the policy of unconditional surrender was never surrendered unconditionally, and was finally implemented against Germany in 1945.[5]

The policy would, if carried out, wipe the German slate clean at the end of the war. How the Allies would write upon it should, ideally, be determined well in advance. Since the Germans were to give their fate over completely to the Allies, the task which faced the planners for postwar Germany was an immensely complicated one. Military occupation had to be planned and territorial provisions drafted. The nature of the postwar German state or states must be determined. The internal and international economic life of the Germans had to be charted. The extent to which Germany should be made to pay the costs of war must be calculated. Punishment of war criminals must be arranged. Measures for the prevention of future German aggression would have to be developed. And, if "unconditional surrender" were to be interpreted in a literal sense, the Allies could blueprint a cultural and social revolution in Germany as sweeping as their divergent philosophies, desires, military power, and geographical proximity to Germany permitted.

EARLY BRITISH PROPOSALS

Britain had taken arms against Hitler's Germany at a time when the United States still basked in the prolonged autumn of benevolent neutrality, and while Stalin was appeasing Germany in a way that made the Munich decisions of 1938 appear less uniquely sinful and stupid than before. In those days Churchill considered

---

[5] Churchill, *Hinge of Fate*, 688; Cordell Hull, *The Memoirs of Cordell Hull*, 2 vols. (New York, 1948), II, 1570-1579.

Stalin "the mortal foe of civilised freedom." By the spring of 1942 military necessity had moderated the Prime Minister's public statements, if not his innermost feelings: "All now depends upon the vast Russo-German struggle," he wrote to Roosevelt on April 1, 1942. Ten months later the battle of Stalingrad altered the European balance of power and the course of history. "I think it inevitable that Russia will be the greatest land Power in the world after this war," Churchill wrote on September 5, 1943, to Jan Christian Smuts. Churchill wrote as one anti-Communist to another. He informed Smuts that his hope lay in a combination of British and American power, which might "put us on good terms and in a friendly balance with Russia at least for the period of rebuilding." A modest goal was thus modestly stated by a war leader who sensed the drift toward a two-power world—and sought doggedly to save in it a large place for a tired Britain.[6]

These attitudes were basic in shaping the thoughts of British planners of peace with Germany, but they were partly counter-balanced by the immediate necessities of the war. The immediate danger remained Germany, not the U.S.S.R. Many officials believed that the Soviet Union would not send troops beyond her pre-1941 territory, and that the Western Allies must try to "persuade her not to relax her efforts." After the war the British wanted the Russians out of Central Europe as fast as possible; but in 1944 they urged them in. Churchill himself has admitted that there was no concern in the first half of 1944 about the size of the German zone of occupation the U.S.S.R. would gain in the process. As late as July 1, 1944—after D-Day—Churchill encouraged Stalin to push on to Berlin. Caught between worry about the Russians and the more immediate dread of Germany, Churchill's strategy was, like Roosevelt's, to postpone basic policy decisions about the future of Germany for as long as possible. Even as late as February, 1945, Foreign Secretary Anthony Eden told his Russian and American colleagues at Yalta that the British War Cabinet had not formally discussed a program for postwar Germany, though

---

[6] Churchill, *Hinge of Fate*, 203; and the 5th volume in his *History of the Second World War: Closing the Ring* (Boston, 1951), 129.

proposals had been studied "on a technical level." [7]

Economic problems were the first to be considered seriously by the British "on a technical level." Under Sir William Malkin, legal adviser of the Foreign Office, a British committee of experts in 1942 began the systematic study of economic aspects of peace with Germany. The British experts were men of ability, experienced in German economic problems. Furthermore, "the spirit of revenge and retaliation had little place in their attitude to the future peace." But they lacked even the most basic policy decision upon which to found a policy: was Germany to be one economy or several states with disrupted economies after the war? In the absence of instructions, these experts necessarily became mind readers: they assumed that postwar Germany would remain "substantially a unitary state," and founded their work upon this supposition.

The Malkin committee explored two major problems in 1942-43, first the future reparations policy to be followed and, secondly, economic measures to prevent future German aggression. On both matters the British experts took moderate positions. They recommended that reparations be collected largely in kind, but some in money payments; that the collection period should be restricted to the immediate postwar years; and that the total amount collected should be kept small. Most important of all, reparations policy would not be used to wreck the German economy, as some proposals for security against German aggression were suggesting. The Malkin group considered two types of measures to hobble Germany's war horse: (1) control and restriction of German imports to prevent key war materials from coming into the country; (2) liquidation of certain branches of the German economy, such as the aviation, oil, and machine tool industries. The experts found the latter method too troublesome, and recommended in favor of import restrictions.

The work of this group of experts was not all in vain. When

---

[7] Ministry of Foreign Affairs of the U.S.S.R., *Correspondence . . . Chairman of the Council of Ministers of the U.S.S.R. . . . 1941-1945*, I, 233; Winston S. Churchill, in the 6th volume of his history of the war: *Triumph and Tragedy* (Boston, 1953), 507-508; Edward R. Stettinius, Jr. (Walter Johnson, ed.), *Roosevelt and the Russians: The Yalta Conference* (Garden City, 1949), 119.

Churchill and Eden finally clarified their policy on reparations and Germany's economic future, their decisions basically matched those of the Malkin committee. But in 1942-1943, as in so many other cases, the experts outstepped their policy makers. The result was inevitable, though frustrating for the experts. An American colleague has been left to sing the expert's lament in place of Malkin, who was killed in an airplane crash in 1945: In the opinion of the experts, the progress they had made was "thrown away" by the failure—or perhaps we should say the refusal—of ministers to study, and take at least a tentative position on, postwar economic questions relating to Germany.[8]

The failure of the British war leaders to act upon the recommendation of their experts was inherent in their own status and that of the war in 1943. Too much depended upon the way the war would end, upon what would happen in Germany before the collapse, and, above all, upon the desires of Britain's allies.

The only concrete policy that could be defined at the top level of government in Britain in 1943 was a proposed division of Germany into zones of occupation for the period immediately after the surrender of Germany. In agreement with his Chiefs of Staff, Churchill created a special Cabinet committee, headed by the Deputy Prime Minister and Labor Party leader, Clement Attlee, to study this problem, and the Attlee committee in the summer of 1943 made its recommendations.

In the Attlee report, the Germany that the world knew from 1945 until 1949—and the Berlin of 1959—could be seen in broad outline. The whole country was to be occupied. It would be divided into three zones of roughly equal size: the British would occupy a northwestern zone, the Americans a southern and southwestern zone, and the Russians an eastern zone. Berlin would become a separate zone, jointly occupied by the three Allies. In thus visualizing and proposing the future relations of the Big Three in a new balance of power in Germany, the Attlee committee remained true to the arch principles of four centuries of British foreign policy: Europe as a whole was to be dominated by no

---

[8] E. F. Penrose, *Economic Planning for the Peace* (Princeton, 1953), 217-224. Penrose was Economic Adviser to the United States Ambassador in London, John Gilbert Winant.

single power, and British maritime interests would be advanced by occupation of Germany's North Sea Coast. More prosaically, it also reflected the reluctance of military leaders to work in combined commands with forces of the other Allies. The War Cabinet approved the recommendations and passed them on for consideration by Britain's allies. The proposals only slowly became the established policy of "the world triumvirate." [9]

Proposals to divide Germany permanently were also advanced in Britain in 1943. The majority of the Cabinet members believed that it was either impossible or undesirable to undo the work of Bismarck, but an active minority kept the question open. The positions of Churchill and Eden roughly reflected the division in the Cabinet, and fluctuated widely in negotiations with Britain's allies. During a visit to Washington in March, 1943, Eden not only stated informally that Poland should annex East Prussia, but said that some form of partition of Germany into several states should be achieved. But in August, 1943, Eden told Cordell Hull at Quebec that he personally was opposed to the dismemberment of Germany, and that he believed "in general, the Cabinet also" was opposed. It would be another matter, he said, if the Germans themselves wished to carry out partition voluntarily. Within four months both Eden and Churchill were to express themselves again more definitely in favor of dismemberment. [10]

EARLY UNITED STATES PROPOSALS

Planning for peace started early in the United States and, before it was completed, led to much conflict between the major departments of the government. The State Department initiated studies on postwar German policy in 1942, the War Department began to work in 1943, and the Treasury was eventually to play an influential and disturbing role in 1944. The Navy, too, was consulted, but took no such significant part in American planning as did the other departments. Congress was not consulted and did not demand a part in wartime planning for postwar Germany. In the

---

[9] Churchill, *Triumph and Tragedy*, 507-508.

[10] Penrose, *Economic Planning for the Peace*, 225-226; Sherwood, *Roosevelt and Hopkins*, 710-714; Hull, *Memoirs*, II, 1233-1234.

last analysis the President himself was to determine the broad lines of policy.

The implementation of any program which might be drafted for postwar Germany was bound to be the responsibility of the Allied armies, at least during the first months after the surrender of Germany. As a result, the War Department insisted upon participation in American planning for the military occupation of Germany. For this task the War Department was woefully lacking in background. Despite the many occupation operations the Army had performed in its past history, only one even approximated in character and scope the tremendous problems which would be faced after the defeat of Germany. That one experience, occupation of the South during the decade of "Reconstruction" after the American Civil War, was rich in lessons that taught "what not to do." But that experience was little known to the officials who ran the War Department in World War II. Though lacking experience and keeping jealous eyes on other planners who showed more initiative and industry, the War Department was slow to begin its own serious study of the German problem.

The Secretary of War, Henry Stimson, had very definite ideas about the proper treatment of Germany. Before 1914 he had learned from his father "to mistrust the Prussians and admire the French." The First World War had further convinced the rising New York lawyer that the Germans were an intrinsically warlike nation. But Stimson's reason held his emotions in tight rein. As Herbert Hoover's Secretary of State in 1931 he had warmly endorsed the moratorium on German reparations payments; and his experiences in 1931 left him leery of the many reparations proposals which were advanced during World War II. Notwithstanding his early reactions to Germany, therefore, Stimson was one of the most conservative of all the wartime planners who determined Germany's future.

Stimson's moderate views were generally shared by John J. McCloy, the Assistant Secretary of War. State Department officials and others have suggested that the Assistant Secretary had no especially constructive ideas concerning Germany in 1943-1944. While he did not press vigorously for the adoption of moderate concepts, he occasionally vetoed radical ones. In February, 1944,

24

an official of the Office of War Information, James P. Warburg, approached McCloy with a proposal that the army of occupation sharply devalue the German currency as a catalytic measure to promote revolution; the Allies could then form a military ring around Germany while the Germans carried out their own settling of accounts and regenerative beginnings. Such a proposal was based upon the assumption that there was a "good Germany," and was not as harsh as many proposals which were heard in those days. Warburg would not partition Germany, nor would he destroy its economy. But such an internal "catharsis" as he proposed would hardly have led to the creation of a viable, democratic German state, and would almost certainly have led to great evil. McCloy rejected Warburg's plan on the grounds that it would "induce chaos." (Warburg is apparently wrong in his postwar assertion that McCloy *"asked"* him "to express an opinion" about occupation plans). At the secretarial level, it seems clear that the War Department was consistently interested in avoiding a harsh policy for Germany. It also was intent upon having a short period of occupation with a minimum of political responsibilities.[11]

But in spite of the views of its chiefs, the War Department "embodied the most baffling contradictions." These contradictions were not simplified by the creation in the spring of 1943 of the Civil Affairs Division within the War Department. One of the functions of this division was to plan the future occupation of Germany. It was headed by Major General John Hilldring, who began his work on April 17, 1943. The Civil Affairs Division resisted the efforts of the State Department to draft in 1943 a comprehensive and long-term program, insisting that the War Department should not merely implement State Department policy, but should help plan it. Perhaps the chief difference between the

---

[11] Henry L. Stimson and McGeorge Bundy, *On Active Service in Peace and War* (New York, 1947), 83-84, 202-208, 567-568; Warburg, *Germany— Bridge or Battleground*, 266-271; and, also by James P. Warburg, *Germany, Key to Peace* (Cambridge, Mass., 1953), xviii. Little is added to Stimson's memoir comments on the German problem by Richard N. Current, *Secretary Stimson: A Study in Statecraft* (New Brunswick, N.J., 1954). But see also Holborn, *American Military Government*, 8-9. A critical survey of military preparations for administration of occupied Germany may be found in Harold Zink, *The United States and Germany* (Princeton, 1957), 5-18.

State Department and War Department planners arose from what Walter L. Dorn has called the "limited liability" concept of the War Department experts. Contemplating a "brief punitive spasm" of about eight weeks of military government, these men would limit it to "basic but essential tasks" directly related to the war.[12]

There was little appreciation for Germany in the Civil Affairs Division. The key staff officers of the division were energetic and influential men recruited from civilian life. One of the more influential officers was John Boettiger, the President's son-in-law. Another was Colonel David Marcus. The son of a Rumanian emigrant grocer, "Mickey" Marcus had climbed from New York's East Side with the help of a rare combination of intelligence, industry, personality, and luck. After graduating from West Point, he had won a law degree. Marcus and Thomas E. Dewey became friends when both served as young Assistant United States District Attorneys during the early thirties. By 1940 Marcus was Commissioner of Correction in New York City under Mayor Fiorello H. LaGuardia. In 1948 he was to be felled by an Arab bullet, after guiding the new Israeli army into being. In 1943-1945 his task was to help draft plans to occupy the German nation. Jewish outrage, aroused by the barbaric practices of Nazi Germany, undoubtedly intensified the sense of purpose with which Marcus approached his work in the Civil Affairs Division. By the time Germany was defeated Colonel David Marcus was Chief of the Planning Branch of the Civil Affairs Division in the War Department. He played a little-known but important part in drafting the terms of surrender and plans for military government for Germany.[13]

---

[12] Penrose, *Economic Planning for the Peace*, 236, 270-271; Dorn, "The Debate over American Occupation Policy," *loc. cit.*, 487. Dorn's article is based in part upon research in unpublished sources, including documents of the Civil Affairs Division of the War Department.

[13] The fullest statement about the career of David Marcus which the author of this chapter has found, and one which mixes errors of exaggeration with general factual accuracy, is that by Lowell M. Limpus, "This Was Mickey Marcus," *Saturday Evening Post*, CCXXI (Dec. 4, 1948), 28-29, 179-181. Of interest but of slight scholarly value is Judith Halperin, Phyllis Kreinik, and Rita Schweitzer, *Mickey Marcus: The Story of Colonel David Marcus* (New York, 1949). See also the short accounts in the New York *Times*, June 12, 1948; *Time*, LI (June 21, 1948), 32; and *Newsweek*, XXXI (June 21, 1948), 66.

The State Department began its consideration of the future peace more than two years before the United States officially entered the war. Secretary of State Cordell Hull on September 16, 1939, appointed Dr. Leo Pasvolsky, a distinguished social scientist of the Brookings Institution, as his special assistant in charge of problems of peace. Serious study of plans for postwar Germany were begun early in 1942 and were reviewed periodically thereafter. The staff specialists who studied German matters were Professor Philip E. Mosely of Columbia University and Professor David Harris of Stanford University. Between these moderate-minded experts and their policymaking chief, Under-Secretary of State Sumner Welles, a wide rift developed. In the summer of 1942 Welles was in general charge of the discussions of peace plans and, as his book of 1944 revealed, was a convinced advocate of the partition of Germany. In the words of one of his experts, he "pushed very hard and there was no one at the proper level to stand up against him." [14]

Generally, Cordell Hull agreed with the conclusions of the experts, but the Secretary of State was not as closely involved in these planning activities as was Welles. Furthermore, Welles and Franklin D. Roosevelt were personal friends of long standing, and Welles occasionally used this friendship to achieve presidential approval of policies to which Hull was either lukewarm or even opposed. The growing friction between Hull and Welles was climaxed early in August, 1943, when Roosevelt, unable to part with Hull because of political considerations, asked the Under-Secretary of State to resign. It is important to note that Welles broke off all relations with the State Department immediately, though his resignation was announced officially only on September 25, 1943. He was replaced as Under-Secretary by Edward R. Stettinius, Jr.[15]

The departure of Welles in August was reflected immediately

---

[14] State Department, *Postwar Foreign Policy Preparation*, 19, 104, 107, 135-139, and 154-155; Philip E. Mosely, "Dismemberment of Germany: The Allied Negotiations from Yalta to Potsdam," *Foreign Affairs*, XXVIII (April, 1950), 488-489; Philip E. Mosely, "The Occupation of Germany: New Light on How the Zones Were Drawn," *Foreign Affairs*, XXVIII (July, 1950), 584n.

[15] Hull, *Memoirs*, II, 1227-1230, 1256.

in State Department planning for Germany. A tentative report on Germany was finished on August 17, 1943, in time for Hull to take it with him to the Quebec Conference between Roosevelt and Churchill in that month. A scholarly memorandum, this report of August 17 weighed the pros and cons of various proposals to partition Germany. While objective in tone, the memorandum tactfully recommended against partition by suggesting that, if left alone "to form a moderate-liberal regime," the Germans might voluntarily "restore some mild form of federal state." At Quebec, Hull learned from Eden that the Foreign Secretary and the majority of the British Cabinet were opposed to forced dismemberment of Germany. After Hull's return to Washington, State Department experts, free to express their own views more forcefully than before, carefully reconsidered and restated their position on partition and other German problems. They performed their work with a sense of urgency, knowing that Cordell Hull would soon meet with Anthony Eden and Vyacheslav M. Molotov in Moscow. With Welles out of the way, the experts now boldly stated their views in a memorandum of September 23 on "The Political Reorganization of Germany." [16]

In this memorandum the experts opposed "the enforced breakup of Germany," arguing that such a partition would "constitute a grave danger to future world order." They favored decentralization within a united Germany, based upon "the living tradition of federalism." And they emphasized the importance of developing in postwar Germany a democratic government which would be able to stand against the attacks of new Pan-German or Nazi movements. Three conditions were needed in order to promote a democratic experiment in postwar Germany, concluded the State Department experts: (1) The United States should foster a "tolerable standard of living" by allowing "the economic recovery of Germany." (2) The peace treaty should leave a "minimum of bitterness." Finally (3)—a precondition stated in words which may yet prove to have been prophetic—the State Department planners called for "harmony of policy between the British and American Governments on the one hand and the Soviet Government on the

---

[16] State Department, *Postwar Foreign Policy Preparation*, 554-557, and 558-560; Hull, *Memoirs*, II, 1233-1234.

other." In case of friction, they warned, Germany would be in a position "to hold the balance of power with disastrous results." This memorandum warned that unwise policies might lead to the establishment of "Russian hegemony in Germany." Secretary of State Hull carried a modified version of this statement, containing its essential points, to Moscow in October. There he distributed it to his British and Russian colleagues (minus the references to Russian hegemony, one may assume). He offered it not as a concrete proposal but "to show the trend of our thinking." [17] Unfortunately, events would show that the State Department ideas were still subject to frustration from above. Though Welles was gone, his powerful friend, the President, remained on the job.

President Roosevelt frequently by-passed the Department of State during World War II. There were many reasons for this. He thought the departmental organization was antiquated, he disliked its devotion to formality and legalism, and he considered its "security" untrustworthy; his most confidential messages for Stalin and Churchill were usually sent by the Navy in its code, not through the Department of State. Furthermore, though Roosevelt had fears as well as hopes about the Soviet Union, he was prepared to go to greater lengths to cultivate good relations with the U.S.S.R. than were some State Department officials.

The President's personality must be considered in this connection. We are told that even as a child the future President had an instinctive "desire to please and an inborn intuition of what means could attain that end." Flattery was one of his common techniques. The Roosevelt "charm" had even been tried out on Adolf Hitler at the beginning of the Nazi dictatorship; Hjalmar Schacht, Hitler's financial wizard, sent the following report to Berlin on May 6, 1933, during an official visit to Washington: "Both at table and afterward, the President gave indication of undoubted sympathy for the person of the Reich Chancellor, and stated that he hoped to see him some time soon." [18] The President's flattery of Hitler quickly turned into an animosity that grew with the passing years,

---

[17] State Department, *Postwar Foreign Policy Preparation*, 194-198; Hull, *Memoirs*, II, 1284-1285.

[18] United States Department of State, *Documents on German Foreign Policy, 1918-1945*, Series C, I (Washington, 1957), 393.

but the inclination toward "personal diplomacy" remained a part of his being. The 1933 comments must be remembered when one reads F.D.R.'s warm approaches to Stalin in World War II. Both were shaped by Roosevelt's personality rather than by sympathy with either Hitler's or Stalin's politics.

In 1943 the President seemed convinced that he could "handle Stalin" in dealings man to man. In any case, such an approach was imperative whenever Roosevelt wished to get action in Russia: the President quickly learned that the Soviet dictator was the only man in the U.S.S.R. who would make quick decisions on important matters, and only the President—or his personal agents—could deal with Stalin effectively. This encouraged Roosevelt to use Harry Hopkins for many diplomatic tasks which normally would have been the lot of the Secretary of State or, in other countries, of the ambassador. All this added up to "personal diplomacy," and caused State Department officials to believe they were being left out of the one function of government which was uniquely theirs, the formulation of foreign policy.

In point of fact the State Department *was* much too often left out of much too much. This tendency to ignore the State Department would culminate in the autumn of 1944 in the drafting of a program for postwar Germany by the Secretary of the Treasury, and temporary acceptance of parts of this program, the "Morgenthau Plan," by the President. This deplorable episode can only be understood against this background of the President's relationship with the Department of State, and his notorious tendency "to adopt suggestions which fitted his own pattern of thought." State Department ideas about Germany fitted awkwardly at best into the President's thought patterns on that subject.[19]

The President by 1943 had given a great deal of consideration to the problems of Germany over a long period of time. As a young boy Franklin Roosevelt lived in Europe a few months out of

---

[19] Sherwood, *Roosevelt and Hopkins,* 661-662, 699, 708-709, 748, 755-757; Stettinius, *Roosevelt and the Russians,* 25; Frank Freidel, *Franklin D. Roosevelt: The Apprenticeship* (Boston, 1952), 23; Churchill. *Hinge of Fate,* 201; statement by W. Averell Harriman in U.S. Senate, 82nd Cong., 1st Sess., *Military Situation in the Far East: Hearings before the Committee on Armed Services and the Committee on Foreign Relations,* Part V, Appendix (Washington, 1951), 3328-3342; Rudolph A. Winnacker, "Yalta—Another Munich?," *Virginia Quarterly Review,* XXIV (1948), 522.

almost every year. At six he was taught to write in German script. When he was nine the young Roosevelt attended a public school in Germany (Baden), the only *public* school in any country in which he was ever enrolled. At fourteen he took a bicycle tour through southwestern Germany with a German tutor, thereby acquiring a fluent speaking knowledge of the language. With his mother and father he drank the heady wine of Wagnerian operas at Bayreuth. Later, at Harvard, he briefly studied German history. All in all, the United States has never had a President who knew more about the German people than did F.D.R. in World War II. Powerful emotions were mixed with this knowledge. He had "formed an early distaste for German arrogance and provincialism," the President told General Lucius D. Clay in March, 1945. During World War I he came to feel that Germany was "a monstrous nation." [20]

By 1941 much had happened to reinforce Roosevelt's hostility toward Germany, and little to change it. The President was deeply concerned about the problem of Germany after the war, talking about it frequently with his wife, with his daughter, with Harry Hopkins, with Henry Morgenthau, Jr., and with his personal Chief of Staff, Admiral William D. Leahy, and others. Roosevelt was anxious as few other men that "it should be made impossible for Germany to start a war" in the future. The President saw little hope in the regenerative powers of the German people. He never took seriously the possibility of an uprising against Hitler, at least not one which would put men in power with whom he would have wished to make peace. Lacking faith in "the other Germany," Roosevelt concluded that harsh restrictions upon Germany would provide the only safe means to prevent German aggression in the future. "Germany understands only one kind of language," he informed Hull on one occasion. But in 1943 he did not think in terms of using American troops to speak the language of power to postwar Germans. The United States would use its force to police Asia (with China) and the Americas, the President remarked

---

[20] Freidel, *Franklin D. Roosevelt: The Apprenticeship*, 22, 30-34, 61n, 332-335; Lucius D. Clay, *Decision in Germany* (Garden City, 1950), 5. See also William D. Hassett, *Off the Record with F. D. R., 1942-1945* (New Brunswick, N.J., 1958), 9, 199-200.

on April 5, 1943. He would leave "the peace of Europe to Great Britain and Russia." [21]

Roosevelt concluded with Welles that Prussia was the chief source of the German problem; "the Prussians cannot be trusted," he told Anthony Eden in March, 1943. The President formed the conviction that German aggression could be prevented only if Germany were partitioned into several states, with Prussia segregated from the rest. The President believed that other measures also would be required. These would include complete and long-term disarmament, enforced by the victors by "police activity"; the denial of aviation construction and even of commercial airlines to Germany; and the annexation of East Prussia by Poland. All these views the President had informally conveyed to the Russians and the British by the spring of 1943. He also believed by October, 1943, that Germany should be forced to pay reparations in labor and equipment, and that the Kiel Canal should be internationalized. But in October, 1943, partition remained his pet scheme for the solution of the German problem.[22]

The President had the good sense to realize, however, that all his ideas about Germany were highly personal ones, and he was hesitant to base definitive policy upon what might be his subjective whimsy. On the other hand, he could not bring himself to accept the moderate ideas of the State Department. Roosevelt thus found himself in a dilemma in which he could only postpone final decisions on any policy toward Germany. His dilemma was most fully revealed in a conference of October 5, 1943. Then, in preparation for his forthcoming meeting with Eden and Molotov, Cordell Hull and his top associates met with the President to review problems which might arise at Moscow. The President stated "categorically" that he was in favor of the partition of Germany into three or more sovereign states. These states would be held together

21 Eleanor Roosevelt, *This I Remember* (New York, 1949), 330-331; Henry Morgenthau, Jr., "Postwar Treatment of Germany," *Annals of the American Academy of Political and Social Science*, CCXLVI (1945), 125; Leahy, *I Was There*, 242; Sherwood, *Roosevelt and Hopkins*, 791; Hull, *Memoirs*, II, 1576; Hassett, *Off the Record with F. D. R.*, 166.

22 Sherwood, *Roosevelt and Hopkins*, 572-573, 708-716; Hull, *Memoirs*, II, 1265-1266; Eduard Benes, *Memoirs of Dr. Eduard Benes, from Munich to New War and New Victory*, Godfrey Lias, trans. (Boston, 1954), 187.

only in *a customs union*. (It is very important to note that Roosevelt even at this point envisaged a healthy economy, not a wrecked one, in the politically restricted Germany of the future.) Hull and his colleagues raised objections against partition.

What followed fully showed the indecisive state of the President's thinking about Germany. Often he recalled his own experiences in Germany, and he did so on this occasion. Hull's account of the President's comments follows:

> He said he had traveled and studied in Germany, could speak German, and thought he knew Germany better than we did. He insisted that partition was the solution. The conversation shifted to other topics, but after a considerable time the President suddenly brought it back to Germany by saying that, after all, it was many years ago that he had become acquainted with Germany and perhaps he didn't know so much about her as he thought. He then said that the whole transitional period would have to be one of trial and error. . . .[23]

"Trial and error"—exactly what the expert planners of both a "hard" peace and a "soft" peace wished to avoid. The President was mentally hung in a quandary between the opposing schools of thought, a position in which many honest and able men have found themselves when confronted by the problem of Germany in the twentieth century. The consequences of Roosevelt's indecision were considerable. Turning first this way and then that, the President gave his subordinates no clear cut policy, and simultaneously failed to accept those proposals which they offered. The fluctuation which Hull noted in October, 1943, was to trouble Morgenthau a year later, and the Russians were to meet it at Yalta. The President's personal inclination was toward a hard peace. But if he ever made hard and fast decisions in these matters he kept them from Stalin up to his death in April, 1945. Until then he played in German matters a role that he knew well, that of an artful dodger. The game undoubtedly annoyed the Russians at times as much as it constantly bothered the American experts.

---

[23] Hull, *Memoirs*, II, 1265-1266; the quotation is by permission of The Macmillan Company, publishers of Hull's *Memoirs*. Leahy, *I Was There*, 187.

EARLY RUSSIAN PROPOSALS

Soviet planning for postwar Germany probably involved less conflict between reason and war passion than did early American planning. In Russia the passion was much greater because of the long record of struggle between Slav and Teuton, and the reason was made colder by the geographical proximity of "the German problem" to the U.S.S.R. The men who ruled the U.S.S.R. had twice faced German invasions in their lifetimes. During the 1920's and again between 1939 and 1941 the Soviet leaders had tried cooperation and even appeasement of Germany; they were reaping the results in World War II, and the lesson was not lost upon them. The Russians faced many problems in planning their part in the postwar world, but the achievement of security against German aggression stood in the forefront of them all. The prospects of achieving or losing this part of the peace must have conditioned Russian planning toward Poland, for example, and toward other issues.

In one basic consideration, Stalin and Roosevelt were in agreement on the problem of Germany. Each in his own way put no faith in the potentialities of "the other Germany." Roosevelt remembered how Wilsonian faith in the German people had been disillusioned. Stalin remembered that the German workingclass, even when strongly socialistic, had nonetheless demonstrated the obedient thought patterns of other Germans. At Teheran and again at Yalta, Stalin was to tell his American and British allies how two hundred German socialists in 1907 had refused to leave a railroad station platform in Leipzig for a scheduled meeting, because there was no official present to punch their tickets. The Soviet leaders remembered how little help Russian radicals got from the German workers in the revolutions of 1905, of March, 1917, and of November, 1917, and how the German workers failed to revolt against the imperialistic Treaty of Brest-Litovsk in 1918. Eduard Benes in January, 1944, returning from a cordial reception in Moscow, confidently reported to Anthony Eden that the Soviet Union "had no thought . . . of procuring a revolution in Germany . . . . " The German "mentality of discipline and obedience" could not be changed, Stalin had concluded. Stalin's emotional complex

34

toward Germany was, in part, that of a disappointed lover, his hatred all the more intense because of hopes spurned by the object of affections. Both desire and frustration preconditioned Soviet planning for postwar Germany in World War II.[24]

Official Soviet discussion of the German problem proceeded on two levels, however, and one must distinguish between the moderate public statements and the secret conversations held with Russia's allies. Molotov, not Stalin, was first to speak publicly after the German invasion in 1941. The careful distinction he made between the German people and their rulers set a pattern which was maintained for more than two years by Soviet public statements. The war had been forced upon Russia by Germany's "bloodthirsty fascist rulers," not by the German "workers, peasants, and intellectuals," Molotov insisted. Stalin seconded this on July 3, 1941, insisting that Russia would fight to liberate not only her own people but the people of Germany, "enslaved by the Hitlerite regime." On February 23, 1942, Stalin publicly denied reports that the aim of the Red Army was to exterminate the German people and the German state. "Hitlers come and go," said Stalin; "the German people, the German state, remain." On November 6, 1942, making a strong bid for the surrender of German armies around Stalingrad, Stalin even proclaimed that the destruction of German militarism was not one of his objectives. To destroy all organized military power in Germany was not only impossible but

---

[24] Sherwood, *Roosevelt and Hopkins,* 782; Standley and Ageton, *Admiral Ambassador to Russia,* 158; Churchill, *Triumph and Tragedy,* 393; Benes, *Memoirs,* 266; Edward J. Rozek, *Allied Wartime Diplomacy: A Pattern in Poland* (New York, 1958), 172. See also: Henry J. Tobias and John L. Snell, "A Soviet Interpretation of the SPD, 1895-1933," *Journal of Central European Affairs,* XIII (1953), 61-66; the article by Snell, "The Russian Revolution and the German Social Democratic Party in 1917," *American Slavic and East European Review,* XV (1956), 339-350; Richard W. Reichard, "The German Working Class and the Russian Revolution of 1905," *Journal of Central European Affairs,* XIII (1953), 136-153; Helm Speidel, "Reichswehr und Rote Armee," *Vierteljahrshefte für Zeitgeschichte,* I (1953), 9-45; and the following volumes: Lionel Kochan, *Russia and the Weimar Republic* (Cambridge, 1954); Gustav Hilger and Alfred G. Meyer, *The Incompatible Allies: A Memoir History of German-Soviet Relations, 1918-1941* (New York, 1953); Edward Hallett Carr, *German-Soviet Relations between the Two World Wars, 1919-1939* (Baltimore, 1951); and Gordon A. Craig and Felix Gilbert eds., *The Diplomats, 1919-1939* (Princeton, 1953), especially 234-281, 344-377, 487-511, and 555-569.

unsuitable *(unzweckmässig)*, he said.[25]

A few days after Stalin sounded this overture to the German Army, the German Resistance leader, Carl Goerdeler, met in a Smolensk forest with a German Field-Marshal, and thought for a time that he had persuaded the general to join the anti-Hitler forces. Two months later an entire German army, with its Field-Marshal (Friedrich Paulus) and twenty-two generals, surrendered at Stalingrad, despite Hitler's specific orders that it should not give up. Events soon proved that propaganda had nothing to do with the surrender at Stalingrad; it was dictated by desperation, not hope. But for the time being it appeared that propaganda might achieve useful results, and it was intensified and given a new twist in 1943. The Russians were not restrained by the Casablanca formula of "unconditional surrender."

In mid-July, 1943, the U.S.S.R. brought together an improbable assembly of German Communist emigrants to Russia, army deserters, and captured German army officers in the so-called "National Committee for Free Germany." On July 19 the first issue of a propaganda newspaper, entitled *Freies Deutschland (Free Germany)*, was issued by this committee and on July 20 it began making propaganda broadcasts over a special radio station which the Soviet Union set aside for its use. When this Soviet-rigged and Communist-run "National Committee" failed to get impressive results, the Russians in September organized an affiliated organization, which they hoped would make more convincing propaganda. This was called the League of German Officers. German Communists in Russia—Wilhelm Pieck, Walter Ulbricht, Erich Weinert, and their supporters—made the propaganda these groups produced, but this propaganda was supervised and ultimately controlled by Soviet authorities. Both organizations urged their fellow Germans to overthrow the Hitler regime and seek peace.

Their appeals could give only vague indications of the kind of peace the Germans might hope to get through such action. Some of the German Communists thought that German unity might be

---

[25] Deutscher, *Stalin*, 487; Wolfgang Steinitz ed., *Stalin Spricht: Die Kriegsreden vom 3. Juli 1941 bis zum 9. Mai 1945* (Stockholm, 1945), 15-16, 44-45, and 70. An English language edition is also available: Joseph Stalin, *The Great Patriotic War of the Soviet Union* (New York, 1945).

preserved if the German people could be persuaded to turn against the Hitler regime and sue for peace. The propaganda caused some desertions from the German Army, but achieved no visible results in Germany. Thus, by November 7, 1943, the nature of Stalin's public pronouncements on Germany changed. Then and subsequently he dropped the distinction between the German people and the Nazi Government. He spoke of "the *German* criminals," not merely "the *Hitlerite* criminals"; he asserted that the Soviet people would not "forgive the *German* barbarians *(Urmenschen)*" for their crimes on Russian soil; and he talked increasingly of the hour of reckoning "in which the *Germans* must be made accountable for their infamous acts in our country." (Author's italics.)[26]

If Stalin's public statements on Germany seemed to change, it may be assumed that his basic intentions remained constant. In 1934 he had told the Seventeenth Congress of the Communist Party in the Soviet Union: "Our orientation in the past and our orientation at the present time is towards the U.S.S.R., and towards the U.S.S.R. alone."[27] This was the spirit in which the Soviet leaders approached planning for postwar Germany in World War II. That spirit, and especially Stalin's anxiety about Germany is revealed by the recently published record of his talk with the leader of free Poland, Stanislaw Mikolajczyk, in Moscow on August 9, 1944. Stalin's words deserve full quotation:

> The Germans will rise again. They are a strong nation. From Bismarck's triumph in 1871, they needed forty years to undertake new aggression. After its failure twenty or twenty-two years of regeneration were sufficient to repeat that once more—this time almost successfully. Now, who knows if after twenty or twenty-five years they will not be once more ready to fight. Yes, Germany is a strong country even though Hitler is weakening it. But the German economic and military staff will survive Hitler. It is our conviction that the danger from Germany may repeat itself. For this reason, the present discussions which are going on

---

[26] Wheeler-Bennett, *Nemesis of Power*, 530, 614-615, 716-718; Andreas F. Lowenfeld, "The Free Germany Committee—an Historical Study," *The Review of Politics*, XIV (1952), 346-366; Steinitz ed., *Stalin Spricht*, 111, 121, 126; Einsiedel, *I Joined the Russians*, 60-204; Leonhard, *Child of the Revolution*, 238-280 *passim*. Both Einsiedel and Leonhard were participants in the "Free Germany" group.

[27] Joseph Stalin, *Selected Writings* (New York, 1942), 311.

in Washington about collective security are so urgent. I am for all possible and impossible repression of Germany.[28]

Stalin might have added that he had been in this mood since 1941. As early as September 28, 1941, Stalin told W. Averell Harriman and Lord Beaverbrook that Germany must be made to "pay for the damage" as part of any postwar settlement. Reparations remained high on the list of Soviet war aims thereafter, and one on which basic differences arose between Russia and the West. In December, 1941, the Soviet Ambassador in London, Ivan M. Maisky, frankly informed Anthony Eden and John Gilbert Winant, United States Ambassador to Great Britain, that his government feared the West would not take harsh enough measures against Germany to render her harmless after the war. Later that month Stalin himself gave Eden in Moscow the first statement of purpose concerning Germany which any of the Big Three made. Stalin stated his aims, and Eden conveyed them to Hull in Washington, as follows: Austria must be made independent of Germany proper; East Prussia must be transferred to Poland; the Rhineland should be detached and made into an independent state or a protectorate; and Bavaria possibly should become an independent state. In addition, Germany should pay reparations in kind, especially in machine tools. Maisky in London and Maxim Litvinov in Washington restated these aims in March, 1943, and they remained the basic objectives of the U.S.S.R. concerning Germany, though they were slightly modified, clarified or supplemented from time to time.

Some war aims which one might have expected to find were conspicuously absent from Soviet statements, both public and private. There was no demand, even in Soviet propaganda, that the capitalistic system be overthrown in Germany. Instead, Stalin on November 6, 1941, proclaimed the remarkable war slogan: "No interference in the domestic affairs of other people!" Furthermore, if Stalin had any imperialistic desire to control Germany in 1943 it played no part in his war strategy. There is much pleasant irony in the fact that Stalin insistently and peremptorily demanded that the British and Americans create a second front in Western Europe, and that critics of American policy have blamed wartime leaders

---

[28] Quoted in context by Rozek, *Allied Wartime Diplomacy,* 247; quoted by permission of the publisher, John Wiley and Sons., Inc.

for not invading the Balkans; for the front in the West inevitably was to place the Ruhr and Scandinavia under the influence of the West. The U.S.S.R. was left bottled up in the Baltic and with control over a smaller and less valuable part of Germany than that which the West occupied at the end of the war. This does not prove that Stalin's foresight was unusually faulty or that he was unimperialistic. It merely shows that Stalin, like the Western leaders, was in 1943-1944 primarily intent upon winning the war and that he was limited in his vision. Victory and postwar security were still his main objectives.[29]

It remained to be seen how far the Western Powers were willing to cooperate with their colleague in the Kremlin in the conduct of such a foreign policy. There was no better place to find out than Moscow. Eden and Hull went there in October, 1943, for the first high-level conference of the three Great Power Allies during the war.

---

[29] Hull, *Memoirs*, II, 1165-1167; Deutscher, *Stalin*, 474, 502; Sherwood, *Roosevelt and Hopkins*, 388; Steinitz ed., *Stalin Spricht*, 33.

Chapter III

BIG THREE TALKS BEGIN

TENSION between Stalin and the Western Allies had run high in 1942-1943, chiefly because the West failed to strike across the Channel in strength at Hitler's Reich. Throughout 1943 Soviet troops had fought alone against the brunt of the power of the *Wehrmacht*. Stalin's scorn for British and American military operations in Italy was turned into political suspicion in August, 1943, after Mussolini was overthrown and a new Italian government prepared to surrender to the Western Powers. Would they also do business with Germans? A noted Soviet journalist asked the American Ambassador in Moscow this question in high disdain. In the first half of September, at the height of Soviet anger at Britain and the United States—always kept decorously secret to preserve public unity behind the war effort—the Russians even entered into secret armistice discussions with Hitlerian agents at Stockholm.

Since Moscow quickly informed the Western Allies of these talks, it must be assumed that it was only using them to gain concessions from its allies. But no chances could be taken with a separate peace; London and Washington remembered the Brest-Litovsk treaties of 1918 as well as the Nazi-Soviet Pact of 1939. Thus, Western leaders went out of their way to conciliate Stalin in the fall of 1943. The United States was especially anxious to do so because it wanted Stalin's help in the creation of an international organization to preserve the peace—the future United Nations. And since the Soviet leader had just acquiesced in the British determination to preserve the Italian monarchy ("almost by return mail," Eden told Stanislaw Mikolajczyk), London was more than usually ready in October, 1943, to soothe the Soviets with concessions. The major quid pro quo for the Russians was to be found in the eastern territories of pre-1939 Poland, which the Red Army was approaching in October, 1943. The Big Three discussions of Germany's future at Moscow and Teheran in the fall of 1943 must be viewed against this background.

Above all, it must be remembered that the West still felt a great need for Soviet cooperation against Germany. In October, 1943, British diplomats in Moscow would be cheered by even a hint from Stalin that the Red Army might be sent on into Germany when Soviet territory was liberated from the dreaded *Wehrmacht*. They feared that a war-weary Red Army might *not* "cross the German frontier" at all, and scarcely thought as yet of limiting its westward advance into Germany. Anxious to retain the Soviet ally, British and American statesmen could not risk challenging Soviet aims for postwar Germany even if they had wished to do so.[1]

THE FOREIGN MINISTERS IN MOSCOW

Three-way talks between Eden, Molotov, and Hull—deputies of the "Big Three"—were held in Moscow, October 18-30, 1943. Behind a facade of amiability, disagreement lurked in the background. But it entered the pourparlers of the foreign ministers only on cat paws, and the ministers reached some important informal decisions concerning Germany's future.

The meetings began auspiciously. Hull privately presented a State Department memorandum of September to Molotov before airing it in the formal three-way conversations, explaining to Molotov that it was not a formal proposal but merely a basis for discussion. As modified, this memorandum suggested that the question of partition of Germany needed further study, but that in any case decentralization and the lessening of Prussian influence

---

[1] See Ministry of Foreign Affairs of the U.S.S.R., *Correspondence . . . Chairman of the Council of Ministers of the U.S.S.R. . . . 1941-1945*, I, 89-177; II, 50-108, especially 84; Feis, *Churchill, Roosevelt, Stalin*, 62-217; Rozek, *Allied Wartime Diplomacy*, 142-146; Peter Kleist, *Zwischen Hitler und Stalin, 1939-1945: Aufzeichnungen* (Bonn, 1950), 265-278; Leonhard, *Child of the Revolution*, 256-258; Norman Kogan, *Italy and the Allies* (Cambridge, Mass., 1956), 18-58. Stalin quickly adjusted to the fait accompli in Italy. On March 13, 1944, Italy's royal government announced the renewal of full diplomatic relations with the Soviet Union. By the end of March the Italian Communist Party was endorsing the monarchy. See also William Strang, *Home and Abroad* (London, 1956), 200.

in Germany was desirable. Molotov took the American memorandum to Stalin. Next day he reported to Hull that his chief was "enthusiastic" about it. "It expresses Russia's thoughts about Germany exactly as if we had expressed them," Molotov informed Hull. "Stalin would like to make this a Russian suggestion."

When this memorandum was discussed in the formal conversation, harmony began to break slightly. General agreement prevailed on many of its points, such as unconditional surrender, occupation of Germany by forces of the three Great Powers, the creation of an Inter-Allied Control Commission, total disarmament of Germany, and the dissolution of the Nazi Party. Moderate disagreement arose, however, when Molotov stated that the Russians regarded the American paper as a *minimum* proposal. Hull tactfully indicated that the United States was not prepared to agree—at least not at this point—to the dismemberment of Germany. At first, he said, there had been general agreement in his government that dismemberment should be required. But mature consideration had revealed arguments both for and against dismemberment. There was, therefore, an increasing tendency in Washington "to keep an open mind on this point."

Eden now proved that the American leaders were not alone in their much publicized tendency to align themselves with the Russians in Big Three conferences. The British also resorted to this diplomatic tactic, designed to assure the Soviet leaders that they were not confronted by an anti-Russian Anglo-American bloc. At Quebec in August, Eden had indicated that he opposed partition. But Eden at Moscow flatly asserted that his government did not wish to see a united Germany survive the war. It was uncertain whether dismemberment should be forced, said Eden, in one of those reservations which may translate "yes" into "no" in diplomacy. But he added that any separatist tendencies inside Germany should be encouraged. The Moscow Conference was able to unite definitely upon only one aspect of the dismemberment problem: It was formally settled that Austria should be separated from the Reich and treated as a liberated area. But the conference also reached agreement upon another proposal which had been made many times during the war without contradiction: East Prussia should be severed from the rest of Germany. It was generally understood that this area would become part of a new Poland.

When the question of reparations was discussed, differences reappeared. Hull proposed that reparations be paid to compensate for the losses of non-military property inflicted by the Germans. This basis of payment would, of course, assure the U.S.S.R. of a major share of any reparations collected from Germany. But Hull also proposed that reparations should be levied against Germany only to the extent that they were consistent with the strengthening of "the postwar world economic and political order," a qualification which would seriously limit the exactions against the German economy. As if to anticipate the demands which were to be raised subsequently by Morgenthau and later by the Russians, Hull insisted that reparations demands should not be used "as a major element of control over Germany's military power." In plain words, they should not be used to de-industrialize Germany. Furthermore, said Hull, payments should be limited to a brief period immediately after the end of the war. Exactly how Eden and Molotov reacted to this statement of the American position has not yet been made known. It may, perhaps, be surmised that Eden fully agreed and that Molotov demurred and put forward a claim to use of German labor. In any case the discussion was very brief and tentative, and there was no agreement, except that reparations payments should be made in goods and services, not in money. Services could only mean enforced labor.

A larger degree of unity was achieved on the future treatment of Nazi leaders and members of the German army who had committed war crimes. Eden argued that legal formalities must be observed; but now it was Hull's turn to agree with the Russians. If he could have his way, the wry old Tennessean said, he would bring the arch offenders before a drumhead court-martial and hang them at sunrise. "As this was translated, Molotov and his entire delegation broke into loud exclamations of approval," Hull later related. But the statement on war criminals that was adopted at Moscow and quickly proclaimed by Roosevelt, Churchill, and Stalin was somewhat less primitive than Hull's comment. It declared that after the war those Germans who were responsible for atrocities would be "sent back to the countries in which their abominable deeds were done in order that they may be judged and punished according to the laws of the liberated countries." Speaking of the German leaders, the declaration added that major criminals, "whose offenses have no particular geographical localisation," would be punished "by joint decision of the Governments of the Allies." Here in incubation, was the idea of the Nuremberg trials of 1945-1946.

It was obvious at Moscow that the formulation of Allied policy toward Germany required further inter-Allied discussion and, indeed, discussion on both higher and lower levels than that of the foreign ministers. On the one hand, numerous technical problems on which there was broad policy agreement needed to be worked out; this task must be carried out by officials subordinate to the foreign secretaries. On the other hand, broad policy decisions could be definitively made only by Roosevelt, Churchill, and Stalin. Thus, planning for Germany would proceed henceforth on three levels: at the top, by the Big Three; at a secondary level, by their foreign ministers; at the "tertiary" level, by subordinates of both. The foreign ministers decided at Moscow to create a special three-power organization, to be called the European Advisory Commission, for work on the tertiary level. This commission would meet in London. Questions could be referred to this body upon the unanimous consent of the three governments. Specifically, the European Advisory Commission was assigned two tasks: (1) it should draft the terms of surrender which should be imposed upon Germany; and (2) it would suggest "machinery required to ensure the fulfillment of those terms." The foreign ministers decided to forward to the European Advisory Commission as a basis for discussion the memorandum which Hull had presented at Moscow.[2]

Clearly, however, basic decisions on these matters could be made only by the chiefs of the three Great Powers. The task of

---

[2] Mosely, "Dismemberment of Germany, " loc. cit., 489; Mosely, "The Occupation of Germany," loc. cit., 582n; Mosely to Snell, Sept. 21, 1955; Hull, Memoirs, II, 1284-1305. The Moscow Declarations of November 1, 1943, are available in Holborn, American Military Government, 132-135, and the declaration on atrocities and war criminals also appears in Department of State, The Axis in Defeat, 3-4. See also Andrew Rothstein, trans., Soviet Foreign Policy during the Patriotic War: Documents and Materials, 2 vols. (London, 1946?), I, 237-245. For a general survey of the Moscow Conference, see Feis, Churchill, Roosevelt, Stalin, 206-234.

clarifying differences of opinion had been performed well by the foreign ministers. The way was now open for the Big Three themselves to meet for the first time to discuss the way to victory and the future of the world.

THE TRIUMVIRATE IN TEHERAN

The location of the first Big Three meeting was symbolic. Seventy miles south of the Caspian Sea, the Iranian capital brought back memories of the days when its country, then known as Persia, was a pawn in the game of great power imperialism before the First World War. In 1907 Tsarist Russia and Great Britain had divided Persia into three zones, a northern zone in which Russian interests were to be supreme, a southern zone in which British interests were to reign, and a "neutral" zone between the two. One of the purposes of the agreement of 1907 was to exclude Germany from both the northern and the southern zones, thus disrupting the famous *Drang nach Osten* of Kaiser William II's genteel empire. Now, in November, 1943, with their thoughts still on Germany, the representative of a new-Russia-with-old-thoughts and the Prime Minister of an old-Britain-with-old-thoughts met with the representative of a power neither would have thought to consult in 1907. It is interesting to note that the Big Three met, at Stalin's insistence, within the northern zone of 1907. With such niceties diplomacy in the grand manner is staged.

The meetings at Teheran quickly revealed the personality of each of the Big Three leaders to his colleagues. "Churchill employed all the debater's arts, the brilliant locutions and circumlocutions, of which he was master." Stalin sat with impassive impatience and "wielded his bludgeon with relentless indifference to all the dodges and feints of his practiced adversary." "A man hewn out of granite," was Roosevelt's description of Stalin at Teheran. Roosevelt himself was left to play the persuasive role he had played so often in domestic politics, that of moderator and arbitrator. The Western statesmen sought to open the sessions with pleasantries. They were cut off short when Stalin's translator, embarrassed, put into English his chief's curt words: "Now let's get down to business."

As the conference proceeded Stalin remained for the most part "correct, stiff, solemn, not smiling," devoted to the doodles he made on pieces of scratch paper and the infinitely careful work of folding them into wads and placing them in his pockets. Roosevelt and Churchill embodied all the genial graces of urbane families and civilizations; at Teheran they faced a rude perfectionist, "a highly intelligent man who spoke well and was determined to get what he wanted for Russia." Roosevelt subsequently complained to a member of his cabinet that early in the conference there was, in Stalin, "nothing human to get hold of." Churchill was fully convinced of Stalin's primitive ruthlessness when, later, the Russian leader proposed a toast to the shooting of some fifty thousand German officers at the end of the war. The President apparently believed that Stalin was joking, and tried to bring the humor of the comment to Churchill by suggesting that only 49,500 officers be executed. Churchill, refusing to see humor in such grim jests, insisted that "mass murder" was not consistent with "our British sense of justice." When the President's emotionally pro-Russian son, Elliott, solemnly agreed with Stalin, the irate Prime Minister left the table, returning only when Molotov and Stalin assured him that the proposal was not meant seriously. Small wonder that during the night Roosevelt suffered from acute indigestion. There were many strained moments at Teheran, as the dissimilar partners in the strange alliance "felt each other out."

Much of Stalin's show of petulance at first was deliberately staged to demonstrate his displeasure because there had been no second front against Hitler's West Wall. As specific issues were presented, he proved somewhat more agreeable, though never wavering from his rigid recourse to the "rights" of the Soviet Union. When the question of the occupation of Germany arose, Stalin indicated that he thought France should have no zone of occupation. He distrusted the French because of their quick collapse in 1940, forgetting that he, far from fighting, was then appeasing Hitler. France was not to be trusted with "any strategic positions outside her own borders in the postwar period," he said. There seems to have been no disagreement about the matter of zones, which the American Chiefs of Staff had studied on the way to Teheran. It was agreed "in principle" that Germany should be divided into three zones for occupation purposes, plus a combined inter-Allied zone in Berlin from which common occupation policies would be administered.

Stalin's concern for Russia was further revealed when he talked about Germany's postwar eastern frontier. Churchill himself proposed, in a gesture that went well beyond the agreement at Moscow, that all German territory east of the Oder River, including much of Silesia, should be annexed to Poland. But Stalin now indicated that not all of East Prussia was to be absorbed by Poland; he himself laid claim to the strategic and ancient German port city of Königsberg, where the first Prussian king had crowned himself and his consort in 1701. The Russian ruler then traced a proposed frontier which, he said, would leave Russia "on the neck of Germany." What he did not point out, because it was plain to see, was that the proposed annexation would also leave the Soviet colossus astride the shoulders of Poland. Churchill's efforts to find out what other territories Russia might want at the end of the war met only the enigmatic answer: "There is no need to speak at the present time about any Soviet desires—but when the time comes, we will speak."

No decision on Russia's claim to Königsberg was reached at Teheran. Instead, Churchill tried to calm Stalin's fear of future German aggression by assuring him, in a private conversation, that Germany would not be able to rise again after the war. Nothing could have whetted Stalin's sense of insecurity—and his appetite for power—more than this revelation of Western complacency, this suggestion that the West might be too lenient toward Germany. On the contrary, said Stalin, Germany would recover in fifteen to twenty years, unless some special precautions were taken to prevent it. Then, without spelling out his proposal, as Morgenthau would do in 1944, Stalin broached a subject which neither the State Department nor the Foreign Office liked. Germany had shown great skill in secretly converting apparently peaceful industries to war production, he said; it would seem that Germany's manufacturing capacity should be reduced.

Stripped of all verbiage, here was the first high-level demand that Germany be de-industrialized, stated boldly by Stalin within weeks of Hull's indication in Moscow that the United States was opposed to such a measure. Furthermore, Stalin indicated at

Teheran that the U.S.S.R. would insist upon taking large quantities of German machinery to make up for what had been destroyed. Stalin also made it known that Russia would require "at least four million Germans" for labor in Soviet reconstruction after the war. At Teheran, far from accepting the idea of de-industrialization, as he eventually would do when his own friend and Secretary of the Treasury proposed it, Roosevelt countered Stalin's suggestion by pointing out that a world organization, if sufficiently strong and effective, would prevent any secret re-armament in Germany.[3]

It was not wise to challenge Stalin with great vigor at Teheran. The old thought that the Russians might make a separate peace with Germany had been revived in mid-1943. When Admiral William Standley returned to Washington from his ambassadorial duties in Moscow in October, 1943, one of Roosevelt's first questions was: "What do you think, Bill, will he make a separate peace with Hitler?" Standley had reassured the President that self-interest would keep Russia in the war. But if, six weeks later, Roosevelt and Churchill were to suggest German policies which seemed contrary to basic Soviet self-interest, there was some possibility that they might drive Stalin into peace with Hitler.

This consideration, plus the need to calm Stalin's anxiety about future German aggression, in some way short of wrecking the economy of Europe, reinforced Roosevelt's own thoughts on Germany; on the last day of the conference the President himself produced some ideas for the dismemberment of Germany. About three months before the meeting, he said, "he and his advisers" had "had a shot at a plan" as a basis for discussion. He did not explain who his advisers were. This proposal may have been drafted by Welles before he resigned, though its details differed considerably from those which Welles subsequently developed publicly. Some of its features were less like those Welles advanced than Morgenthau's suggestions of September, 1944, but there were

---

[3] Sherwood, *Roosevelt and Hopkins*, 776-798; King, *A Naval Record*, 515-517; John R. Deane, *The Strange Alliance: The Story of Our Efforts at Wartime Co-operation with Russia* (New York, 1947), 40; Hassett, *Off the Record with F. D. R.*, 226; Frances Perkins, *The Roosevelt I Knew* (New York, 1947), 83-85; Churchill, *Closing the Ring*, 359-360, 373; Elliott Roosevelt, *As He Saw It* (New York. 1946), 188-189; Leahy, *I Was There*, 197-198, 205-206; Holborn, *American Military Government*, 22-23; Rozek, *Allied Wartime Diplomacy*, 275.

basic differences between both of these proposals and those which Roosevelt advanced at Teheran. The authorship of the Teheran proposals remains obscure. One thing is certain: the State Department, as it existed in November, 1943, almost certainly neither drafted nor approved the partition plan which Roosevelt presented at Teheran. Probably it was his own invention.

Roosevelt's plan for partition embraced internationalization of some of the fragments of Germany. The Kiel Canal, Hamburg, the Saar, and the Ruhr should all be placed under the control of the future United Nations, the President suggested. Then a reduced Prussia would become one of five states, which would be carved out of the remains of Germany. When Roosevelt introduced his plan, he described those five states as "autonomous." Later, however, when Stalin said that Germany should be "broken up so that she could not reunite," Roosevelt assured him that his proposal offered a means of doing just this. Besides a rump Prussia, the four German states of the future would be composed of: (1) Hanover and the northwest; (2) Saxony "and the Leipzig area"; (3) Hesse-Darmstadt, Hesse-Cassel, and the area south and west of the Rhine; and (4) Bavaria, Baden, and Württemberg. Implicit in Roosevelt's scheme was the assumption that Austria, too, should become an independent state, as had been agreed at Moscow.

To this Churchill expressed the only sane reaction, and he did so in American slang: "The President has said a mouthful!" He, too, believed that Prussia should be severed from the rest of Germany, but he would treat the rest gently while following a harsh policy toward Prussia. "South Germans," said Churchill, "are not going to start another war," and he wished to make it "worth their while to forget Prussia." Churchill then revealed his desire for a stronger German state than either Stalin or Roosevelt wanted. The Prime Minister proposed a plan (which Eden has denied he ever approved) whereby the southern states of Germany should be joined with *Austria and Hungary* to form a "Danubian Confederation." What the British had helped put asunder in 1918—the Hapsburg realm—Churchill now proposed to bring back into modified existence. "All very good, but insufficient," Stalin asserted. He was opposed to any confederation; if there were Germans in it, they would dominate it, and the menace of a powerful Germany would arise again. Stalin refused to recognize any substantial differences between the Prussians and other Germans; all Germans fight "like fierce beasts," he said. Besides, dismemberment must *mean* dismemberment, Stalin insisted; it would be much better "to break up and scatter the German tribes" than to leave them united in any way. Even if partition were carried out completely the Germans would seek to reunite, and must be prevented from doing so by economic measures and even force, if necessary. In any case, said Stalin, neither Austria nor Hungary could be incorporated in any combination with the states of Germany proper.

Stalin was still thinking of Soviet security against German aggression, and possibly also of Soviet power in the Balkans after the war; Churchill was thinking of the great void which the destruction of Germany would leave between "the white snows of Russia and the white cliffs of Dover." At the end, Churchill insisted that all this discussion must be regarded as only a tentative survey of "a vast historical problem." Stalin agreed. And that marked the end of Big Three top-level discussion of the Roosevelt scheme for partition, or any other such specific proposals. But throughout the war the idea of partition "in principle" was kept alive. Even Churchill, in summing up the discussions at Teheran for his colleagues, stated that the Big Three were agreed that Germany should be "decisively broken up into a number of separate states"; that East Prussia and the area east of the Oder should be "alienated forever and the population shifted"; that Prussia itself should be "divided and curtailed"; and, finally, that the "Ruhr and other great centres of coal and steel must be put outside the power of Prussia." [4]

These important principles were not put in the form of a binding agreement. And beneath the surface of cordiality, some of the Americans took careful note of the meaning of Stalin's comments. Within days after the Big Three had parted amidst gener-

---

[4] Churchill, *Closing the Ring*, 400-403; Churchill, *Hinge of Fate*, 689-690; Sherwood, *Roosevelt and Hopkins*, 790-798; Hull, *Memoirs*, II, 1234; Deutscher, *Stalin*, 513; Pogue, *The Supreme Command*, 165; Standley and Ageton, *Admiral Ambassador to Russia*, 498; Feis, *Churchill, Roosevelt, Stalin*, 246-287; Ernst Deuerlein, *Die Einheit Deutschlands: Ihre Erörterungen und Behandlung auf den Kriegs-und Nachkriegkonferenzen 1941-1949* (Frankfurt etc., 1957), 36-44.

ous farewells, one of the American participants stated his conclusion that the Stalin-Molotov program for the future would leave the Soviet Union "the only important military and political force on the continent of Europe. The rest of Europe would be reduced to military and political impotence." [5] Roosevelt himself noted a number of storm signals at Teheran. Some months afterward, he told the leader of the Polish government-in-exile that it was difficult to negotiate with Stalin, that Stalin had impressed him at Teheran as "a realist," although not as "an imperialist or communist." The President added that Stalin was "terribly clever" and "obviously very suspicious." [6] Meanwhile, Stalin's suspicions had been made plainer: just six weeks after the Teheran Conference *Pravda* published a report which suggested that the British were negotiating a separate peace with Germany behind Russia's back. As if to provide a basis for Soviet mistrust, General George S. Patton, Jr. in April, 1944, stated indiscreetly that the United States and Britain would run the postwar world.

It is a tribute to the military menace and the evil of Hitler's Germany that the strange "Triple Alliance" of World War II held together until the Reich lay in ruins. As long as the Reich stood, the luxury of schism was one the Big Three could ill afford.

THE CIVILIAN EXPERTS IN THE POLICY VACUUM

Much was discussed at Teheran, but nothing had been definitively decided, so far as the future of Germany was concerned. The experts remained as uncertain as ever about the basic questions which daily confronted them. Hampered though they were, they none the less continued their planning activities, and even intensified their efforts after Teheran.

In the United States, State Department consideration of the future of Germany in January, 1944, became the function of the high-level Post-War Programs Committee, which operated under the direction of Edward R. Stettinius. This committee held sixty meetings between January and November, 1944. Before June 21, 1944, Philip Mosely attended twenty-eight meetings of this committee, and David Harris attended twenty altogether. Working

---

[5] Quoted anonymously by Feis, *Churchill, Roosevelt, Stalin,* 275.
[6] Rozek, *Allied Wartime Diplomacy,* 221.

under the responsible officials of the Department of State, these men were the experts who studied the German problem; their attendance suggests the effort expended in the State Department in reexamining its basic ideas concerning Germany. Slowly, "a comprehensive series of recommendations on both transitional and long-range United States policy toward Germany" was approved in the spring of 1944. Early in May the Post-War Programs Committee summed up its recommendations in a fifteen-page memorandum, which was approved by Secretary of State Hull in July, 1944. Soon afterward Hull was to inform Morgenthau that no one had ever shown him the record of the Teheran Conference. This may be true, though it is known that Roosevelt discussed the conference at length with Hull. In any case, the State Department memorandum of May-July, 1944, recommended against the partition of Germany, repeating the arguments against it which the State Department memo of September, 1943, had advanced.

On August 4, 1944, the State Department's Executive Committee on Economic Foreign Policy approved a statement on American economic aims concerning Germany. This memorandum called for (1) limited control of the German economy; (2) elimination of Germany's economic domination over Europe; (3) eventual reabsorption of Germany into the world economy; (4) short-term collection of reparations in kind—and in current production rather than in capital equipment; and (5) the maintenance of German production at a level sufficient to maintain a minimum standard of living. The State Department position on Germany thus underwent no important changes between September, 1943, and August, 1944. In its moderation it remained as far from approval by the President as it had been in the previous year; and even farther, in fact: for the State Department was after December, 1943, only one unit in the mechanism of Washington planning for postwar Germany.[7]

It will be recalled that the Moscow Conference of October, 1943, decided to create a special committee, the European Advisory

---

[7] Department of State, *Postwar Foreign Policy Preparation*, 208-210, 229, 367; Mosely, "The Dismemberment of Germany," *loc. cit.*, 490; and John L. Chase, "The Development of the Morgenthau Plan through the Quebec Conference," *Journal of Politics*, XVI (1954), 326-328.

Commission, to study German problems on the "tertiary" level. To feed instructions to the American representative on this commission in London on political and military questions concerning Germany, a special inter-departmental committee was organized in Washington. This "Working Security Committee" consisted of representatives of the State, War, and Navy departments until September, 1944, when Treasury Department representatives entered. Until then, the Working Security Committee was often used as a funeral parlor for State Department proposals; after September 15, it became a forging furnace in which Treasury Department concepts were fused with those of the State and War Departments into a curious amalgam of ambiguously harsh policy toward Germany.

Before the entrance of Treasury representatives, the State Department experts on Germany encountered most trouble in the Working Security Committee from the officers of the Civil Affairs Division of the War Department. The State Department experts (Mosely until June 21, 1944, and Harris, thereafter) were well prepared. The officers of the Civil Affairs Division, who were reluctant even to participate at first, reflected little preparation— even ignorance, some would say—for the large job of planning toward Germany. The first task at hand was that of proposing a zonal division of Germany for purposes of occupation. Mosely in mid-December, 1943, presented a State Department proposal which would carve the Reich into three zones, make Berlin a joint-occupation zone, and provide for a definite corridor between Berlin and the Western zones of occupation. In the Working Security Committee the Civil Affairs Division officers first insisted that the delineation of zones of occupation was a military matter. In the discussion that followed they offered only disagreement with the State Department proposals. The Army officers indicated in January, 1944, that they expected the Red Army to conquer all of Germany east of the Rhine River, and suggested that the zones of occupation should be determined by the relative military positions of the three armies at the end of hostilities. When State Department representatives recovered from their amazement at this proposal they argued that it was clearly not in the interest of European

53

and American security that "all or nearly all of Germany should pass under Soviet control." [8]

ORIGINS OF TWO GERMANIES AND THE ISLAND OF BERLIN

While this debate was developing in Washington the European Advisory Commission was stalemated in its work for want of instructions to the American representative. This commission held its first meeting on December 15, 1943, and began serious work on January 14, 1944. From then until it was dissolved in August, 1945, the E.A.C. was to hold twenty formal and ninety-seven informal meetings, most of them concerning Germany, many of them fruitless, and all of them with insufficient instructions and cooperation from Roosevelt.

Serving on the European Advisory Commission (E.A.C.) was a job calculated to breed frustration and despair. During the Yalta Conference the Soviet representative on the commission, Fedor Tarasovich Gusev, was teased by Stalin for "always being glum and serious and for never cracking a smile," personality deficiencies which might well have been intensified at London in 1944. Gusev doubled as E.A.C. member while serving as Soviet Ambassador to London. The British Government was ably represented on the commission by Sir William Strang, a professional diplomat who was in close touch with Eden and constantly supported by the Foreign Office. Strang was the only member of the commission who had no other responsibilities. The United States was represented by John Gilbert Winant, Ambassador to London. In Strang's words, Winant was "a self-tortured soul, noble and passionate, inarticulate, deceptively simple, the pattern of honour." Strang adds, however, that Winant's chief advisers amply compensated for his shortcomings as a negotiator. During the first half of 1944, Winant's political adviser was George F. Kennan, whose name in 1947 was to become a synonym for the policy of "containing" the Soviet Union in the "Cold War." Kennan's successor in June, 1944, was Philip E. Mosely. Mosely brought to London considerable Washington preparation for the frustrations that faced him there, but he proved

---

[8] State Department, *Postwar Foreign Policy Preparation*, 211-225.

to be highly skilful at negotiating with Soviet representatives.

Since instructions about zones of occupation were not available from Washington, in January, 1944, the British Foreign Office submitted to the European Advisory Commission the proposals that had been developed by the Attlee committee in 1943. Eastern Germany—about 40 per cent of the territory, 36 per cent of the population, and 33 per cent of the productive resources of the German Reich of 1937—would be occupied by the Red Army. The Soviet zone would extend at the most western point to about a hundred miles east of the Rhine River. It would include any German territories that might be won by Poland after the war. (Without the areas Poland administered after 1945 this area comprehended only about 23 per cent of the German land area of 1937.) Northwestern Germany, including the great coastal ports and the Ruhr, would be occupied by British forces. The United States Army would control the Saar and southern Germany. Berlin would be under joint occupation—much as it was actually to be still in 1959—inside the Soviet zone of occupation and with no specific corridors between Berlin and the western zones.

The U.S.S.R. on February 18, 1944, indicated its general acceptance of the zone of occupation thus offered, and approved the joint occupation of Berlin; but Gusev quibbled about the exact line of demarcation between the Soviet zone and the British zone in the northwest. Doggedly and for two months the Soviet representative sought in the European Advisory Commission to secure the little Baltic island of Fehmarn as part of the Soviet zone. The British argued that it really belonged with the province of Schleswig-Holstein, and by perseverance, had their way. But Strang recalls "little discussion and early agreement" about the general location of the western boundary of the Soviet zone of occupation. It was the product of a British draft, not a Russian demand, and was "agreed upon without great difficulty," although it restricted Russian power to the Baltic Sea.

Winant caused no trouble in the determination of zones, but Washington did. It was often apparent that the American representative was embarrassed by "unresolved disagreements" about policy among governmental agencies on the Potomac. Forwarded to Washington, the British draft was rejected by the President and his military advisers. Apparently Roosevelt felt that it gave Russia too much of Germany as a zone of occupation. On the "Iowa" en route to the Teheran Conference the President had discussed zones for Germany with military aids who based their presentation on a map prepared by the Joint Chiefs of Staff. This map set forth a Soviet zone of occupation well to the east of that provided for in the British plans. At about the same time, according to Herbert Feis, the President had sketched on the back of a used envelope his ideas for the occupation, and on it he drew the boundary between the Soviet and the Western zones much more to the east than the British plan had proposed. The President also had other reservations about the British plan. He feared that the proposed occupation of southern Germany by American troops might cause the United States to become embroiled in Balkan problems. Furthermore, he seemed to some of his advisers to be obsessed with the idea that France would soon be torn by revolution, and preferred a zone to which he would have access without going through France. For all these reasons, he urged that Britain occupy the southern zone and *all* of Austria as well, leaving the northwest to the United States. (Only at the beginning of 1945 would the United States definitely agree to participate in the occupation of Austria.)

At the end of February, 1944, the Civil Affairs Division officers in the Working Security Committee suddenly produced a map showing a division of Germany which they said the President himself had authorized. It was very much like the one which Roosevelt had studied on the "Iowa" and perhaps like the one he had crudely sketched. Berlin itself became the dividing line between East and West on this map, and a line drawn due west from Berlin divided western Germany into northern and southern zones, without any regard whatsoever for the state frontiers within Germany, or for transportation, communication, or any other essential considerations. The Western Powers would have direct access to the German capital according to this map. If Civil Affairs Division talk of Soviet occupation as far west as the Rhine had seemed pro-Russian, this plan was equally as anti-Russian, and would inevitably create trouble if it were presented before the Soviet representative in the European Advisory Commission as an American proposal. Only 22 per cent of 1937 Germany would fall under

Soviet military occupation under this plan.

In London, Ambassador Winant refused to present this proposal unless he was provided with further commentary upon it. But the Civil Affairs Division of the War Department refused to elaborate upon the plan. This deadlock lasted for many weeks. Then, in April, with Anglo-American forces not yet even in France, and with Soviet armies moving westward, Roosevelt approved the zone for Russia which the British had proposed and Moscow had accepted. The Joint Chiefs of Staff approved the line of demarcation on April 28, and American approval in the European Advisory Commission was announced on June 1. Except for slight alterations, it became the line of zonal division in 1945. Afterward, as zones became states, this line came to divide the two Germanies the world has known since World War II. Without intending to do so, the wartime allies in the spring of 1944 had taken the first step toward the present partition of Germany. (See map, p. 160.)

Their action gave hostages to fortune in another way. No specific provisions were made for access to Berlin—deep within the Soviet zone—from the west. The military authorities thought it premature to specify which transportation facilities they would want (some would be bombed out) and Ambassador Winant may have thought that pressing the matter would create misunderstanding with the Soviet Union. The basis was thus laid amidst clever intentions for the bleak Western position in the Berlin crisis of 1948-1949 and in the subsequent crisis of 1958-1959.[9]

Long after June, 1944, the President continued to refuse to accept the rest of the British plan for occupation. His insistence upon having the northwestern zone—which Stimson, McCloy, and Stettinius thought a mistake—delayed final decisions for many more months. Meanwhile, invasion plans for D-Day had been drafted upon the assumption that Britain would occupy northwestern Germany. Thus British forces landed and moved across France on the left flank of Eisenhower's armies in the summer of 1944.

As D-Day approached, the necessity of defining the policies to

---

[9] Strang, *Home and Abroad*, 199-216; Mosely, "The Occupation of Germany," *loc. cit.*, 582-595; Churchill, *Triumph and Tragedy*, 507-508; Stettinius, *Roosevelt and the Russians*, 221; Hull, *Memoirs*, II, 1611; Stimson and Bundy, *On Active Service*, 568-569, 575; Feis, *Churchill, Roosevelt, Stalin*, 360-365. See also Hassett, *Off the Record with F. D. R.*, 154.

to be followed upon the collapse of Germany became all the more pressing. In addition to its work on the problem of zones of occupation, the European Advisory Commission also faced the task of developing an organizational arrangement for the joint control of Germany as a whole. Furthermore, it had to draft a surrender document for Germany to sign at the end of hostilities. The first of these tasks was basically completed by the Europeon Advisory Commission in the month before the great invasion fleet put out from England for the Cherbourg Peninsula: in May, 1944, a charter for inter-Allied control of Germany was tentatively accepted, providing that the commanding general of each occupation force in Germany would sit on a control council for Germany as a whole.

Drafting the surrender instrument required more time. In trying to decide how much to put into it, the E.A.C. faced the perennial and fundamental questions that hampered the making of policy throughout the war: What must be decided quickly? What decisions should be postponed in the interests of allied wartime unity? Generally speaking, the discussions in the E.A.C. typified the contemporary broad policy of each of the Great Powers. The United States and the U.S.S.R., anxious above all to maintain the united front against Germany, wished to draft a brief surrender document. The United States would declare in sweeping generalizations the right of the Allies to reorganize Germany's political, economic, and social life. It is interesting in retrospect that the Soviet representative opposed this, arguing that the surrender document should stick to military questions and leave the others for post-surrender definition. Gusev was chiefly interested in providing that *all* German soldiers should be taken prisoners of war by the Allied armies. When Winant and Strang raised technical objections to this, the Soviet representative asserted that they were being "tender to Fascism and to German militarism." The British, thinking of the postwar period and fearful lest they face obligations greater than their power, insisted that the surrender instrument should spell out in detail the postwar political and economic treatment of Germany.

After long debate, the European Advisory Commission finally adopted a compromise document, proposed by the British. This surrender document must be viewed as an epitome of the "policy of postponement" from above, and the making of plans in a policy vacuum from below. Its very refusal to face the fact that the collapse of Germany would create a balance of power problem in Europe was an impressive if painfully indirect acknowledgment of the problem. This draft surrender document provided that Germany should be disarmed. It left the disposition of German prisoners of war to be determined later, and by each Allied army as it saw fit. Consistent with the unconditional surrender policy, it would proclaim that the Allies assumed supreme political authority in Germany. And, most important though most vague, it announced that the Allies would impose after the surrender "additional political, administrative, economic, financial, military and other requirements" upon the Germans.[10]

The surrender document was accepted in the European Advisory Commission on July 25, 1944. Progress on difficult problems had been made since January in the European Advisory Commission, and it was expected to continue. But trouble lay dead ahead. Two weeks later the Secretary of the Treasury of the United States was to descend upon England. When he left, Americans on the European Advisory Commission knew that their past problems would pale before those of the future.

The commission had developed a considerable degree of inter-Allied cooperation during its brief existence. The Soviet representative had been troublesome; but at times he had been more helpful than the American representative could be, because "the War Department and the White House on several occasions held the EAC at a standstill." In a spirited and convincing defense of the Commission, Winant's Economic Adviser, E. F. Penrose, has stated that "in the last resort the main obstacle to greater accomplishments by the commission came from the indecisiveness of the heads

---

[10] The above account is based upon the best sources as yet published on the work of the E.A.C.: Strang, *Home and Abroad*, 209-216; Holborn, *American Military Government*, 22-27; Mosely, "The Occupation of Germany," *loc. cit.*, 591-594; Penrose, *Economic Planning for the Peace*, 229-292. John Gilbert Winant's *Letters from Grosvenor Square: An Account of a Stewardship* (Boston, 1947), treats only the early period of his service in London and does not cover the period of E.A.C. The surrender document of July 25, 1944, is presented in United States Department of State, *The Conferences at Malta and Yalta: 1945* (Washington, 1955), 110-118. For the agreement on control machinery as finally approved see *ibid.*, 124-127 (hereinafter cited as *Yalta Papers*).

of state and leading ministers on some of the issues relating to Germany and their stubborness." With this verdict history will not argue. The painfulness of this "postponement policy" at the top level to the experts is reflected in Penrose's additional comment:

> The future historian will look back in wonder on those times during which an outstanding American representative was appointed to an important post abroad on a commission which the United States had taken a leading part in establishing, and was left stranded without instructions on the policy that he should follow, without freedom to propose a policy of his own, and without a mandate to comment on the policies proposed by other member countries.[11]

The source of Winant's problems lay partly in interdepartmental wrangling in Washington. But the nature of the wartime alliance was a greater problem than maliciousness or lack of foresight on the Potomac. Any Big Three agreement on Germany's future would have had to be—before 1945—an agreement upon Russia's terms. The West could not risk the loss of Soviet power against Hitler. Later, with troops in Europe, the West could bargain better. This implies, of course, that Roosevelt's strong hope for Soviet cooperation in the postwar era was tempered by realistic considerations. One brief comment Hopkins made about Eden's visit to Washington in March, 1943, should be remembered here: "We discussed at some length, the political effect of our troops being in Italy as against France at the time of the collapse of Germany and, while both Eden and the President thought it would not be as advantageous, it was better than not being there (on the Continent) at all." [12] Was it the policy of Franklin Roosevelt in dealing with the Russians to practice what his famous uncle had preached, to speak softly but to carry a big stick? One must ponder words like those of Hopkins, and even more so those that Under-Secretary of State Stettinius spoke in mid-June, 1944, to Stanislaw Mikolajczyk on the Polish grievances against Moscow: "Neither Great Britain nor America can take a firmer stand against the Soviet Union. . . . But I am convinced that in the not too distant

---

11 Penrose, *Economic Planning for the Peace*, 233; quoted by permission of the publisher, the Princeton University Press.

12 Sherwood, *Roosevelt and Hopkins*, 712; quoted by permission of the publisher, Harper and Brothers.

future, maybe in a month or two, or maybe six months from now, the general situation undoubtedly will change; and when it changes, the whole attitude of the United States to Russia will change completely." [13]

When Stettinius spoke, the Anglo-American invasion of the continent was only a few days old, and no progress was being made. Upon its development would depend the change in the "general situation" which Stettinius foresaw.

BRITISH AND AMERICAN MILITARY PLANNERS

In the absence of clear-cut policy from above, basic policy plans or assumptions were made in 1944 by many different groups and at several different levels. The duplication of effort which resulted from this was unfortunate enough. But the great gulfs that developed between the thinking of these various groups, and the personal, jurisdictional, and philosophical conflicts that eventually developed because of this lack of policy at the top and duplication of effort below were even more tragic consequences of the policy of postponement. All this is illustrated by the history of the efforts of British and American army officers to evolve an occupation policy for Germany in 1944. Soon these military planners had even greater cause for concern than did the European Advisory Commission; for they would be affected by the entrance of Secretary Morgenthau into the planning process in August, 1944.

A report compiled by Supreme Headquarters, Allied Expeditionary Forces (SHAEF) in April, 1944, showed that seventy-two studies on problems of the armistice and the first phase of the occupation of Germany were then being undertaken by various groups of military planners. At the top Anglo-American military level, planning for the occupation in its broadest outlines was a function of the Combined Chiefs of Staff, meeting in Washington. Since long-range policy was undefined, the Combined Chiefs of Staff could only plan policies for the period between the penetration of Germany by Eisenhower's forces and the formal surrender of Germany. They embodied their decisions in a partial draft of a pre-surrender directive which was sent to General Eisenhower on April 28, 1944.

[13] Rozek, *Allied Wartime Diplomacy*, 223; quoted by permission of the publisher, John Wiley and Sons, Inc.

This directive was rounded out in May by the addition of statements on financial and economic policies, but these were subsequently to be sharply modified to meet the wishes of the Treasury Department. Meanwhile, the possibility of securing Soviet acceptance of the directive to Eisenhower for use in Russian areas of occupation was explored in the European Advisory Commission.

The directives of April and May gave promise of a strict but humane occupation. The Supreme Commander of the Anglo-American armies was to conduct a "firm" administration; he was to arrest *high* Nazi leaders and government officials; he was to take steps leading to the dissolution of the Nazi Party; the German courts were to be purged of Nazis; and no political activity "of any kind" was to be allowed, except by special permission of the Supreme Commander. But Eisenhower was further directed to provide for the revival of German agricultural production. In addition, the possibility even of imports to prevent chaos was provided by the statement that Eisenhower was to arrange for the Germans to receive minimum amounts of food and other supplies as needed "to prevent disease and unrest." Public utilities were to be restored to full operation as soon as possible. Coal mines should be operated as fully as transportation facilities permitted. This set of directives of April and May, 1944, was the primeval and more humane nucleus of the policy directive which later became known as JCS 1067. The harsher coloration of the far more important policy document of 1945 was to show not only what could happen in the evolution through six generations or so of the same general species of government paper; more specifically, it would reflect the impact of the Treasury Department upon the shaping of occupation policy.[14]

By the time Eisenhower received the 1944 directives from Washington and paratroopers under his command had begun the long-awaited invasion of France, military government officers under his command had virtually completed a basic handbook on military government for Germany. This was the work of about 150 English and American staff planners, mostly civilian experts in uniform, who were assembled in the so called "German Country Unit." They, too, worked without instructions about what policy would—or

[14] Pogue, *The Supreme Command*, 347. The directives to Eisenhower are published in Holborn, *American Military Government*, 43, 135-143.

should—be. Because these men knew Germany, and because they expected to be assigned to responsible military government posts in the defeated Reich, they assumed a policy of moderation and produced a handbook that called for "constructive action." Eisenhower gave their preliminary draft his blessing and sent a copy on to the Secretary of War in June, 1944.

This *Handbook for Military Government in Germany* insisted that it would be the task of the armies in Germany to "see that the machine works and works efficiently." It called for retention of the centralized German administrative system. It would carry out some de-industrialization, but would retain and rehabilitate on a peacetime basis sufficient light and heavy industry to make Germany a self-supporting nation and, even more significant, to keep the entire European economy on "a reasonably even keel." Not only should Germany be self-supporting, but she should retain a relatively high standard of living: even through imports, if necessary, her citizens should be provided with an average of 2000 calories per day per person, several hundred more than the average Frenchman, Dutchman, Pole, or Yugoslav was able to get in mid-1944 under German control.[15]

The *Handbook* offered a glimpse of a very different kind of occupation than that which actually was to be conducted from 1944 through 1947. Its fate provides additional proof of the great difficulty of planning a rational, constructive peace amidst the passions of war. In early August its third—and supposedly final—edition was ready and awaiting distribution. But at this point the Secretary of the Treasury of the United States entered into the planning. The result was an onslaught which the *Handbook,* as it stood then, could not survive. The net effect of the onslaught would be to bring the experts more into line with the thinking of the Big Three as this had been revealed during the conference at Teheran.

---

[15] Carl J. Friedrich and associates, *American Experiences in Military Government in World War II* (New York, 1948), 219-220; Harold Zink, *American Military Government in Germany* (New York, 1947), 19-20, 42-43, 131-132; Henry Morgenthau, Jr., "Our Policy toward Germany," New York *Post,* Nov. 26, 1947.

Chapter IV

THE MORGENTHAU PLAN

ON July 22, 1944, Secretary of the Treasury Henry Morgenthau, Jr. addressed the United Nations Monetary and Financial Conference at Bretton Woods which his special assistant, Harry Dexter White, had been instrumental in organizing. "I take it as an axiom," the Secretary told the gathered delegates, "that after this war is ended no people—and therefore no government of the people —will again tolerate prolonged or widespread unemployment." To prevent this, said Morgenthau, a revival of trade was indispensable. Further, "long term financial aid must be made available at reasonable rates to those countries whose industry and agriculture have been destroyed by the ruthless torch of an invader or by the heroic scorched earth policy of their defenders." [1]

That this forecast of things to come was not meant to be applied to Germany some of the Secretary's listeners already knew. The rest of the world was to find it out in September. Just two weeks after he made this speech Morgenthau went to England on a flight which was to influence radically the entire development of wartime policy toward Germany, bringing it out of the constructive directions in which some of the experts had started and into line with the temper of the times.

ORIGINS OF THE "MORGENTHAU PLAN"

Henry Morgenthau was one of many men of prominence in World War II whose basic political ideas were strongly colored by their experience in the Wilson era. Morgenthau's distrust of

---

[1] United States Treasury Department, *Annual Report of the Secretary of the Treasury on the State of the Finances for the Fiscal Year Ended June 30, 1945* (Washington, 1946), 341.

Germany dated at least from World War I. Some of the notions of his plan are reminiscent of Georges Clemenceau. A long and somewhat Jeffersonian interest in agriculture also seems to have influenced his views on the German problem. Henry Morgenthau was a specialist on agricultural problems before coming to Washington. He edited the magazine *American Agriculturalist* between 1922 and 1934, and served as Conservation Commissioner and Roosevelt's adviser on agricultural problems when F.D.R. was governor of the state of New York.

Morgenthau's long record of official association with the President was supplemented by a close personal relationship. They were neighbors in Dutchess County, New York, and Eleanor Roosevelt has recalled that, though she made few new friendships in Washington, the Morgenthaus "continued to be close friends." She has called Morgenthau "Franklin's conscience." Morgenthau has described the President as "the man I admired and loved second only to my father."

Morgenthau has also stated that when the President "wanted something personal and original to be done, he would often turn to me to work out the ways and means." If the President asked the State Department to prepare a plan, and he didn't like the results, he was caught in a highly awkward position. If Morgenthau did it, and the President did not like it, "that ended it," Morgenthau has plausibly recounted. Roosevelt had used Morgenthau to explore the possibility of establishing diplomatic relations with the U.S.S.R. in 1933, when the State Department was "unsympathetic if not hostile to the whole idea." Much to the annoyance of Secretary of State Cordell Hull, Morgenthau often meddled in foreign policy matters during the thirties. As early as 1934 Morgenthau and the President were discussing the "inhuman policy" of Nazism.[2]

It is possible, therefore, that the President himself might have initiated Morgenthau's interference in planning for postwar Germany. But Morgenthau has not contended that this was the case, and the opposition of the President in 1943 to some of the

---

[2] Henry Morgenthau, Jr., "The Morgenthau Diaries," *Colliers*, CXX (Sept. 27, 1947), 11-13, 80-82; and *ibid.* (Oct. 4), 20-21, 45-49; (Oct. 11), 20-21, 72-79; (Oct. 18), 16-17, 71-75. See also Eleanor Roosevelt, *This I Remember*, 332, 350; Hull, *Memoirs*, II, 1073, 1379; Hassett, *Off the Record with F. D. R.*, 3, 74, 137, 163, 266, 269, 292, 306, 307, 319.

Morgenthau ideas, notably de-industrialization, has already been noted. The evidence at hand suggests rather that the Secretary of the Treasury acted on his own initiative, and then was quick to take advantage of his close personal connection with the President in achieving his objectives. The result was far from edifying. It was indeed a tragedy, as one economist has written, "that one who did so much on so many issues on the side of the children of light should have injured his record by siding with the children of darkness on another great issue directly affecting the lives and well-being of millions of people." [3]

According to the Secretary of the Treasury's postwar account, his involvement in planning for Germany began quite unexpectedly on August 5, 1944, when he left the United States on a flight to England on other matters. As he settled down for the tiresome hours ahead, an assistant (Harry Dexter White) "pulled out of his briefcase" a copy of a State Department memorandum on German reparations. "I settled back to read it, first with interest, then with misgivings, finally with sharp disagreement," recalled Morgenthau later. He thereupon determined to find out all he could about plans for Germany, he has stated. [4]

It is possible that in a general way Morgenthau had been kept abreast of official planning in Washington for some time before he made this trip. As Morgenthau's deputy, Harry White had served on the State Department's inter-departmental Executive Committee on Economic Foreign Policy for several months. Both White and Morgenthau were chiefly involved in international problems in the summer of 1944 and may have given little time to developing plans for the occupation of Germany. White, however, was present at the meeting on August 4, when the Executive Committee on Economic Foreign Policy formally adopted the relatively moderate policy recommendations on economic policy toward Germany which have been summarized above (see page 52). The memorandum of August 4 was almost certainly the document which Morgenthau's assistant "pulled out of his briefcase" as the airplane was "swinging out over the Atlantic" on August 5.

---

[3] Penrose, *Economic Planning for the Peace*, 243.
[4] Morgenthau in the New York *Post*, Nov. 24, 1947.

There is reason to conclude that White, if not Morgenthau, also knew the general nature of discussions in the European Advisory Commission; for L. C. Aarons, a Treasury Department official attached to the American Embassy in London, busied himself with many matters which were not strictly financial in nature. Furthermore, through Colonel Bernard Bernstein, White and possibly Morgenthau kept up with the progress of SHAEF planning on the future of Germany. Bernstein, a former Treasury official, headed the Finance Division of the SHAEF Civil Affairs Division. It is established beyond any doubt that Bernstein at least occasionally submitted drafts of Army planning papers to White or Morgenthau by way of Aarons. It was Bernstein who sent Morgenthau the copy of the Anglo-American German Country Unit's preliminary *Handbook* on military government in Germany. Probably Morgenthau knew relatively little about these things, for he delegated much responsibility to his staff. In any case, he indicated in England and later that what he learned in August came as a profound shock to him.[5]

In England, Morgenthau and his assistants lunched and talked with General Eisenhower on August 7. The Secretary lost no time in making plain his interest in plans for the occupation of Germany. Financial policy in occupied Germany should be designed to show that country no advantage, he told the Supreme Commander. Eisenhower, apparently embarrassed by the Treasury Secretary's attempt to interfere in Army policy planning, indicated that he had been too busy with the invasion to be "specifically concerned with the future economy of Germany," but he reassured Morgenthau that he had "an able staff section working on the problem." This, of course, was precisely what worried the Treasury delegation. When Harry Dexter White criticized Army planning for being too mild, Eisenhower insisted that he personally believed that Allied policy should leave "no room for doubt as to who won the war." He said that he favored harsh measures, including the requirement of reparations and the control of key industries. He apparently

---

[5] Hammond, "JCS 1067 Policy for Germany," 47, 113-117; Friedrich and associates, *American Experiences in Military Government in World War II*, 219-220; Morgenthau in the New York *Post*, Nov. 24, 1947; Harold Zink to Snell, Oct. 6, 1955.

also indicated that he had no desire to "bolster" the German economy. But Eisenhower has stated that he also told Morgenthau that he opposed "choking off natural resources," and that he thought the idea of flooding the Ruhr mines was "silly and criminal."

Eisenhower, Morgenthau has stated, told him that those who wanted a soft peace with Germany hoped to make the Reich once again into "a bulwark against Russia"; that he personally believed that Russia had "all she could digest," and that the best cure for the paranoia of the Germans was to let them "stew in their own juice." Morgenthau thus has left the impression that Eisenhower was quite as completely anti-German as Morgenthau himself was. Morgenthau even suggested after the war that his own belief in a harsh treatment of Germany was derived at least in part from Eisenhower. But another participant in the discussion, Morgenthau's own public relations assistant, Fred Smith, has acknowledged Eisenhower's additional comment that fears of Russia were not completely lacking in foundation. "This is a problem," the Supreme Commander stated, "because the strength of Russia is fantastic."

It would appear that the Secretary's intervention had some influence upon Eisenhower's approach to occupation problems. The Supreme Commander on August 23 advised the Anglo-American Combined Chiefs of Staff in Washington that he would probably be unable to assume responsibility for maintaining and controlling the German economy. This statement may have been prompted by Eisenhower's assumption that he would find Germany in such economic chaos that maintenance and control would be impossible. But it seems far more likely that he anticipated a policy squabble brewing in Washington which was certain to make it risky, if not impossible, for him to assume responsibility for the maintenance of the German economy.[6]

---

[6] There are three accounts by participants of the Eisenhower-Morgenthau luncheon conference. Eisenhower's account omits reference to certain aspects of the discussion which both Morgenthau and his public relations assistant cite; but there are significant discrepancies between the accounts of the latter two. See: Morgenthau in the New York *Post*, Nov. 24, 1947; Fred Smith, "The Rise and Fall of the Morgenthau Plan," *United Nations World*, *II* (March, 1947), 32-38; Dwight D. Eisenhower, *Crusade in Europe* (Garden City, 1948), 287. See also Pogue, *The Supreme Command*, 353-354.

According to Morgenthau's postwar account, this visit with Eisenhower first set him to thinking about an effective plan for the treatment of Germany. "Ideas," he has written, "were percolating in my own mind. As a farmer myself, I knew that people who lived close to the land tended to tranquil and peaceloving lives. . . . Why not make Germany a nation predominantly of small farmers?" To this, he added the idea of dismembering the Reich—into "small agricultural provinces." That a Germany robbed of industrial resources and factories would be powerless to wage modern war was evident. Whether the humanitarian instincts of the Western world or even hard-headed consideration of the economic future of Europe as a whole would allow such a drastic restrictive measure as the de-industrialization of Germany remained to be seen. Morgenthau lost no time in trying out the idea upon his British and American hosts.

Morgenthau found that Churchill had more immediate economic problems than those of Germany to consider. Churchill explained England's acute need for continuing American financial support, both during and after the war, and suggested that Morgenthau, as Secretary of the Treasury, was "becoming rather hard" in his attitude toward Britain. According to Fred Smith, Morgenthau's companion and assistant, it was precisely at this point that Morgenthau unexpectedly introduced Churchill to his ideas about the treatment of Germany. Two factors may have entered into this approach to Churchill. For one thing, Morgenthau, a proven friend of wartime Britain, saw the crippling of German industrial production as a means to relieve British industry of postwar competition. If this should solve Britain's long-range economic problems, she might not need turn to the United States for financial assistance after the war; and the British might respond favorably to Washington's desire for freer trade. Secondly, Britain's need for dollar credits could be used as a lever to move the Prime Minister into a harsh policy for Germany.

Continuing his preliminary soundings of official British opinion on policy toward Germany, Morgenthau approached the Conservative Chancellor of the Exchequer, Sir John Anderson, a man whom Churchill once described as the "Home Front Prime Minister." Morgenthau found that Anderson was worried about Russian power in postwar Europe; he wanted to allow the Germans to continue to manufacture non-military items after the war, and opposed the idea of "small agricultural provinces." Foreign Secretary Anthony Eden, on the other hand, admitted to Morgenthau that a soft peace with Germany would arouse Russian suspicions.[7]

Morgenthau and his party next presented their concepts before American representatives on the European Advisory Commission. On August 12 Ambassador Winant, Mosely (Political Adviser) and Penrose (Economic Adviser) drove out into Wiltshire at Morgenthau's invitation to spend the day at the country house which the Morgenthau party was using during the visit to England. Once at the Morgenthau place, the E.A.C. representatives found that Colonel Bernard Bernstein, the former Treasury official whom many viewed as a Treasury Department "agent" in the SHAEF Civil Affairs Division, had also been invited. Penrose, at Morgenthau's request, reviewed British economic planning for postwar Germany in considerable detail. At the end of his discourse Morgenthau asked if the British were likely "to forget and forgive speedily" after the war. Penrose replied that the British were "not a vengeful people." Morgenthau then heard a report from Bernstein about Anglo-American military planning, which, as he later recounted, "confirmed my fears about the Army." From Ambassador Winant, Morgenthau learned that the European Advisory Commission was proceeding upon the assumption that Germany should remain united after the war.

Then, after a pleasant lunch, the officials assembled on the lawn and listened to the first full-dress exposition of the "Morgenthau Plan." Morgenthau laid down the general groundwork; Harry Dexter White buttressed the walls, doing as good a job as could be done of making the edifice economically sound. The setting was nearly perfect. From a pastoral afternoon in southeastern England to visions of a rustic Reich the imagination could wander easily, untroubled by sticky problems of reality beyond the Channel. However, the vista unfolded of a rural Reich was occasionally broken by the hard arguments of a man who knew both Russia

---

[7] New York *Post*, Nov. 25, 1947; Smith, "The Rise and Fall of the Morgenthau Plan," *loc. cit.*, 33; Winant, *Letter from Grosvenor Square*, 214; R. S. Sayer, *Financial Policy, 1939-45* (London, 1956), 469.

and the ways of European power relationships. Philip Mosely repeatedly interrupted White to challenge his economic logic or his political assumptions, and to impress upon him the power-political implications of his suggestions. Mosely argued that if the Allies should attempt to "smash and run" the German economy, the Germans would be driven into dependence upon the Soviet Union, for they would be denied the only alternative, integration into the Western world. Mosely bluntly suggested that the United States had not fought two world wars "in order to turn over Germany, and with it all of Europe, to Soviet control."

White had long since won a reputation for his "rasping truculence," but he did not reply directly to Mosely's arguments. Thus Mosely was left to wonder whether the Treasury proposals reflected merely naivete or devious purposes. One thing is apparent: Mosely tried to show White and Morgenthau that their proposals would benefit the U.S.S.R.

This meeting left the Americans from the European Advisory Commission in a despondent mood indeed. Winant "quickly perceived that an inter-agency row was in the making" and that it might frustrate all the constructive work of the E.A.C. Hoping to secure decisions on several matters before the Secretary of the Treasury returned to Washington, Winant on August 19 sent a lengthy telegram directly for President Roosevelt. He specifically urged that broad policy instructions be provided, especially regarding reparations, in order that E.A.C. deliberations might be facilitated. Winant anticipated heavy Soviet reparations demands, and wished to negotiate an early settlement with Russia, one which would not create economic problems in the future United States zone of occupation. He urged that discussions of the partition of Germany be delayed. But Morgenthau arrived in Washington three days before Winant's telegram. The Ambassador never received a reply from the President.[8]

---

[8] New York *Post*, Nov. 25, 1947; Penrose, *Economic Planning for the Peace*, 244-247, 271; Mosely, "The Occupation of Germany," *loc. cit.*, 595-596; Mosely to Snell, Sept. 21, 1955. For White's "rasping truculence" see R. F. Harrod, *The Life of John Maynard Keynes* (New York, 1951), 538, 557-558. The Winant telegram (more like 1000 words than 7000, as has been suggested) may be consulted in the Historical Division of the Department of State.

Just before leaving Britain, Morgenthau again talked with Anthony Eden, informing the Foreign Secretary that the E.A.C. was assuming that Germany would remain united. At this point, after Morgenthau had already formulated the basic concept of "small agricultural provinces," Eden showed him the records of the Teheran Conference. These records reinforced Morgenthau's position, for they showed that Roosevelt had talked at Teheran in terms of partition, though no formal decision had been reached. They also showed Morgenthau, if he had not already known it, that Stalin had favored heavy reparations and de-industrialization at Teheran. The Secretary of the Treasury was now prepared to round out and polish his own basic ideas about Germany into a "plan," which he would be able to present in Washington as an embodiment of the will of the Big Three at Teheran.[9]

Morgenthau returned to Washington on August 17. He went almost immediately to see Cordell Hull and commented upon his findings in England. Hull informed Morgenthau that he had "never been permitted to see the minutes of the Teheran Conference." When asked what he proposed to do about Germany, Hull replied that he was not given "a chance to do anything," that he was "not told what is going on"; he had been informed that the planning of post-surrender policy toward Germany was "a military affair." It is possible that Hull was trying through these comments to fend off Morgenthau's intervention into State Department affairs. But Morgenthau may well have been encouraged by the comments to proceed with his own plans for Germany.

Morgenthau also lost no time in going to his powerful friend. On that same August 17, 1944, F.D.R. told press representatives that Germany must be occupied by Allied armies, even though the Germans should "collapse internally or surrender unconditionally before we cross their borders." Germany would not this time escape the military occupation she had "dodged by the Armistice in 1918." Was it mere coincidence that the President spoke in this way on the day Morgenthau returned to Washington, or had the Secretary of the Treasury already talked to Roosevelt? In any case, on this same August 17, the Morgenthaus rode from Washing-

---

[9] New York *Post*, Nov. 26, 1947.

ton to Hyde Park with Roosevelt. Morgenthau himself has told of seeing the President on August 18 and that he proved to be in "a cordial mood." When Morgenthau reported the evidence of British "softness" toward Germany which he had encountered, the President assured him that in thirty minutes with Churchill he could "correct all this." "We have got to be tough with the German people, not just the Nazis," said Roosevelt. Thus receiving assurance again that the President favored a harsh peace, Morgenthau apparently decided to bring to Roosevelt's attention the fact that American officials entrusted with the task of planning Germany's future were not acting in accordance with presidential wishes. Meanwhile, the Secretary appointed a special Treasury Department planning committee "to draft the Treasury's analysis of the German problem." The committee was headed by Harry Dexter White. White was assisted by two Treasury lawyers, John Pehle and Ansel Luxford.

When Morgenthau again called upon the President on August 25, he brought with him the Army's *Handbook for Military Government in Germany*. For years Morgenthau had insisted that his own staff should present only short memoranda to him. Knowing the President's heavy schedule and impatience with time-consuming approaches, Morgenthau now provided a brief memorandum in which were quoted the most constructive comments that appeared in the *Handbook*, all of which Roosevelt would be likely to interpret as pro-German. The President read the memorandum on the spot. It aroused his interest. He was noncommittal, but kept both the memorandum and the *Handbook*. Then the President and Morgenthau talked with Stimson and James Forrestal, Secretary of the Navy. He had "just heard" about the Army *Handbook* for Germany, Roosevelt said, and thought the plan was too soft. The Germans should be allowed "simply a subsistence level of food," the President stated, a level not higher than "the lowest level of the people they had conquered." If American help were needed to bring German subsistence up even to this level, army soup kitchens would be sufficient for the purpose. Stimson demurred, but Roosevelt continued in the same vein. He finally announced that he would appoint a special cabinet committee, composed of the State, War, and Treasury secretaries, to "consider the problem

of how to handle Germany *along the lines that he had outlined.*"
(Author's italics.)[10]

On August 26 the President put his oral statements into "a
stinging memorandum" to the War Department, a copy of which
was sent to Hull. "This so-called 'Handbook' is pretty bad,"
Roosevelt began. The President demanded to know who was responsible for the *Handbook,* and indicated that "all copies should
be withdrawn" if it had not already been distributed as approved
policy. The President repudiated the idea that the German people
were not responsible for Nazi crimes. It was important, he said,
that "every person in Germany should realize that this time Germany
is a defeated nation." Defeat must be impressed upon the German
people so fully that they would "hesitate to start any new war."
"The German people as a whole," he continued, "must have it
driven home to them that the whole nation has been engaged in
a lawless conspiracy against the decencies of modern civilization."

With this strong statement of the President's own desires in
their files, both Hull and Stimson were put on notice that the
State and War departments must develop tougher attitudes toward
Germany or expect to be by-passed in policy formulation. Since
State, not War, normally regarded policy formulation as its task,
the President's memorandum chiefly represented a challenge to
Hull's jurisdictional powers. Even if Morgenthau had retired from
the field at this moment, it is virtually certain that his campaign
would have shown some successes. State and War Department
planning would undoubtedly have been altered somewhat to bring
it into harmony with the President's forcefully stated views.[11]

But Morgenthau's action of late August was only the beginning
of a sustained campaign which was continued within the new
cabinet committee. The President picked Harry Hopkins to coordinate the work of the cabinet committee on Germany, and
Hopkins on September 1 undertook to explain to Hull some of
Morgenthau's objections to previous State Department planning.

---

[10] *Ibid.,* Nov. 25-26, 1947; Walter Millis ed., *The Forrestal Diaries*
(New York, 1951), 10; Hassett, *Off the Record with F. D. R.,* 264, 266.

[11] Hull, *Memoirs,* II, 1602-1603; New York *Post,* Nov. 26, 1947;
Stimson and Bundy, *On Active Service,* 569; Roosevelt to the Secretary
of War, Aug. 26, 1944, copy in Historical Division, Department of State.

Then, with Morgenthau's criticisms in mind, H. Freeman Matthews and James W. Riddleberger of the State Department reexamined in detail the previous State Department studies of Germany. Matthews and Riddleberger summed up State's policy once more in a memorandum to be presented to the cabinet committee. This proposal continued to resist both de-industrialization and forced partition, and it won Cordell Hull's approval.

Riddleberger, Chief of the State Department's Division of Central European Affairs, presented the proposal on September 2 to a committee of deputies of the War, State and Treasury secretaries, who met with Hopkins in his White House office. It was at this meeting that Harry White presented the plan for Germany which his Treasury committee had drafted during the previous week. The report of September 1 which he introduced on September 2 differed in only one important respect from the memorandum which soon was to become notorious as the "Morgenthau Plan": White would separate the Ruhr from Germany but leave most of its industry intact; Morgenthau would soon insist that the Ruhr, like the rest of Germany be stripped of all heavy industry.[12]

THE "MORGENTHAU PLAN"

The White-Morgenthau plan as it finally evolved was a remarkable historical document. Some have viewed its vengeful sentiment as an understandable manifestation of strong Jewish animus against Germany; still others have interpreted its pro-Russian features as proof of Communist influence in high places in Washington. But in this connection it is well to remember that a conservative Englishman, Lord Vansittart, had earlier proposed much the same future for Germany without being called a "Red." One thing is certain: whether judged in terms of morality and humanitarianism or in terms of *Realpolitik,* the Morgenthau-White plan has not won much favor since 1945.

According to this "Program to Prevent Germany from Starting a World War III," the Germans were to be completely demilitarized. They would lose to Denmark or to an international authority the Kiel

<hr>

[12] Hull, *Memoirs,* II, 1604-1608; copy of Treasury Department's program for Germany, Sept. 1, 1944, Historical Division, Department of State.

Canal and the provinces of Schleswig and Holstein; and the Ruhr and Rhineland industrial areas were to be internationalized. France would annex the Saar coal area and adjacent territory as far east as the Rhine River. Poland was to receive much of Silesia and that part of East Prussia which the Soviet Union did not annex. The rest of Germany would be divided into two independent states, each of which would be organized internally on a federal basis. Bavaria, Württemberg, Baden, and smaller provinces of the south and southwest would constitute one state. The remains of Prussia, Saxony, Thuringia, and smaller provinces of the north would be combined in a second German state.

Germany was to become an agriculturalized "geographical expression." The Ruhr and the surrounding region would, according to Morgenthau's departure from the White draft, be "stripped of all presently existing industries" and "so weakened and controlled that it can not in the foreseeable future become an industrial area." This de-industrialization was to be accomplished in two ways: (1) by the closing of all mines; and (2) by dismantling and transporting "all industrial plants and equipment not destroyed by military action . . . to Allied Nations as restitution." Eventually all Germans would be removed from the Ruhr, to prevent any movement for reunion with Germany. The area would be resettled by French, Belgian, Dutch, "and other" workers. Many of the industrial plants and equipment in the two remaining German states would likewise be distributed to "devastated countries" as reparations, a formula under which Russia would receive the major share. Other reparations would be paid by the seizure of Germany's foreign assets, and by "forced German labor outside Germany."

Implementation of the White-Morgenthau plan would have left the Soviet Union in position to dominate Central Europe. Germany, according to this proposal, would be subjected to a long-term occupation by "Germany's continental neighbors." A list of these "neighbors" indicated that Russia, though not an immediate neighbor, would provide occupation troops. Great Britain, which was separated from Germany only by the North Sea, was not on the list. United States troops were to remain in Germany for a "relatively short time." Sweeping social reforms were to be achieved under the auspices of the foreign armies of occupation.

76

Large estates were to be broken up and "divided among the peasants." Workers in heavy industries would be settled upon farms, Morgenthau subsequently explained. How? Morgenthau simply dismissed this question as "a German problem." All education was to be terminated until the entire school system could be reorganized, and appropriate teachers and textbooks secured. Meanwhile, during the occupation period the German people were to be given no outside aid in their efforts to sustain themselves.[13]

The Morgenthau-White plan has often been summarized; its motivation has yet to be satisfactorily explained. It is possible that it never can be clarified definitively. Nevertheless, various explanations have been offered. One is that Morgenthau hoped to help Britain by suppressing the industry of a competitor. Morgenthau himself advanced this as a motive in talking with Roosevelt in September, 1944. But it would seem that White possessed a sufficient knowledge of economics to see the fallacies of this kind of reasoning. The most superficial explanation offered by critics of the Morgenthau Plan is that Morgenthau and White, as Jews, sought vengeance for an angry Jehovah. The fact that these men and many of their assistants were Jewish certainly cannot be dismissed. But too many other Jews showed greater degrees of realism or mercy to make this interpretation altogether convincing. In fact a German Jewish refugee economist, M. J. Bonn, is among the vigorous critics of the plan. Bonn has suggested that "the Soviets should remember Mr. Henry Morgenthau, Junior, and present him with the Order of Lenin."

This hints at another primitive but tempting interpretation which others, less responsible than Bonn, have presented more emotionally and at greater length. These critics base their arguments almost exclusively upon their assumption that the draftsman of the plan, Harry Dexter White, was a member of a Communist spy ring. "A plain common traitor—highly esteemed by Secretary Morgenthau—was the principal author of the criminal policy," one critic has written. This thesis rests chiefly upon statements by two

---

[13] The White-Morgenthau plan is presented in much the form in which it was taken to Quebec in mid-September; see Henry Morgenthau, Jr., *Germany is Our Problem* (New York etc., 1945), frontispieces; and see 23, 50.

one-time Communist witnesses before Congressional committees that White provided information to a Communist spy ring. But neither Elizabeth Bentley nor Whittaker Chambers would state flatly while testifying that White was a Communist, and both indicated that the information they received from his office came through employees there, not directly from White. This part of the testimony of Bentley and Chambers is not altogether convincing to the scholar who applies to it the tests of historical criticism. Later, in his book, Chambers stated without qualification that White was "a Soviet agent." Yet, three days before he died of a heart attack, Harry Dexter White told a Congressional committee that he had never been a Communist or even a near-Communist. He denied ever having known Elizabeth Bentley or Whittaker Chambers. In answer to specific questions White stated that he would not knowingly have employed members of the Communist Party in important governmental positions. Confronted by such contradictory evidence as that at hand, the historian can only suspend judgment in this question. Surely, if a man is to be judged innocent until proven guilty, the benefit of the doubt remains with White until evidence is made public that proves the allegations which have been made against him. White may have been, in fact, a clever traitor. But the evidence now available to the conscientious researcher does not prove it beyond doubt.[14]

Yet, there is no doubt that the Morgenthau-White plan for Germany would have been decisively pro-Russian in its effects. Its timing may also seem to have been pro-Russian. It was

---

[14] The Jewish interpretation is suggested by Hull, *Memoirs*, I, 207-208, 472; Penrose, *Economic Planning for the Peace*, 248, 253, and others. The thesis of Communist influence is suggested cautiously by M. J. Bonn, "The Economics of Fear," *Annals of the American Academy of Political and Social Science*, CCXLVI (July, 1946), 142, and strongly by the following: Norbert Muhlen, *The Return of Germany: A Tale of Two Countries* (Chicago, 1953), 10, 12; Felix Wittmer, *The Yalta Betrayal: Data on the Decline and Fall of Franklin Delano Roosevelt* (Caldwell, Idaho, 1953), 64, 98; G. F. Hudson, "The Harry Dexter White Case," *The Twentieth Century*, CLV (Jan., 1954), 22-35; *Life*, XXXV (Nov. 23, 1953), 29-35; and Whittaker Chambers, *Witness* (New York, 1952), 500 and *passim*. The thesis of Communist motivation is presented in its most irrational form in the "footnoted hate" of John Beaty, *The Iron Curtain over America* (Dallas, 1951), 79 and *passim*. In contrast to these loose allegations, see White's seemingly unambiguous testimony in U.S. House of Representatives, 80th Congress, 2nd Session, *Hearings before the Committee on Un-American Activities* (1948), 877-906.

pressed upon Roosevelt and Churchill just when Western military successes provided military bargaining power in future negotiations with the Soviet Union. Eisenhower's forces by late August had liberated Paris and had driven almost to the German frontier. British intelligence reports since July had been speculating that Germany might soon be forced into submission. In fact, by the time Roosevelt and Churchill would meet at Quebec in September, 1944, they believed that Germany might conceivably surrender "within a matter of weeks or even days." Suggestions abounded that the Germans might deliberately fall back, leaving the way clear for British and American forces to gain control over Germany, forestalling Russian occupation. It was an opportune moment, so it may be argued, for a pro-Soviet faction to seek to commit Britain and the United States to a plan which would break the mine props of continental industry, and leave the ruins under the military domination of Russia.

But not even the nature of the plan and the timing of its presentation prove that it was drafted under Communist influence. For all this circumstantial evidence of a Russian orientation there are counter-arguments. Russian armies were also rolling in August-September. At the end of August the Red Army entered Bucharest; Bulgaria capitulated; and on September 2 Finland also asked for an armistice. The near future promised to strengthen the military bargaining power of the U.S.S.R. as well as that of the West. A case can be made that the timing of the Morgenthau Plan was anti-Russian, not pro-Russian. The substance of the Morgenthau Plan remains disturbing. But to this it may be argued that the most obviously pro-Russian aspect of the plan, the proposal to leave Soviet troops as the chief occupation forces in Germany, can be explained by two considerations: (1) Roosevelt himself had indicated as early as the fall of 1943 that the United States troops would be withdrawn from Europe in about two years after the war ended, and British troops would be needed for the Pacific War; and, perhaps as a result of this, (2) the plan was based on the assumption that future German aggression could be prevented only by leaving separate German agricultural provinces under the Russian knout. To Morgenthau, according to his own statements, the prevention of future German aggression was the most important goal of the war.[15]

But after all this is said, it must be noted that at times Morgenthau was pro-Russian as well as anti-German. In 1933 he had enthusiastically worked for the diplomatic recognition of the U.S.S.R. In talks with Roosevelt and in his book of 1945, instead of considering and rejecting rationally the objective arguments for moderate plans for Germany's future, Morgenthau vigorously condemned the advocates of such plans; their "real motive," he said, was a desire to build up a bulwark against Communist Russia.[16]

Morgenthau's views toward the U.S.S.R. may be further illustrated by an incident that occurred on the eve of the Yalta Conference. Throughout the year 1944 the Treasury Department had given consideration to the development of a plan to provide economic assistance to Russia in her postwar recovery efforts. As late as January 1, 1945, it appeared that the Russians were reluctant to ask for aid. But two days later they gave ample evidence that bashfulness no longer held them back. In a request of January 3 Molotov asked for the extension of a loan of six billion dollars at annual interest of only 2¼ per cent, the credits to be repaid over a period of thirty years. In return the U.S.S.R. would buy manufactured goods from the United States—at a special price of "20% off the government contracts" for all orders placed before the end of the war. Coming only one month before the Big Three would meet at Yalta the Soviet proposal looked like a demand. In a memorandum to the President, dated January 10, 1945, Morgenthau proposed that the United States provide the Soviet Union with a loan of ten (instead of six) billion dollars, to be paid back over a period of thirty-five years (instead of thirty) and at interest of 2 per cent (instead of 2¼ per cent). These terms can be evaluated all the better if it is remembered that our total Lend-Lease supplies to Russia during the entire war amounted to about eleven billion dollars in value.

---

[15] Sherwood, *Roosevelt and Hopkins,* 818; Morgenthau, *Germany Is Our Problem,* 89-101; New York *Post,* Nov. 24, 1947; Pogue, *The Supreme Command,* 349; John Ehrman, *Grand Strategy* (London, 1956), 398, volume V of the British series, *History of the Second World War.*

[16] Hammond, "JCS 1067 Policy for Germany," 117-118.

Both the Russians and Morgenthau strongly suggested that the proposed credit was in the economic interest of the United States. At a time when economic experts were groping for a system that would mitigate or even prevent a postwar depression, the loan and the resulting Soviet orders would probably help to keep "our own economy going." The proposal can, of course, be interpreted as evidence of Morgenthau's friendship for the Soviet Union. However, it is also possible to contend that Morgenthau's proposal for a Russian loan arose from his hatred and distrust of Germany. His proposal of aid to Russia indicated a way in which the Russians could avoid keeping the German economy productive; if they were assured of supplies from the United States, they would have no reason to wish reparations in current production from Germany. Morgenthau's proposal of aid to Russia was, therefore, in close harmony with his demands that Germany be de-industrialized.[17]

From all this the following inconclusive remarks about Morgenthau's motivation may be made: (1) he wanted to cripple Germany permanently; (2) he wished to strengthen the U.S.S.R. as a means of crippling Germany without a long Anglo-American occupation. It is, of course, true that there were other ways of preventing future German aggression than by leaving Russia in command of the continent of Europe. That the Plan did not advocate other means does not prove that it was Communist inspired, however. Public opinion polls indicated that in December, 1943, about 51 per cent of the people of the United States trusted the U.S.S.R. and only 27 per cent of those who were polled stated that they definitely distrusted Russia. By November, 1944, distrust had increased (35 per cent of those polled indicated distrust), but even then about 47 per cent of the American people still trusted Russia, if the polls of the National Opinion Research Center are accepted as an index to public opinion. It is significant to note in this connection that not even the Republican presidential candidate, Thomas E. Dewey, criticized Soviet motives and actions during the 1944 campaign. While criticizing the influence of Communists at home, Dewey on November 1, 1944, specifically stated that "the question of communism in our country has nothing whatsoever to do with our

---

[17] *Yalta Papers*, 309-324.

Allies any more than it has to do with where a man was born." [18]

It was precisely in this campaign season, when sentiment favorable to Russia and opposed to Germany ran highest in America, that the Morgenthau Plan was developed. Morgenthau's desire for a strong Russia as an alternative to an aggressive Germany was shared by vast numbers of non-Communist Americans in the year 1944.

THE QUEBEC AGREEMENT

The really big question about the Morgenthau Plan remains to be answered: How was Roosevelt—and even Churchill—brought to accept the White-Morgenthau plan "in principle" on September 15, 1944?

On September 2, while the Roosevelts took tea with the Morgenthaus at Hyde Park, deputies of the cabinet secretaries met in Washington. At this meeting Harry White revealed the Treasury proposals. The draft at that time called for the separation of Ruhr industry from Germany, not its destruction. Even so, the discussion which the White proposals provoked revealed the tremendous differences between departments. McCloy and Hilldring of the War Department opposed the Treasury proposals, as did Riddleberger and Matthews of the State Department. It appears that Harry Hopkins also opposed the Treasury proposals, at least in certain significant points. But Hopkins at this time had little influence upon the President, and perhaps none at all. In any case it was obvious that the Treasury attitude was close enough to the President's own views to command respect. Thus, at McCloy's suggestion, the committee of deputies on September 2 agreed to instruct the State Department to draft a new memorandum, *which all three departments might be able to accept and submit to the President as the recommendations of the cabinet committee.*

The Labor Day week-end at Hyde Park continued, but the President was not able to escape from the German problem. While the State Department staff tried to reconcile impossibly divergent concepts, Roosevelt saw a new movie on Woodrow Wilson's life. Thereupon, on September 4 F.D.R. had his secretary look up

---

[18] Bateman, "The Election of 1944 and Foreign Policy," 141-143; Westerfield, *Foreign Policy and Party Politics*, 188-189.

Wilson's World War I comments on peace. At about the same time the State Department finished the new proposal it had been instructed to prepare. Next day—September 5—Hull presented it to the first regular meeting of the cabinet committee in his office.

The State Department proposal of September 4-5 bent toward the Treasury in several ways. Instead of opposing partition outright, State now suggested that the decision on partition be postponed, and added that no attempts should be made to discourage any spontaneous German movement for partition. The Department of State also conceded that the United States should not interest itself in building up a strong German economy after the war. The last paragraph of the State Department's memorandum, which concerned the German economy, was phrased in a highly ambiguous fashion, obviously in an attempt to win approval for it as a compromise without flatly accepting the Treasury proposals: "(1) the standard of living of the German population shall be held down to subsistence levels; (2) German economic position of power in Europe must be eliminated; (3) German economic capacity must be converted in such a manner that it will be so dependent upon imports and exports that Germany cannot by its own devices reconvert to war production." By whose standards would "subsistence levels" be defined? Would point two mean de-industrialization? To the State Department it merely meant that Germany would surrender the economic domination over Europe which it had established by military force. Point three might suggest the possibility of emphasis upon agriculture. But as State interpreted it, point three would merely mean that the German policy of autarchy would be ended.

It is most important to bear in mind the interdepartmental background of this memorandum and of Hull's personal position on September 5. The position he then assumed necessarily differed from his and the State Department's previous and subsequent attitudes, because the Secretary was seeking to get a compromise memorandum which men of radically different viewpoints could adopt. These circumstances caused Stimson, who had not been present at the meeting of September 2, to conclude that there was little difference between the Morgenthau and Hull positions. And Morgenthau himself has recalled that, upon returning from his Labor Day vacation in Dutchess County, "State's position seemed to be nearer ours than the War Department's." It appears that Hull at this time gave at least temporary lip service to the idea of wrecking "the immense Ruhr-Saar area of Germany," and that Hopkins, who was also present, would have prevented the manufacture of steel in the Ruhr. It is important to note that even in this, his most cooperative moment, Hull never approved the proposal to de-industrialize Germany as a whole. But Stimson was left alone to repudiate altogether the economic provisions of the Morgenthau Plan. For him, this was the most "difficult and unpleasant meeting" of four years in Washington. Morgenthau, who was encouraged by the shift in the State Department position, remembers the meeting more pleasantly; the Secretaries merely disagreed as honorable men, in "an attempt to break the logjam," he has recalled.[19]

Hull's strategy in these meetings failed. His efforts were inconsistent with his previous and subsequent positions, and a detailed account would probably detract from the reputation of the longtime and weary Secretary of State. It would surely show him attempting out of jurisdictional expediency to compromise with a policy whose principles he and his department disapproved.

Following the conference of September 5, Stimson circulated a memorandum in which he repeated in writing his opposition to the Morgenthau-White economic proposals concerning Germany, and those which Hull had presented in his latest draft. Stimson wrote that he could not conceive of the transformation of the Saar and the Ruhr into agricultural provinces. He believed the effort was not likely to succeed and that "enormous general evils" would arise from an attempt to convert "such a gift of nature into a dust heap." Furthermore, if keeping the German standard of living at the "subsistence level" were to mean keeping it at "the edge of poverty," Stimson opposed this policy, too. "Such a program," he wrote, would "create tension and resentments far outweighing any immediate advantage of security and would tend to obscure the

---

[19] Hassett, *Off the Record with F. D. R.*, 269, 271; Sherwood, *Roosevelt and Hopkins*, 812, 818, and 832; Hull, *Memoirs*, II, 1304-1309; Stimson and Bundy, *On Active Service*, 569-571; Morgenthau in the New York *Post*, Nov. 28, 1947; and Riddleberger's account of the meeting of September 2 in *Yalta Papers*, 160-163. Cf. Dorn, "The Debate over American Occupation Policy in Germany," *loc. cit.*, 491.

guilt of the Nazis and the viciousness of their doctrines and their acts." Whatever the views of the Civil Affairs Division in the War Department might have been, Stimson and McCloy in the September showdown of 1944 made clear their opposition to the Morgenthau Plan and in fact any significant compromise with its economic proposals.[20]

On September 6 the cabinet committee met with the President. Morgenthau continued to press his point of view. Going beyond White, he demanded that the industries of the Ruhr be destroyed. Stimson remained firm against this and Hull once again moved into almost complete opposition against a harsh peace. Roosevelt himself indicated that he believed the Ruhr industry should be left productive; it would be needed to provide raw materials for the British steel industry, since Britain would be "in sore straits after the war." Stimson sensed that he was making some progress in his efforts to prevent the adoption of a hard policy. Apparently Morgenthau sensed the same thing, for he asked for another meeting with the President on September 9.

This meeting revealed Morgenthau's keen knowledge of the President's personality. In his new memorandum for this meeting, the Secretary answered the President's arguments of September 6 not by attacking the aim that Roosevelt had presented, aid to Britain, but by seeking to show that his own plan for Germany was the best way to achieve the President's aim. Morgenthau argued that it was a fallacy that Europe needed a strongly industrialized Germany. The destruction of Ruhr industry would actually aid Britain economically, he reasoned, because it would enable the British to take over German markets and thus cure "the alleged English depression" in coal mining. The most fallacious thing about all this was, of course, Morgenthau's argument that Europe did not need a healthy German economy. But Roosevelt was intrigued by the idea. "That is the first time I have seen anybody say that," he exclaimed. And according to Morgenthau he added: "All the economists disagree, but I agree with that."

Hull talked relatively little during the meeting. He was obviously being by-passed by the President in the conduct of foreign

---

[20] Stimson and Bundy, *On Active Service*, 570-573.

relations to a very great extent, having been given no invitation to the approaching Quebec Conference until this meeting of September 9. Even then he was given only a perfunctory one which he declined, as he was obviously expected to do. Stimson continued his battle for a reasonable policy, but it seemed pretty clear to the depressed Secretary of War that he was losing. The September 9 meeting of the cabinet committee reached no decision and it was the last to be held before the President departed for his meeting with Churchill at Quebec. There, on September 12, without the countervailing arguments of either Hull or Stimson, Roosevelt sent Morgenthau a telegram: "Please be in Quebec by Thursday, 14 September, noon." [21]

Roosevelt's "Quebec dispatch" of 1944 may well go down in German history as wryly reminiscent of Bismarck's "Ems dispatch" of 1870, the one helping to make modern Germany, the other signalling plans for its destruction. Morgenthau arrived in Quebec in time for tea on September 13. The stage was set for him to climax his efforts by converting an obstinate Churchill.

That evening Roosevelt asked Morgenthau to present the Morgenthau Plan for Germany orally before the British. It is highly important that we notice Morgenthau's own account of Churchill's first reaction:

> I had barely gotten under way before low mutters and baleful looks indicated that the Prime Minister was not the most enthusiastic member of my audience. . . . I have never seen him more irascible and vitriolic than he was that night. . . . He was slumped in his chair, his language biting, his flow incessant, his manner merciless. I have never had such a verbal lashing in my life.

Churchill made it plain that he was not convinced that the destruction of the Ruhr would benefit Britain's economy: it would mean chaining Britain to "a dead Germany," he replied.

Had Germany's future been the only subject under consideration at Quebec, it seems certain that Churchill's original reaction to the

---

21 *Ibid.*, 573-574; Morgenthau in the New York *Post,* Nov. 28, 1947; Hull, *Memoirs,* II, 1602; Eleanor Roosevelt, *This I Remember,* 332; statements by Stimson of Sept. 9, 1944 (in pencil) and Sept. 15, 1944, against the Morgenthau Plan, copies in Historical Division, Department of State.

Morgenthau Plan would have remained unaltered; it certainly reflected his previous position and the attitude he was to take at Yalta in 1945. Suggestions that he was won over by the argument that Britain would acquire German iron and steel markets are not convincing and are made without evidence to substantiate them. It seems clear, therefore, that Churchill was won over to part (not all) of the Morgenthau Plan by one major consideration and a secondary one. The secondary consideration was the concession finally made by Roosevelt that Britain would occupy the northwestern part of Germany, and that this would include the Saar as well as the Ruhr. The United States would occupy the southern zone. This concession was made, it would seem, only after Churchill accepted the Morgenthau economic principles, and Roosevelt's reluctance to make the concession probably encouraged the Prime Minister to give way to Morgenthau. Roosevelt insisted upon the following stipulations, which were to be worked out technically before American approval of the zones of occupation became final: (1) the United States was to occupy and control, within the British zone, the enclaves of Bremen and Bremerhaven, and (2) the United States was to be guaranteed rights and facilities for transportation and communication through the ports of Bremen and Bremerhaven across the British zone, to the United States zone of occupation in the south. According to Churchill there was general agreement at Quebec that "it was too early as yet to provide for a French zone in Germany."

The major reason for Churchill's acceptance of Morgenthau's economic program for Germany remains to be noted. Churchill had come to Quebec in quest of assurance that the United States would extend financial aid to Britain even beyond the end of the war. This, in fact, was "uppermost in his mind," Morgenthau has recalled. But the United States wanted Britain to reduce or eliminate her preferential tariff system as a condition of further aid. As a result, Churchill had some difficulty in convincing Roosevelt that aid should be given with no strings attached. At one point, in half humorous desperation, the Prime Minister blurted out: "What do you want me to do? Get on my hind legs and beg like Fala?"

It was finally decided at Quebec that a special Anglo-American committee should be created to arrange an agreement on postwar

American aid for Britain. Morgenthau was named to serve as chairman of this committee, a development which inevitably left him in a strong position to bargain with Churchill. All of this may seem to suggest that Churchill was in effect bribed to accept the Morgenthau Plan. In a literal sense, he was not. There was no need for Morgenthau to make an offer and for Churchill to accept, or for White to make a deal with Churchill's adviser, Lord Cherwell, as has been suggested. The hard facts of the situation were understood well by both the Prime Minister and the Secretary of the Treasury. As the Prime Minister told Eden, "If it is between the British and German people, I am for the British. . . . " Churchill's memoir comments on the Morgenthau Plan, though understandably brief, are most revealing in this connection: "At first I violently opposed this idea. But the President, with Mr. Morgenthau—from whom we had much to ask—were so insistent that in the end we agreed to consider it." [22]

Even the opposition of Eden was not sufficient to forestall the "dollar diplomacy" victory that awaited the Secretary of the Treasury at Quebec. After others failed to draft a memorandum to his liking, Churchill himself on September 15 dictated a statement which incorporated in general terms Morgenthau's economic proposals. Churchill has written that his approval of the memorandum was subject to "the full consideration of the War Cabinet." This in no way absolves Churchill of responsibility for the agreement of September 15, which Churchill and Roosevelt both initialed; technically, all acts of the Prime Minister were subject to Cabinet approval. The memorandum initialed at Quebec included the following provisions: (1) Russia and other devastated countries should be authorized "to remove the machinery they require in order to repair the losses they have suffered"; (2) heavy industries (defined as the chemical and electrical, as well as the metallurgical

---

[22] Mosely, "The Occupation of Germany," *loc. cit.*, 596-597; Sayer, *Financial Policy, 1939-45*, 469; Morgenthau in the New York *Post*, Nov. 28-29, 1947; Morgenthau in "The Morgenthau Diaries," *Colliers*, CXX (Oct. 18, 1947), 75; Morgenthau, "Postwar Treatment of Germany," *loc. cit.*, 126; Hull, *Memoirs*, II, 1613-1614; *Time*, LXII (Nov. 23, 1953), 23; Ehrman, *Grand Strategy*, V, 516; Churchill, *Triumph and Tragedy*, 156-157, 160, 510, and 514; *Yalta Papers*, 137; Clay, *Decision in Germany*, 11.

industries) in the Saar and the Ruhr would be "put out of action and closed down"; (3) these provinces should be placed under some form of international control to prevent their re-industrialization; and, most sweeping in its potential implications, (4) the proposed program for the Saar and Ruhr "looked forward to" the conversion of Germany into a country which would be "primarily agricultural and pastoral in character." [23]

What the memorandum of September 15 said was impressive, and few readers noted what it left unsaid. The Quebec memorandum failed to provide for the partition of Germany into two states, as Morgenthau had proposed; in fact, a close reading of the Quebec memorandum might have suggested that Churchill had included a forecast of a united state: Germany, shorn of the Ruhr and Saar, was to be converted into *"a country* primarily agricultural and pastoral in character." (Author's italics.) And it should also be noted that the Quebec economic formula was a very general one. It was now certain that Germany would be de-industrialized to some extent, but how much? What would the loose phrase *"primarily* agricultural and pastoral" be made to mean? That 90 per cent of the Germans must plow, milk cows, and listen to the twitter of birds? Or that as much as 49 per cent of the population would be allowed to engage in trade and industry? (About two thirds of the German people lived in urban areas on the eve of World War II.) Obviously the answers to these questions could be found only in future detailed negotiations.

Thus, though the Quebec formula represented a partial retreat from the policy of postponement, the policy was by no means surrendered altogether. How much territory was Germany to lose? How much was Germany to pay in reparations? How? To what countries? Was Germany to be partitioned or left united? What was to be the extent of de-industrialization in Germany? All these fundamental questions remained open after the Quebec Conference, as they had been kept open during the preceding three years. The Morgenthau Plan was never to be adopted in its entirety by the government of the United States, nor even by the President.

---

[23] New York *Post*, Nov. 29, 1947; Churchill, *Triumph and Tragedy*, 157; *Yalta Papers*, 137-138.

IMMEDIATE REPERCUSSIONS OF THE QUEBEC AGREEMENT

Yet, the general effects of Morgenthau's victory were impressive and quickly felt in Washington. Morgenthau's success and his new prestige tremendously strengthened the bargaining power of the Treasury Department representatives and all other advocates of a harsh peace. In interdepartmental negotiations Treasury representatives were able to win many concessions, especially during the month of September, for they could and did insist that not only the President but even the Prime Minister had approved some of their basic views. The general effects upon military plans for the occupation of Germany were immediate and lasting. It seems safe to conclude, therefore, that the Quebec formula approximately achieved what the President desired it to achieve.

Military developments cast a spell of urgency over the efforts to revise United States policy toward Germany in mid-September, 1944. Allied forces had penetrated the Reich near Aachen; General Montgomery was insisting to Eisenhower that the Ruhr, and possibly even Berlin could be taken if Eisenhower would only "put every single thing into the left hook and stop everything else"; and, though Montgomery's vain requests were risky, there seemed a possibility that the fall of Hitler's Germany would not be long delayed. Complicating thought, somewhat, the press carried new reports that Germany was seeking a separate peace with Russia and the Soviet Government on September 23 confirmed the rumors. The same issue of the New York *Times* that reported the rumor of separate peace efforts also reported increasing Soviet fears that the West would "take too easy an attitude toward Germany after the war." To be prepared in the event that Germany might fall at any moment, the State Department in September sent Robert D. Murphy, with the rank of ambassador, to act as Political Officer for German Affairs with SHAEF. Murphy's previous service in similar activities in North Africa and Italy had convinced many liberals and leftists that he was an instrument of reaction; some flatly called him a fascist. Thus, Murphy's appointment to implement State Department policy in Eisenhower's name undoubtedly

90

caused advocates of harsh measures to redouble their efforts.[24]

The impact of the Quebec memorandum was first felt at the planning level within the interdepartmental committee which had grown out of the Working Security Committee. Treasury Department representatives now sat with representatives of the War Department's Civil Affairs Division and the State Department. Spurred on by the thought that Germany might fall at any moment, Treasury representatives demanded that the economic and financial directives for the occupation of Germany which had been sent to Eisenhower in the spring should be revised in the light of the Quebec agreement. Four meetings between September 2 and September 22 were devoted to this question of the interim directives. State Department representatives fought against the Treasury demands until the Quebec meeting made it impossible to resist them any longer. The crucial meeting of the committee was held on September 17. It ended with a major Treasury victory.

By slight changes in the wording of the interim directives, their fundamental meaning was sharply altered in the new drafts of September 17. The earlier drafts provided that Germany should receive the minimum foodstuffs necessary "to prevent disease and unrest"; the new drafts called for only enough "to prevent *serious* disease and *serious* unrest." (Author's italics.) The new directives also called for much more complete de-Nazification. The Supreme Commander was instructed to remove from office and to arrest Nazis and Nazi sympathizers who held "important and key positions" in industry, finance, education, and the press, as well as those in the government, in the courts, and in party positions. The new directives provided categorically that: "All schools and universities will be closed." They were to be reopened only after changes in personnel, curricula, and textbooks could be carried through.

In the next few days the drafts were polished. Colonel Mickey Marcus seems to have dictated the final version of the basic directive, and it met with the warm approval of the Treasury officials. "I told Jack McCloy that the directive . . . was an excel-

---

[24] Pogue, *The Supreme Command*, 95-96, 289-295; Hull, *Memoirs*, II, 1462; New York *Times*, Sept. 17, 1944.

lent job," Harry White recorded. "He said, 'You like it?', and I said, 'Yes, very much'." The harsher drafts were adopted finally by representatives of the three departments, meeting as the cabinet committee in an all-day session on September 22 in the Pentagon. Treasury representatives now declared that the harsh proposals had been approved by President Roosevelt. With the War Department and the Treasury Department now working together, State Department opposition was forestalled. Hull, however reluctantly, approved the directives as being "prepared by the War and State Departments and concurred in by the Treasury Department." The directives marked, therefore, another compromise of principle by Hull to protect the semblance of departmental prerogative. Probably it was an inevitable compromise. In any case it was one in which the Civil Affairs officers of the War Department shared responsibility; Colonel Marcus in particular talked more like Morgenthau than like his own chiefs, Stimson and McCloy. It is important to note that the new interim directives adopted on September 22, bearing the strong imprint of the Treasury Department, were basic drafts of the long-term directive which, after long and painful debate, would become known in 1945 under the title of "JCS 1067." Meanwhile, the interim directives were forwarded to General Eisenhower for implementation as the conquest of the Reich proceeded.[25]

Morgenthau subsequently used all his influence in direct negotiations with the British to make certain that they did not abandon the Quebec principles. Going far beyond financial matters, he continued to encroach upon State Department prerogatives in discussions in Washington with John Maynard Keynes and with Lord Cherwell, who was one of Churchill's four or five closest advisers. Somehow Morgenthau got possession of a British draft statement on Germany of about a hundred pages in length, dated September, 1944. In October he prepared a sharp commentary on the British draft. Assistant Secretary of War John J. McCloy tried to per-

---

[25] Hull, *Memoirs*, II, 1616; State Department, *Postwar Foreign Policy Preparation*, 369; Hammond, "JCS 1067 Policy for Germany," 84-89; and compare *Yalta Papers*, 143-154 with Holborn, *American Military Government*, 135-143, for the changes made in the interim directives; see also *Yalta Papers*, 136-143; Dorn, "The Debate over American Occupation Policy in Germany," *loc. cit.*, 494-495.

suade Morgenthau not to give this critique to Lord Cherwell, but all in vain; Morgenthau presented the memorandum to Lord Cherwell just before he left for England. He also sent a copy of it to the State Department, claiming that he had given it to Lord Cherwell with War Department approval.

In his strong critique, Morgenthau insisted that the British should abandon their own draft and accept the interim directives which had just been prepared under his influence. He insisted more specifically that the following matters were not treated adequately by the British draft, and were all essential to any long range program: (1) the elimination or destruction of German heavy industry and controls to prevent re-industrialization; (2) territorial reduction of Germany, especially separation of the Ruhr; (3) partition; (4) decentralization; (5) restitution and reparation levies; (6) reorganization of German education; (7) agrarian reforms; and (8) punishment of war criminals. The British were left to ponder over these suggestions while wondering whether they would get an extension of credit or not. It was not until the end of the year that a new Lend-Lease arrangement was worked out between Britain and the United States, and then only after "two months of very hard work" by Morgenthau's committee.[26]

Meanwhile American advocates of a moderate peace had launched their counter offensive as soon as Morgenthau returned triumphant to Washington. Their best ally had not been present at Quebec, nor did he participate in the conferences in Washington which followed. He sat in Moscow, but his armies in the autumn of 1944 began to shape the future of Central Europe.

---

[26] *Yalta Papers*, 163-165, 174; Sayer, *Financial Policy, 1939-45*, 470-474; Harrod, *The Life of John Maynard Keynes*, 588-591.

Chapter V

THE HESITANT RETREAT FROM VENGEANCE

QUITE early after September 15 both Churchill and Roosevelt reversed their Quebec positions in the debate about Germany's future. The explanation for the change seems clear: Soviet policy in the autumn of 1944 was unquestionably the best ally of those who favored a moderate policy for postwar Germany.

In August, 1944, friction between East and West reached a new high over Poland. On August 1, seeking to confront the approaching Red Army with a native regime, the underground army in Warsaw of the Polish government-in-exile began a major rising against German control. Though Russian troops were within ten miles of Warsaw, they ignored the Polish patriots for weeks, allowing German forces to slaughter thousands. Churchill and Roosevelt both asked Stalin to help the gallant Poles, but their requests met with a cold reception. Stalin only denounced the Warsaw Poles as "power-seeking criminals." Then he repented slightly. On September 13, as Roosevelt and Churchill met at Quebec, a few Soviet planes actually sought to drop food to the people of Warsaw. The gesture may have aroused new hope at Quebec, but nothing really helpful was done for Warsaw. On October 2 Polish resistance in Warsaw collapsed amidst the most brutal repressive measures by the Germans. The back of the pro-Western Polish Home Army was thus broken. Three months would pass before the Red Army "liberated" Warsaw.

The Russian failure to help Warsaw turned pro-Soviet sentiment into a mixed feeling of wonder and hostility among great numbers of British and American fighting men. Western statesmen found still more cause for concern in other Soviet policies in this period. In August and September, 1944, the Red Army occupied parts or all of Finland, Rumania, Bulgaria, Yugoslavia, and Hungary. In each of these areas the Russians acted unilaterally. To Western protests, Moscow frankly and bluntly replied that it was simply acting as the Anglo-American forces had acted in 1943 in Italy. Meanwhile, at the Dumbarton Oaks Conference on the creation of the future United Nations (August 21 - October 7), the Soviet representative had demanded sixteen seats in the General Assembly. And he had uncompromisingly resisted United States proposals for the use of veto power in the proposed Security Council of the U. N.

These diffuse developments, all of them in progress before the Quebec Conference, were not vividly brought into focus until mid-September. They must have nagged at the President's mind during the week after his return to Washington. By September 18 Hull was urgently asking the American Ambassador to Moscow if the U.S.S.R. had decided to renounce its policy of cooperation with the Western Powers.

From Moscow—acting independently of Hull—Ambassador W. Averell Harriman and George Kennan, Counsellor of the United States Embassy, on September 19 dispatched a careful and critical joint analysis of current Soviet policies. Then on September 20, in response to Hull's query of the eighteenth, they sent an even longer report. In these documents they suggested that the U.S.S.R. was becoming more certain that it could win the war and confident that it could do without the help of the West if necessary; that Moscow would prefer continued cooperation, but would try to cooperate on its own terms. Harriman and Kennan thought it might be necessary to match Stalin's disregard for American ideas with a similar disregard for his.[1]

It is ironical evidence of bureaucratic time lags that Morgen-

---

[1] Convenient surveys of the events of August-September, 1944, may be found in John L. Snell and others, *The Meaning of Yalta: Big Three Diplomacy and the New Balance of Power* (Baton Rouge, La., 1956), 14-24, 91-103, 133-136, and Feis, *Churchill, Roosevelt, Stalin*, 378-390, 409-437. See the exchanges in Ministry of Foreign Affairs of the U.S.S.R., *Correspondence . . . Chairman of the Council of Ministers of the U.S.S.R. . . . 1941-1945,* I, 249-259; II, 156-163.

thau's ideas first registered their full impact at lower levels of planning in London and Washington during the fall of 1944. But the ominous behavior of the Russians in Central Europe and the diplomatic impasse in negotiations over this and United Nations questions inevitably put high-level planning for Germany's future in a new perspective. By September 29 Roosevelt was telling Hull that "we have to remember" that the Russians would "do more or less what they wish" in the part of Germany they would occupy. Was it really wise to weaken Germany completely with the Russians already uncooperative in Central Europe? The fall of 1944 was characterized by a retreat from vengeance planning.

But retreat to what? In Washington the Joint Chiefs of Staff still hoped for Soviet help in the war against Japan and Western armies were barely inside Germany. It was still impractical to challenge the Russians in a showdown. What, then, could be done? Roosevelt suggested the answer in his messages to Stalin and Churchill on the eve of the Prime Minister's trip to Moscow in October: he hoped that no decisions on important questions would be reached until all three could meet. In the fall of 1944 the only alternative to vengeance planning for Germany was still what it had been earlier: the policy of postponement was revived in the aftermath of Quebec.

THE POLICY OF POSTPONEMENT REVIVED

On September 20 Secretary of State Hull was host to a meeting of Stimson and McCloy, Morgenthau and White, and H. Freeman Matthews of the State Department to hear Morgenthau's account of his successful negotiations at Quebec. At the end of the meeting Hull expressed his disapproval of "the way such vital matters were settled without any consultation with our Government experts or regard for what has gone before." Stimson likewise made no effort to conceal his disapproval. In fact as soon as he had heard about the developments at Quebec, Stimson had sent to the President a protest memorandum, which was drafted largely by McCloy. The Quebec agreement was neither fair to the Germans nor good for the rest of the world, "either economically or spiritually," stated the McCloy-Stimson protest; it would be, in fact, "a crime against civilization itself" to implement the agreement. Hull, too, protested directly to the President, stating that the Morgenthau Plan was an impossibility. Hull told Roosevelt he was "satisfied" that the British had been won over only by the lure of American financial aid. And the Secretary of State reminded the President that his own Department was "the organ of the Administration set up to negotiate with foreign Governments." Roosevelt said little; he seemingly had not realized the implications of the memorandum he had initialed at Quebec, but he remained noncommittal.[2]

Then someone informed the columnist Drew Pearson of the Churchill-Roosevelt agreement at Quebec. The news was leaked gradually in the press during the three days after September 21. On September 24 the Sunday edition of the New York *Times* carried a roughly accurate report under the following headline: "MORGENTHAU PLAN ON GERMANY SPLITS CABINET COMMITTEE; SECRETARY OF THE TREASURY WOULD CONVERT COUNTRY TO SMALL AGRICULTURAL HOLDINGS." With this, the Morgenthau-White plan, at least in its boldest particulars, became public knowledge; it remained to be seen whether or not it would become a political issue in the presidential election campaign, which was then well underway.

Press reaction to the Morgenthau Plan was generally unfavorable, and important newspapers were highly critical. The New York *Times* attacked it as unrealistic. The leaders of five associations of American engineers protested to the State Department that Germany could not be kept in "economic and industrial subjugation." Repercussions in England were immediate and hostile. The London *Spectator* editorialized that the Morgenthau Plan "would find little support" in Britain; "to destroy German productive capacity and markets would be fatal folly." The plan was attacked in the House of Commons, where a Labour Party member pointed out that it would "lead to a general lowering of the standard of living throughout Europe." In Germany the news from Washington reenergized morale as nothing else which had happened since 1941. Paul Joseph Goebbels and other German propagandists

---

[2] *Yalta Papers*, 136-141; Hull, *Memoirs*, II, 1614-1618; Stimson and Bundy, *On Active Service*, 578.

seized upon the news as proof of a capitalist-Jewish coalition which was bent upon destroying the German nation in the interests of Communist Russia.[3]

Roosevelt, confronted by evidence of American misgivings about the Morgenthau proposals and worried about their impact abroad, now shifted his position abruptly. On September 27 he assured Stimson that the press had exaggerated, that he had not intended to make Germany "a purely agricultural country."

Roosevelt also publicized his new, *los von Morgenthau,* attitude. Perhaps he realized that he would not be likely to alienate Jewish voters if he declared his independence of Morgenthau. For many reasons, American Jews had voted Democratic by overwhelming majorities in each presidential election since 1932; in 1944 as much as 90 per cent of the Jewish vote was to go to Roosevelt. If Roosevelt was fully aware of his strength among Jewish voters (and it may be assumed that he was) then two conclusions may be drawn: (1) his approval of major parts of the Morgenthau Plan at Quebec had not been simply a bid for Jewish support; and (2) he would need have little fear of repudiating the plan, at least in part.[4] In any case, on September 2 the President asked Leo T. Crowley, head of the Foreign Economic Administration, to coordinate and speed up the various plans for economic policy toward Germany which had thus far evolved in the departments of State, Commerce, Treasury, War, and Navy, in the Office of Strategic Services (OSS), and in Crowley's own Foreign Economic Administration. Under Crowley's direction a study would be made of the extent to which specific branches of German industry should be reduced. Roosevelt's request that the Foreign Economic Administration concern itself with the problem marked an indirect and partial repudiation of the Morgenthau Plan. The President went even further when he publicly announced on September 29 that the State Department, not the Secretary of the Treasury, would

---

[3] Friedrich and associates, *American Experiences in Military Government in World War II,* 223; *Spectator,* CLXXIII (Sept. 29, 1944), 277; Stimson and Bundy, *On Active Service,* 580.

[4] Stimson and Bundy, *On Active Service,* 580; Lawrence H. Fuchs, "American Jews and the Presidential Election Vote," *American Political Science Review,* XLIX (1955), 386.

"study and report upon the problem" of Germany's future.[5]

On the same day, while castigating the unknown person who had leaked the Quebec news to the press, the President informed Hull that "no one wants 'complete eradication of German industrial productive capacity in the Ruhr and Saar'." He suggested that his objective in those areas was "complete control," not destruction of industry. He implied that his broader objective had been to aid Britain's economic recovery. Most significant, he indirectly indicated now that he was not contemplating the destruction of German industry outside the Ruhr and the Saar. Yet, he added:

> In regard to the Soviet government, it is true that we have no idea as yet what they have in mind, but we have to remember that in their occupied territory they will do more or less what they wish. We cannot afford to get into a position of merely recording protests on our part unless there is some chance of the protests being heeded.

In this there was a suggestion that the President had initialed the Quebec memorandum in an effort to reassure the Russians that their interests would be respected. There was also here a suggestion that the main de-industrialization which the President actually favored was that which he would in any case be unable to prevent: that which the Soviet Union might carry out on its own in eastern Germany.[6]

In these days Roosevelt explained to Stimson and others that he had never intended to turn Germany into an agrarian state. He sought to shirk responsibility for the whole affair: Henry Morgenthau had "pulled a boner," Roosevelt told his Secretary of War on October 3, and he agreed with Stimson's misgivings that people might attribute Morgenthau's ideas to "racial" motivations. Incredible as it may seem, the President assured Stimson that they were "not apart" on the Morgenthau Plan. When Stimson read him the all-important passages of the Quebec agreement, the President seemed "frankly staggered." He had "no idea" how he could have initialed the agreement, he said; and in a statement which marked

---

[5] B. U. Ratchford and Wm. D. Ross, *Berlin Reparations Assignment: Round One of the German Peace Settlement* (Chapel Hill, 1947), 33-38: Holborn, *American Military Government*, 40-42; Bateman, "The Election of 1944 and Foreign Policy," 138.

[6] F. D. R. to Secretary of State, Sept. 29, 1944, *Yalta Papers*, 155.

either a terrible memory or disingenuous tactics, the President said that "he had evidently done it without much thought." Under the impact of public reaction, Morgenthau, meanwhile, agreed to desist in pressing for the adoption of his views until "after the election." Then, he stated, he fully intended "to get back into the German picture in a big way." [7]

Hull was encouraged by Roosevelt's apparent change of mind. He now sought to win the President over to a State Department program which remained true to the essential principles of previous planning, while making modest compromises with Morgenthau's desires. This program was incorporated in a State Department memorandum of September 29 which Hull on October 1 presented personally to the President. The State Department advocated demilitarization, de-Nazification, control of German industry and trade, and a standard of living which would afford no luxuries. Decentralization was to be encouraged, and spontaneous tendencies toward partition should "not be discouraged." On the other hand, no decision should be made to partition Germany "until we see what the internal situation is and what is the attitude of our principal Allies on this question." Only those factories which were "incapable of conversion to peaceful purposes" were to be destroyed, a proposal very different from Morgenthau's wish to destroy all factories which *might* be converted from peaceful output to war production. Finally, education was to be controlled, not halted, according to the State Department memorandum of September 29.[8]

This memorandum revealed that the Morgenthau Plan had not made any great impression on the State Department's planning. Probably because he still thought State Department policy was too moderate and because he still wished to give no offense to the Russians by appearing soft toward Germany, the President took his own good time in thinking through Hull's memorandum and answering it. Probably he concluded quite early that the best way out of the September cul-de-sac was to return to his original policy

---

[7] Stimson and Bundy, *On Active Service*, 580-581; Stettinius, *Roosevelt and the Russians*, 40; Sherwood, *Roosevelt and Hopkins*, 818-819; *Yalta Papers*, 165. Stimson's notes of an intimate talk with Roosevelt, Oct. 3, were sent to the Department of State for custody on Oct. 4, 1944; Historical Division, Department of State.

[8] Hull, *Memoirs*, II, 1618; *Yalta Papers*, 156-158.

of postponement. The wisdom of such a move was made even more apparent on October 18, when the Republican presidential candidate, Thomas E. Dewey, in a major foreign policy address implied that the administration's policy toward Germany was prolonging the war unnecessarily; it had strengthened the German will to fight, said Dewey.[9]

Two days later—October 20—the President answered Hull's memorandum at last. Roosevelt's answer was hailed by Hull and Stettinius as a victory for the Department of State. In actuality this memorandum was a victory for the policy of postponement. In the memorandum to Hull on October 20 the President insisted, probably with Russia in mind, that there were "some matters" in regard to planning for Germany's future that led him to believe that "speed on these matters is not an essential at the present moment." He added, significantly, that he did not like to make "detailed plans for a country which we do not yet occupy." He agreed, therefore, that no decision should be taken to partition Germany. He insisted that the aircraft industry specifically must be altogether destroyed. And he refused to commit himself to the State Department's moderate proposals concerning education and economic objectives. A careful comparison of the Hull and Roosevelt statements reveals clearly that the President still personally desired a harsher program for Germany than that which the State Department proposed. But he had come a long way from Quebec.

On the same day the President's memorandum was signed, Cordell Hull entered Bethesda Naval Medical Center, a very ill man. Out of consideration for the President he delayed his formal resignation until after the November elections. On December 1, 1944, the Under-Secretary of State, Edward R. Stettinius, formally became his successor.[10]

The day after he sent his postponement proclamation to Hull, Roosevelt made it public in an altered form. Dewey had to be

---

[9] Bateman, "The Election of 1944 and Foreign Policy," 110-111; Westerfield, *Foreign Policy and Party Politics*, 188-189.

[10] President to Secretary of State, Oct. 20, 1944, *Yalta Papers*, 158-159; Hull, *Memoirs*, II, 1621-1622, 1715-1716; State Department, *Postwar Foreign Policy Preparation*, 347.

answered, and the occasion was a speech before the Foreign Policy Association in New York on October 21. The President's comments on Germany were general and brief. They sounded moderate, but the public could interpret them as harbingers of either a harsh or a soft policy toward Germany. "We bring no charge against the German race, as such, for we cannot believe that God has eternally condemned any race or humanity," the President affirmed. "The German people are not going to be enslaved. . . . But it will be necessary for them to earn their way back . . . into the fellowship of peaceloving and law-abiding nations." Quite clearly this was neither acceptance nor rejection of the Morgenthau Plan. Dewey also neither accepted nor rejected it. Both candidates played upon the strong feelings against Germany which then prevailed. Dewey himself publicly favored internationalization of the Ruhr and Allied supervision over the remaining German industry. He complained that the Morgenthau Plan was made outside the State Department and was made public, not that it was too harsh. It seems fair to conclude, therefore, that plans for Germany never became a major issue in the campaign of 1944. Roosevelt was returned to office by an absolute majority of 53.4% of the total votes cast in November, 1944.[11]

While Roosevelt groped his way back to the policy of postponement, Churchill traveled to see "Uncle Joe" in Moscow. Amidst their preoccupation with other concerns, Churchill and Stalin discussed "the merits and drawbacks of the Morgenthau Plan." Churchill summarized the results of the Moscow discussion in a telegram to Roosevelt the day after the President spoke before the Foreign Policy Association. The telegram of October 22 illustrated that the British Prime Minister as well as Roosevelt sought at times to appease the Russians:

> We also discussed informally the future partition of Germany. . . . Contrary to his previously expressed view, he [Stalin] would be glad to see Vienna the capital of a federation of south-German states, including Austria, Bavaria, Württemberg, and Baden. As you know, the idea of Vienna becoming the capital of a large Danubian federation

---

[11] New York *Times*, Oct. 22, 1944; Bateman, "The Election of 1944 and Foreign Policy," 137-139, 382, 389.

has always been attractive to me, though I should prefer to add Hungary, to which U. J. [Uncle Joe] is strongly opposed.

As to Prussia, U. J. wished the Ruhr and the Saar detached and put out of action and probably under international control and a separate state formed in the Rhineland. He would also like the internationalization of the Kiel Canal. *I am not opposed to this line of thought.* [Author's italics.]

Churchill added that no "fixed conclusions" were reached in these matters. He and Stalin agreed at Moscow that the Morgenthau Plan should be subjected to further discussion in the European Advisory Commission, and that final decisions should only be reached at the forthcoming Big Three meeting.[12]

Thus, just when Roosevelt retreated from his Quebec position, at least in public, Churchill led Stalin to think that Russian ambitions in Germany might find fulfillment. By indicating his informal approval of partition, he went well beyond the memorandum which he and Roosevelt had initialed at Quebec. Part of the explanation for this may be found in the fact that Churchill was still uncertain about the extension of American credits; the Morgenthau committee was still considering that question. Churchill's efforts to secure some division of power between Russia and the West in eastern Europe probably made him unusually willing to talk of a harsh peace with Germany while at Moscow. For all these reasons, it would seem, Churchill indicated that he was "not opposed" to principles which were essentially those Stalin had advanced at Teheran and earlier, and which Morgenthau and White had presented in the "dog days" of 1944 in Washington. Churchill's telegram left Roosevelt unmoved from the policy of postponement into which he had withdrawn in October. "Your statement is most interesting," he advised Churchill in noncommittal fashion on October 22. "We should discuss these matters together with our Pacific war effort at the forthcoming three party meeting."

Stettinius, meanwhile, continued to try to win presidential approval of instructions to the European Advisory Commission. On November 11, the elections over, Stettinius presented Roosevelt

---

[12] *Yalta Papers,* 159-160; Churchill, *Triumph and Tragedy,* 240-241.

with a new draft statement on reparations: "You will note as I promised, it is only seven pages," he advised the President. The document touched on matters that went much beyond the reparations issue. The State Department now advised the President that inter-Allied agreement on policy toward Germany should be sought within the E.A.C., and insisted that the need for such agreement was urgent. Its forebodings forecast the future:

> . . . British, Russian and American attitudes on the question show major divergencies which, if allowed to persist, would begin to be reflected in widely different policies at an early stage in the occupation of Germany. Such differences, in turn would lay the basis for new European rivalries and endanger the effectiveness of an international security organization. . . .
>
> Complete identity of methods and objectives in the several zones of occupation is unnecessary and unattainable; it is essential, however, in the economic as in other fields, that the policies carried out in each zone be such as to facilitate a solution of the German problem in a fashion which is acceptable to all major powers and to Germany's neighbors.

The State Department's memorandum then sketched briefly the major differences over Germany's future that had appeared among the Allies. The Russians, it warned, intended to go farther than the British in removing industrial owners and landowners from their "present positions of control." The Russians also intended to take heavy reparations from Germany to aid their own economic reconstruction. The British, on the other hand, were chiefly interested in placing controls on the German economy to restrain future competition; they did not want to wreck the economy and did not demand heavy reparations payments. On one issue the State Department proved to be wrong: because the Russians were demanding reparations from Germany's postwar production, the memorandum suggested that Russia would not demand "sweeping deindustrialization." This, of course, might have been put in as one more State Department attempt to counter the Morgenthau argument; but it was also a logical error at the time, in view of the seemingly contradictory Soviet proposals for the economic future of Germany.

104

The State Department proposed that the United States should support the British and the Russians to some extent. Economic controls, economic disarmament, and reparations for the U.S.S.R. were approved. But the memorandum then established some important and moderating reservations. Our occupation forces, it advised, must "prevent development of a chaotically unmanageable economic situation." Initially they must offer the German people "the lowest standards of health, diet and shelter compatible with the prevention of disease and disorder," but this rigorous treatment would be relaxed when "political tendencies within Germany" warranted relaxation. The United States would approve the removal of some capital equipment as reparation; but generally, the Department of State concluded, "We should favor a short program of heavy reparations payments, derived largely from current German production." [13]

On November 22 Stettinius repeated substantially to the President the recommendations of November 10, and on November 29 sent him an up-to-date survey of British views on the economic treatment of Germany. "British officials seem strongly opposed to sweeping measures of de-industrialization and extreme impoverishment of Germany," Stettinius advised the President. To this Roosevelt replied on December 4 in perhaps his most important statement of the war on economic plans for Germany. Apparently because he did not wish to arouse either Morgenthau or Stalin, the President indicated that his statement should be kept confidential. His views were cryptically stated as follows:

(1) That in the Economic Treatment of Germany we should let her come back industrially to meet her own needs, but not to do any exporting for sometime and [until] we know better how things are going to work out.

(2) We are against reparations.

(3) We do want restitution of looted property of all kinds.[14]

Though the President thus partly revealed his thoughts on economic matters to Stettinius, he refused to provide policy instructions on these major issues to the United States representatives on

---

[13] *Yalta Papers,* 160 n; 165-171.
[14] *Ibid.,* 174.

the European Advisory Commission. These were matters which the State Department officials should keep "in the linings of their hats," he stated on December 4. The European Advisory Commission was not to be allowed to negotiate an occupation policy for Germany. Perhaps, as Walter L. Dorn has suggested, this resulted from the President's determination "to prevent the initiative in policy-making from passing imperceptibly to the British and the Russians." [15] But another consideration may well have overridden this one. The President was still determined to postpone Big Three decisions concerning Germany until the war ended. Concerning Germany's future frontier with France, for example, Roosevelt on December 6 advised Churchill: "It appears to me at the present time that no advantage to our common war effort would result from an attempt to settle this question now and that its settlement subsequent to the collapse of Germany is preferable." [16]

Thus, for four more months after October, 1944, the United States representatives on the European Advisory Commission could only discuss occupation details. They were forced to work under a pall of uncertainty about their own government's position in important German matters. Again, the understandable frustrations of the experts made it impossible for them to judge objectively the situation in which they found themselves. "During these months of 'no policy'," Mosely has recalled, "Winant was unable to press for Allied agreement on a broad range of agreed policy in preparation for the surrender of Germany, for he had no backing from Washington for this effort." But Mosely would be the first to agree that no instructions were better than specific instructions to accept the Morgenthau Plan—or Soviet demands. In view of the military situation of December, 1944, specific terms favorable to Russia constituted the only practical alternative to delay of policy decisions. It was a perceptive editorialist who wrote in the *New Statesman and Nation* on the eve of the Yalta Conference that "fear of being suspected by other Allies of 'softness,' or even of wanting to make a deal with Germany, has paralysed planning."

---

[15] *Ibid.*, 174; Dorn, "The Debate over American Occupation Policy in Germany," *loc. cit.*, 488.

[16] Churchill, *Triumph and Tragedy*, 258-259; *Yalta Papers*. 291.

Roosevelt's return to the policy of postponement must be viewed in the light of these circumstances.[17]

FRANCE AND THE ZONES FOR GERMANY AND BERLIN

The chief accomplishment of the European Advisory Commission between the Quebec and Yalta conferences was the revision of plans for the occupation zones of Germany in accordance with the the Roosevelt-Churchill agreement of September. This work was affected in important ways by the reemergence of France as a national entity. On October 18 General Charles de Gaulle's liberation government demanded that France be given representation on the European Advisory Commission and a zone of occupation in Germany.

In August, 1944, the British had already begun to call for French participation in the occupation of Germany. Roosevelt had not shown favor for the idea, however, and was even slow to recognize de Gaulle's regime as the de facto government of France. Western concern over Soviet behavior in September and October may have helped bring a change in Roosevelt's attitude toward France. In any case, Churchill was scarcely back in England when he was suddenly advised that the United States would recognize de Gaulle as head of a provisional government of France. On October 21 Moscow was just as abruptly notified of the American decision. With Churchill strongly championing de Gaulle's demand for a part in shaping the future destiny of Germany, on November 11, 1944, it was agreed that his provisional government should share in the work of the E.A.C.

At this stage of the war Stalin was strongly opposed to giving France a zone of occupation in postwar Germany. Nor had Roosevelt yet given his approval. To avoid embarrassments, therefore, a revised zonal agreement in E.A.C. was quickly drafted before the French actively joined in the work of the Commission. The basic decisions at Quebec were developed into more detailed terms, completed by the E.A.C. on November 14.

The E.A.C. agreements provided that a somewhat enlarged southwestern zone of Germany would be occupied by the United

---

[17] Mosely, "Dismemberment of Germany," *loc. cit.*, 491; *New Statesman and Nation*, XXIX (Jan. 27, 1945), 51.

States. The northwestern zone, as the British had wished, would be occupied by the United Kingdom. Within the northwestern zone, the United States would control the ports of Bremen and Bremerhaven, and the United States should be given transit facilities through British-held territory to the American zone of occupation.

The Soviet-British-American agreements of November 14 also delineated the sectors of occupation within Greater Berlin. The November amendment of earlier plans was very specific about the areas each ally was to occupy:

North-Eastern part of "Greater Berlin" (districts of Pankow, Prenzlanerberg, Mitte, Weissensee, Friedrichshain, Lichtenberg, Treptow, Köpeneck) will be occupied by the forces of the U.S.S.R.:

North-Western part of "Greater Berlin" (districts of Reinickendorf, Wedding, Tiergarten, Charlottenburg, Spandau, Wilmersdorf) will be occupied by the forces of the United Kingdom:

Southern part of "Greater Berlin" (districts of Zehlendorf, Steglitz, Schöneberg, Kreuzberg, Tempelhof, Neukölln) will be occupied by the forces of the United States of America.

No provision was yet made for French participation in the occupation of Berlin. Much more fateful, no provisions for transit facilities between the western zones of Germany and the city of Berlin were written into the E.A.C. agreement. The sins of omission of 1944—for which the military authorities were chiefly responsible—would lead to great anxieties in the crisis winter of 1948-1949 and again ten years later in the Khrushchev era.

Another E.A.C. agreement reached on November 14 sought to provide a system of unified control over Germany. This agreement, the British representative has recalled, was reached without acrimony between September and November, 1944. The agreement provided that the zone commanders of Great Britain, the Soviet Union, and the United States would exercise supreme authority in their respective zones. But the three commanders would sit together in a "Control Council" in Berlin to establish—by unanimous decisions—common policy in matters concerning Germany as a whole. Specific provision was made for joint policy in Berlin. It was now up to the Big Three themselves to approve the work of the experts. That approval would be forthcoming—with no significant changes except for allowing France a share in the occupation of Germany—at the Yalta Conference.[18]

With these agreements drafted, the way seemed open for the admission of a French representative to the European Advisory Commission. René Massigli, French Ambassador to London, took his place there on November 27. This move—reflecting French preoccupation about future relations with the ancient enemy—marked the first important success in French foreign policy after recognition of the provisional government. It only whetted the Gallic appetite. What French leaders wanted was frankly admitted, as it had been by other rulers of France since the seventeenth century: Foreign Minister Georges Bidault publicly spoke of the Rhine as "this French river." In speech after speech de Gaulle summed up his chief desires: "the definite presence of French power from one end of the Rhine to the other, the separation of the left bank of the Rhine and the Ruhr basin from the future German state, or world of states." In 1958-1959 de Gaulle would talk like a constructive statesman. In 1944 he spoke like a cross between Clemenceau and Joan of Arc. What he then desired was nothing less than "another Peace of Westphalia, which had once set the seal on the division of Germany into petty principalities and vassal states." [19]

For his fellow Frenchmen as for de Gaulle, the German problem in the winter of 1944-1945 was "the center of the universe." A few months earlier the French Resistance movement had held out hope of more modern and rational approaches to the German problem. As late as September, 1944, the *Mouvement de Liberation Nationale* (M.L.N.) distributed thousands of copies of its declaration that the way to prevent future German aggression lay in European political and economic federation. By December, 1944, this notion was losing some of its earlier appeal. General de Gaulle insisted

---

[18] Marcel Vigneras, *Rearming the French* (Washington. 1957). 317, 322; State Department, *Postwar Foreign Policy Preparation*, 344; *Yalta Papers*, 300-304, 118-127, and 688; Mosely, "The Occupation of Germany," *loc. cit.*, 598; Churchill, *Triumph and Tragedy*, 252-253.

[19] Herbert Luethy, *France against Herself*, Eric Mosbacher, transl., (New York, 1955), 340; *Yalta Papers*, 283-309 *passim*.

that annexations were not only desirable but possible: the way to the Rhine, he suggested, lay through the gates of the Kremlin.

Russia and France were "united by history and geography in an indissoluble community of interests," de Gaulle told the French people. None greeted his nationalistic and eastern-oriented out-pourings with louder applause in those days than did the French Communists, who went beyond de Gaulle in their "bloodthirsty calls for revenge on Germany." By flying to Moscow, de Gaulle might hope not only to win the Rhine but also to consolidate the most disparate political elements of France behind his leadership. At the beginning of December, he went. Stalin entertained de Gaulle with his best "vodka diplomacy," and agreed to sign with the French a treaty of alliance. Stalin flattered (and frightened) his visitor by discussing with him the kind of peace the Russians thought was needed in eastern Europe. Stalin proposed to de Gaulle that Poland should win Silesian territory as far west as the Neisse River as well as East Prussia (except for Königsberg). Stalin also tried to persuade de Gaulle to recognize the puppet regime he was grooming for the government of Poland. In close consultation with the Western Allies, de Gaulle held out against this—even at the cost of his own ambitions for France: Stalin proved to be only an interested and noncommittal listener when de Gaulle presented his request for the Rhine. The Soviet leader hastened to inform Churchill and Roosevelt that no bargains had been struck at Moscow and that in discussing the Rhineland he had "stressed the difficulty of the problem."[20]

As the year 1944 ended, the French used their position in the European Advisory Commission to push their immediate postwar desires in Germany. France should be allowed to participate in the signing of the German surrender document, and a French text

---

[20] C. H. Pegg, "Die Résistance als Träger der europäischer Einigungsbes-trebungen in Frankreich waehrend des zweiten Weltkrieges," *Europa-Archiv*, VII (1952), 5197-5206; Konrad F. Bieber, *L'Allemagne vue par les écrivains de la Résistance Francaise* (Geneva etc., 1954), 150-160; Churchill, *Triumph and Tragedy*, 258-259; *Yalta Papers*, 288-309, 572; Feis, *Churchill, Roosevelt, Stalin*, 473, 477; Ministry of Foreign Affairs of the U.S.S.R., *Correspondence . . . Chairman of the Council of Ministers of the U.S.S.R. . . . 1941-1945*, I, 271-281; II, 170-172. For French concern about the expansion of Soviet power see *Yalta Papers*, 299-300, 956-957. Public aspects of de Gaulle's state visit are documented in Rothstein, trans., *Soviet Foreign Policy during the Patriotic War*, II, 185-196.

should be equally as authentic as texts in Russian and English; France should be allocated a zone of occupation in western Germany and a Berlin sector; France should also share in the central Allied control authority in Germany. It appeared at this time that French leaders did not wish to see Germany "reduced to economic misery since they believe that this would inevitably breed trouble." They did, however, favor the separation of the Ruhr from Germany proper and the elimination of German "war industries and near war industries." The French government also wanted at least the right to occupy the Rhineland, and there was "every likelihood" that the French would "try to make their occupation permanent." When it learned unofficially that the Yalta meeting was in the offing, the provisional government of France on January 13, 1945, formally and strongly requested the right to meet with "the other great allied powers"; and the de Gaulle government hinted that it might not be bound by decisions affecting Germany which were made in its absence.

The French desire to meet with the Big Three was not honored. But upon recommendation of the Department of State, the President by January 19 had "approved in principle" the French desire to participate in the occupation of Germany. Another important decision had been taken at the end of December. On December 28 an interdepartmental committee, the State-War-Navy Coordinating Committee, had advised Roosevelt that it was "in the best interests of the U. S. that France resume her traditional position as a principal power capable of playing a part in the occupation of Germany and in maintaining the peace in Europe." With de Gaulle talking of fifty French divisions by the end of 1945, and the Joint Chiefs of Staff predicting that the French would "make every effort to obtain arms from any source," the President in January approved increased United States military aid to France.[21]

In German questions, therefore, the Big Three were slowly becoming three-and-a-half. The haughty leader of France would not be allowed to participate in the Yalta Conference, but his Western patrons would there seek decisions in favor of the proud nation de Gaulle so staunchly represented. The revival of France

---

[21] *Yalta Papers*, 292-309; Vigneras, *Rearming the French*, 337.

promised to complicate the military occupation of Germany, but not to ease its pains for the Germans.

POLAND DEMANDS A SHARE OF EASTERN GERMANY

The problems of a reemerging Poland also influenced Big Three planning for the future of Germany. Throughout 1944 it had become increasingly and painfully apparent that the Soviet Union would insist upon keeping after the war the eastern territories of the prewar Poland which the Red Army had grabbed in 1939. Churchill and Roosevelt—the latter even more reluctantly than the Prime Minister—essentially agreed to this, seeking only slight modifications in the frontier in Poland's favor. Despite the protests of the Polish government-in-exile in London, it was almost certain that the future frontier of Poland would run very close to that "Curzon Line" which Western statesmen in 1919 had proposed as an ethnic boundary between the Polish and the Russo-Ukraine populations.

The Polish government-in-exile, while not wishing to part with Polish eastern territory, was quite anxious to absorb eastern German provinces. Hard pressed by Churchill to accept the Curzon Line as an eastern frontier, Polish Foreign Minister Tadeusz Romer at the end of January, 1944, asked Anthony Eden and President Roosevelt if Poland could count upon winning all German territory east of the Oder River. Romer let it be known that this should include "the territory of the Free City of Danzig, and the entire territory of East Prussia," that the German cession should be permanent, and that a rump Germany should be required to absorb all the German-speaking people who lived in these areas. Both Roosevelt and Eden replied vaguely. At Moscow in October, 1944, Stanislaw Mikolajczyk, head of the Polish government-in-exile, expressed an interest in the partition of Germany, and sought reassurance from Churchill and Stalin that Poland would win German territory after the war. He demanded that the German city of Stettin be included and that Polish forces should participate in the postwar occupation of Germany.

Back in London, Mikolajczyk discussed the matter with his cabinet. One member, General M. Kukiel, expressed a sage misgiving which events have proven well-founded. Counselling against taking too much German land, Kukiel warned that the Germans later were sure to demand its return; that "Poland would not be able to count on a Western guarantee of support, so Poland would have to rely on the Soviet Union." Other members of the cabinet supported Mikolajczyk's position in favor of gains from Germany. But the cabinet was unable to agree to recognize the loss of territories in the east of Poland to the Soviet Union. Believing that a Polish-Soviet agreement was necessary to prevent the Russians from installing their own puppet regime in Poland, Mikolajczyk late in November resigned as premier of the government-in-exile.

Stalin seems to have decided at about this time to go ahead with the installation of a satellite government in Poland, brought in with the baggage of the Red Army. With such a government in control of Poland, there would be no danger to the Soviet Union in the annexation of additional German territory by the new Poland. In Moscow, Ambassador W. Averell Harriman was quick to detect the new trend. "I am somewhat concerned over the expanding concept of the Soviet Government in connection with the future western frontier of Poland," Harriman telegraphed Washington on December 19. Harriman noted that in Stalin's discussions with de Gaulle the Soviet czar had gone beyond his previous proposals and had talked of giving Poland all of Germany east of the Oder and the "lower Neisse" rivers. Harriman warned that such a line would require the removal and resettlement of "several million more Germans" than the six million Churchill had previously talked of moving to rump-Germany from Polish-won territories.

On December 27 Stalin went a step further, announcing to Roosevelt his intention of recognizing his puppet-Poles in the "Committee of National Liberation" as the Polish provisional government, completely ignoring the pro-Western Polish government-in-exile in London and the interests of the West in postwar Poland. Roosevelt and Churchill were quick to register vigorous protests against such action, but to no avail. On January 5, 1945, Moscow bestowed full diplomatic recognition upon the "Warsaw Government" which the Red Army had installed in power.

In view of the bestiality of the German treatment of Poles during the war, a political renaissance of the London regime in Poland would have been an awesome enough harbinger of things to come for Germans. Stalin's puppets would be even more bent on revenge, because their demands would be instruments for the achievement of Soviet power in Central-Eastern Europe.[22]

Thus, while Roosevelt and Churchill had beaten a partial retreat from the vengeance policy of Quebec, the troubled revival of national governments in Poland and France bolstered the arguments of those who favored harsh treatment for the German Reich. Meanwhile, ironically, lower-level military officials of the United States belatedly began absorbing the Morgenthau doctrine which the President himself had already in large part renounced.

THE MORGENTHAU PLAN AT EISENHOWER'S HEADQUARTERS

Military planning for the occupation of Germany was continued in England while on the continent the occupation was actually beginning.

The Anglo-American "German Country Unit," which had prepared the military government *Handbook* on Germany in 1944, had not survived the month of August. It has been suggested that this organization had to be abolished in order to avoid arousing Soviet suspicion that the British and Americans were combining against Russian interests. It would be interesting to know whether or not Morgenthau had any part in securing the orders which dissolved it. In any case, the "German Country Unit" was broken up. To function as planning units and potential military government cadres, a "United States Group, Control Council for Germany" was created between August and October, 1944, and a similar British organization was developed. Many of the officers who had served in the Anglo-American "Germany Country Unit" found positions on the new Group Control councils. Their hope that the

---

22 Rozek, *Allied Wartime Diplomacy, passim,* especially 198, 274-275, 284-285, 295-296; Wolfgang Wagner, *Die Entstehung der Oder-Neisse-Linie waehrend des zweiten Weltkrieges* (Stuttgart, 1953); *Yalta Papers,* 202-226; Charles F. Delzell in Snell and others, *The Meaning of Yalta,* 75-97; Elizabeth Wiskemann, *Germany's Eastern Neighbours: Problems Relating to the Oder-Neisse Line and the Czech Frontier Regions* (London etc., 1956), 70-83. For criticism of the Wiskemann volume see Michael Freund, "Die Oder-Neisse-Linie," *Geschichte in Wissenschaft und Unterricht,* VIII (1957), 393-404.

Soviet Union might send a parallel planning group to London to help draft coordinated plans never materialized.

The struggle to define policy within the United States Group, Control Council for Germany was so stormy that it was commonly called by participants "the battle of Bushy Park," after the name of the London suburb in which it was fought out. After the Quebec Conference much of the previous planning done in England was scrapped; but the controversial *Handbook,* after a few minor changes, was in fact issued to military government personnel. Then "significant personnel changes" were effected in the United States Group, Control Council for Germany. Colonel Bernard Bernstein, Morgenthau's friend, became Director of the Finance Division of the reorganized United States Group, while retaining his position as chief of the Finance Division of the Civil Affairs Division of SHAEF. Thereupon, "many new recruits for his office arrived from the Treasury Department." Furthermore, Bernstein constantly kept Morgenthau informed of planning developments at Bushy Park, with or without the knowledge of his superior officers. Some of the "old hands" on the Group Control Council requested transfers in protest; but this expression of their disgust with developments only speeded them up.

In the late fall and early winter preliminary drafts of the new general policy directive—the future "JCS 1067"—began to arrive at Bushy Park from Washington, and became the basis for the planning efforts of the United States Group, Control Council for Germany. These preliminary drafts had been hammered together in interdepartmental conferences in Washington, and reflected the wide differences that existed among the planners there. Interpreting them caused endless controversy among the planners in Bushy Park. Generally, however, the new draft directives were considerably harsher than earlier Army assumptions in England had been.

Most of the division chiefs in the United States Group, Control Council, opposed the more drastic policy which now flowed from Washington, insisting that it would breed "chaos, discontent, and political radicalism." But the "revolt of the division chiefs" was quickly quelled by instructions from above that they should view the drafts of JCS 1067 as commands. The interpretation given to this emerging directive, JCS 1067, at the top level within the United States Group was "essentially in line with the original Morgenthau memorandum." In the last analysis the SHAEF Civil Affairs Division held veto power over the decisions of the Group Control Council, and this situation somewhat confused planning.

The Civil Affairs Division of SHAEF insisted that the future American zone of occupation in Germany should be administered as exclusively as possible by the United States Army, with little or no regard for overall control from Berlin. But without overall control and integrated Allied policy no constructive policy in Germany could succeed. Thus, purely professional desires of Army officers to jump the red-tape traces of inter-Allied cooperation militated in favor of a harsher program for Germany in the winter of 1944-1945. To make sure that instructions from above continued to be harsh, Colonel Bernstein returned to Washington in January, 1945. There, in a series of conferences with Treasury officials, Bernstein helped draft financial and other provisions for the post-surrender policy directive for Germany which would eventually be known as JCS 1067. A tentative draft of the financial section of this directive, reflecting Treasury demands, was completed in Washington on February 12, the day after the Yalta Conference ended.[23]

ROOSEVELT AND CHURCHILL ON THE EVE OF YALTA

As 1944 became 1945, both the Treasury Department and the State Department sought the President's definite approval for their diverse programs for Germany. Neither succeeded in getting specific commitments, but it is certain that in this period the State Department won an extended hearing for its proposals. Two events served to increase the influence upon the President of State Department planning for Germany: (1) the State Department won allies in the new "State-War-Navy Coordinating Committee," created in 1944; (2) improved liaison was achieved between the State Department and the President.

---

[23] Friedrich and associates, *American Experiences in Military Government in World War II*, 219-220, 224-236; Hammond, "JCS 1067 Policy for Germany," 113-117; Zink, *American Military Government in Germany*, 42-43; Zink, *The United States in Germany*, 21; James Stewart Martin, *All Honorable Men* (Boston, 1950), 24-25.

The new State-War-Navy Coordinating Committee brought increased contact among moderate-minded leaders of the three departments which opposed Treasury Department demands. This committee gave considerable attention to the problem of Germany on the eve of the Yalta Conference. At its meeting on January 16, 1945, James Forrestal, Secretary of the Navy, bluntly indicated his disapproval of: "(a) mass murder of the Germans; (b) their enslavement; of (c) industrial devastation of the country." Secretary of War Stimson concurred in Forrestal's remarks. It may be assumed that the sentiment of this group was frequently conveyed to the President by Edward R. Stettinius, for the Secretary of State talked with the President "many times" during the weeks just before Roosevelt departed for Yalta. Contact was also maintained between the State Department and the White House by Charles E. Bohlen, the future Ambassador to the U.S.S.R. Harry Hopkins, worried about the lack of contact between Roosevelt and the State Department, had secured Bohlen's appointment as a special liaison officer late in 1944. An experienced Foreign Service Officer, Bohlen had served in the American Embassy in Moscow and as Roosevelt's translator during the Teheran Conference. Bohlen participated in the drafting of State Department policy memoranda in preparation for the Yalta voyage, placed these before the President from time to time, and then worked with Roosevelt at Yalta as a special translator.[24]

Through Stettinius and Bohlen, State Department experts drafted and presented to the President between November 10 and January 18 voluminous reports on every issue which conceivably might arise at the forthcoming Big Three conference. These memoranda indicated the attitudes which the State Department believed the governments of Britain and Russia (and, in the case of the German problem, France) took toward these issues, and recommended positions which the President should take on them at Yalta. The President gave considerable attention to the proposals concerning Germany as they were developed. The entire set of pre-conference

---

[24] Millis ed., *The Forrestal Diaries*, 25; Stettinius, *Roosevelt and the Russians*, 29-30; U. S. Senate, 83rd Congress, 1st Session, *Nomination of Charles E. Bohlen: Hearings before the Committee on Foreign Relations, March 2, and 18, 1953* (1953), 7, 116.

papers was then assembled and Stettinius presented them to the President on the morning of January 18. Among the specific recommendations for the agenda at Yalta, Stettinius suggested that the President should seek to obtain "Soviet-British agreement to the short term political and economic treatment of Germany" as outlined in the collected memoranda. The President was much impressed by the collected papers, and gave instructions that they be kept in his cabin during the forthcoming sea voyage.[25]

The major paper concerning Germany in this collection, which came to be called the "Briefing Book," was dated January 12. It showed that the State Department continued to fear the possibility that the Russians might work unilaterally in Germany to accomplish their own type of social and political reforms and to maintain long-range control through a puppet government. Thus, the State Department recommended strongly that overall inter-Allied administration of Germany be achieved: "The establishment of comprehensive military government," it prophetically and hopefully suggested, "would prevent the . . . undesirable development of the importation into Germany of a substantially ready-made provisional government perhaps recognized by and functioning under special foreign auspices." The State Department, among its short-term proposals, recommended the demilitarization of Germany and the destruction (*not* seizure by the occupying powers) of German war materials, and the destruction (*not* removal) of plants and machines which were "incapable of conversion to peaceful uses." No aircraft production would be allowed. The Nazi Party, all Nazi laws, and Nazi semi-official institutions, such as the Labor Front, should be dissolved. Some two million "active Nazis" should be removed from public and semi-public offices, but civil servants among the remaining four million "nominal" members of the N.S.D.A.P. might be used by the occupation authorities in their operations if they were efficient and obedient. Desiring not to leave democratic Germans stigmatized by association with the victors, as had happened after 1918, the State Department recommended against allowing anti-Nazi Germans to take over the government immediately. All war criminals and "the principal political malefactors" should be

25 Perkins, *The Roosevelt I Knew*, 390; *Yalta Papers*, 165-201.

arrested. Educational reform should be sought "as unobtrusively as possible" within the existing German educational machinery, when it was purged of Nazi influences.

The chief long-range objective of the United States in Germany should be, according to these Department of State papers, "the assimilation of the German people into the world society of peace-loving nations." This could only be accomplished through positive measures. In these papers Germany's repudiation of militaristic and ultranationalistic ideologies would depend in the long run upon "the psychological disarmament of the German people, tolerable economic conditions, and the development of stable political conditions." The State Department memoranda recommended that measures for the control of Germany should be as simple and as few in number as would be compatible with safety. It warned against an "indefinitely continued coercion of so many millions of technically resourceful people." The State Department recommended that the President oppose "the forcible partition of Germany," insisting that dismemberment would not take the place of safety controls. It cautioned that disruption of the German economy would cause the decline of the general European standard of living, not merely that of Germany. It called for decentralization within Germany, including the division of Prussia into "several medium-sized states," but warned against carrying even decentralization too far: "the traditional democratic groups in Germany have generally favored a greater unification of the Reich," it rightly remembered.

The State Department recommended in this memorandum of January 12 that Germany's frontiers be made essentially the same as those the Treaty of Versailles had established in 1919, except that Poland should acquire "East Prussia (except for the Koenigsberg area), the former Free City of Danzig, German Upper Silesia, and the eastern portion of Pomerania possessing an area of approximately 6,812 square miles." The State Department had known for some time that the U.S.S.R. would "insist on the annexation of a substantial portion of East Prussia," including Königsberg, and on January 8 the Deputy Director of the Office of European Affairs recommended to Stettinius that the United States should agree to this demand. The desire for Soviet cooperation in the war against Japan encouraged the willingness to make this concession.

119

The Briefing Book paper concerning Poland made it clear that the President should *resist* demands that Poland receive territory which would include the cities of Stettin in Pomerania and Breslau in Silesia. In other words, the Department of State recommended against what has become known as the "Oder-Neisse line."

The Briefing Book papers on Germany recommended economic disarmament and controls on German trade and industry. But they also called for "allied acceptance of large responsibilities for guidance and reorientation of German economic life, including the prevention of an unmanageably chaotic economic situation in the initial period after defeat." During the early post-defeat period, the occupation authorities "should take no steps to provide a higher living standard than is required for prevention of disease and disorder." But agreement should be sought on the definition of this minimum "and the measures to be taken, if necessary, to assure such a minimum." Two clauses in the State Department's commentary on these recommendations reflected Morgenthau's impact upon policy, and left an ambiguity for Roosevelt to clarify in any way he might choose at Yalta: (1) "the heavy industry sector of the German economy could be substantially contracted during a control period in ways which will aid the recovery and industrial development of other European countries without crippling Germany's capacity to meet the basic needs of her population"; and (2) the future reparations program should be small and of short duration, but might allow the "transfer of existing German capital equipment rather than of current German output." [26]

Inclusion of these clauses was an unspecified and reluctant but obvious concession to the Secretary of the Treasury. Morgenthau himself reopened the Treasury campaign to determine German policy in January, 1945. Fully aware of the advantages of having the last word with the President before he departed for Yalta, Morgenthau on January 10 strongly recommended to the President that Germany be deprived of her heavy industries, arguing that "the real motive" of those who opposed his concepts was the desire to build up Germany as a bulwark against Communism. Morgenthau may have noticed the difference between building up

---

[26] *Yalta Papers,* 178-190. See also *ibid.,* 447-455, for concern about Soviet policies.

Germany as a threat to the U.S.S.R. and refusal to tear Germany apart, which would open the way for Soviet domination, but he failed to suggest anything in between.

Morgenthau got a certain amount of outside support in the last skirmishes on the Potomac before Yalta. On January 10 Leo Crowley's Foreign Economic Administration presented to the President the interim report on the economic treatment of Germany which Roosevelt on September 28 had requested it to prepare. Crowley's F.E.A. report disagreed with the Morgenthau doctrine that all German heavy industry should be eliminated, but advocated a generally harsh treatment of the defeated Reich.

The Foreign Economic Administration's interim report of January 10 was, above all, a cautious, tentative, and ambiguous document. It tended to recommend controls rather than destruction of German industry. It frowned on "a thoroughgoing political, cultural or industrial dismemberment of Germany." It recommended a form of "economic and industrial disarmament" that would do "a minimum of damage to the economic fabric of Europe. . . ." It thus contemplated the supervision of German coal production, not its radical curtailment. But it foresaw the continuation of some industrial disarmament for an "indefinite" period and would eliminate some industries, including "any substantial war potential in the aircraft industry. . . ." It called for additional study of proposals to separate the Ruhr and areas east of the Oder River from Germany as a step toward economic disarmament. All in all, the F.E.A. interim report was not so much a body of recommendations as a prospectus for further research. It pointed to the lack of up-to-date information on German industry, and cautioned that such information would not be obtainable until hostilities were ended. The net effect of the F.E.A. report must have been in favor of postponement of basic decisions concerning Germany's postwar economy and reparations.[27]

---

[27] Hammond, "JCS 1067 Policy for Germany," 117-118; Holborn, *American Military Government*, 42; Strauss, *Division and Dismemberment of Germany*, 76-78; United States Foreign Economic Administration, *A Program for German Economic and Industrial Disarmament: A Study Submitted by the Foreign Economic Administration (Enemy Branch)* to the U. S. Senate, 79th Congress, 2nd Session, Subcommittee Monograph No. 6 of the Subcommittee on War Mobilization of the Committee on Military Affairs, 2 vols. (1946), I, x; II, 379-410.

One wonders how Morgenthau reacted to the F.E.A. interim report. The State Department papers on Germany inevitably aroused his anguish and bitter opposition. Apparently these papers were given to the Treasury officials by the Department of State, for they sent their stinging critique of the documents directly to the Department and in all probability Morgenthau made known to the President the Treasury's opposition to the State Department memoranda. To prevent Germany from starting a new war within a generation she must be made weak and kept weak, the Treasury critique insisted. "Any program which has as its purpose the building up of Germany as a bulwark against Russia and communism will inevitably lead to a third World War." It was important to deprive Germany of her chemical, metallurgical and electrical industries, and equally as important "to build up heavy industry in the liberated countries surrounding Germany." Equipment moved from the Rhine-Ruhr area would help in this respect.

Was the Treasury fully aware of the implications of its proposals? The answer was in this memorandum: "In this way the whole balance of industrial power in Europe will be shifted so that Germany will no longer be the dominating power in Europe." The conclusions of the Treasury Department deserve full quotation. "After careful study," it advised, "we completely reject the following propositions":

(a) The fallacy that Europe needs a strong industrial Germany.

(b) The contention that recurring reparations (which would require immediate reconstruction of the German economy) are necessary so that Germany may be made to pay for the destruction she has caused.

(c) The belief that the removal or destruction of all German armament industry would in itself prevent Germany from waging another war.

(d) The illogical assumption that a "soft" peace would facilitate the growth of democracy in Germany.

(e) The fallacy that making Germany a predominantly agricultural country, with light industries but no heavy industries, would mean starving Germans.[28]

---

[28] *Yalta Papers*, 175-176.

Clearly the lines were sharply drawn between the Department of State and the Morgenthau clique. The President at Yalta could step on one side or the other, or continue to straddle the line of division.

Consideration was given in Washington in January to one other problem concerning immediate post-surrender policy in Germany. The President early in January, 1945, asked his adviser and friend, Judge Samuel Rosenman, to systematize previous study of the problem of treatment of war criminals. International legal action against the war criminals was then considered the only conceivable alternative to summary execution.

Rosenman, Secretary of War Stimson, and Attorney General Francis Biddle, meeting on January 18, found quick agreement upon their basic assumptions:

> The criminality of the German leaders and their associates does not consist solely of individual outrages, but represents the result of a systematic and planned reign of terror within Germany, in the satellite Axis countries, and in the occupied countries of Europe. This conduct goes back at least as far as 1933, when Hitler was first appointed Chancellor of the Reich. It has been marked by mass murders, imprisonments, expulsions and deportations of populations; the starvation, torture and inhuman treatment of civilians; the wholesale looting of public and private property on a scale unparalleled in history; and, after initiation of "total" war, its prosecution with utter and ruthless disregard for the laws and customs of war.
>
> We are satisfied that these atrocities were perpetrated in pursuance of a premeditated criminal plan or enterprise which either contemplated or necessarily involved their commission.[29]

By this time about one thousand cases of offenders had been docketed by an inter-Allied War Crimes Commission, meeting in London. What was to be done with the persons against whom retribution had been promised? Rosenman, Stimson, and Biddle agreed that some form of legal action should be taken. Stettinius also gave his approval. Stimson presented the case for legal action

---

[29] United States Department of State, *Report of Robert H. Jackson, United States Representative to the International Conference on Military Trials* (1949), 4-5.

before Roosevelt on the next day, and the President assented during a hurried conversation, just before leaving Washington for the long voyage to Malta and Yalta.[30]

In Great Britain, meanwhile, the terroristic V-1 and V-2 bombs had aroused more hatred of the Germans late in 1944 than any German actions during the war. Simultaneously, in the winter of 1944-1945 irrefutable evidence rapidly was accumulated to prove that the German concentration camps had all but institutionalized scientific, systematic, and senseless mass murder. All this, plus the "Battle of the Bulge" of December, 1944, significantly weakened the remaining rational barriers against public hatred of the enemy in Europe. The passions of war were rampant in Britain as never before on the eve of the Yalta Conference, just when rationalism and moderation were more than ever needed. "I have been struck at every point where I have sounded opinion at the depth of the feeling that would be aroused by a policy of 'putting Germany on her legs again'," Churchill wrote to Eden on January 4, 1945.

In this same letter, the Conservative Prime Minister advised his Conservative Foreign Secretary and political heir apparent that new elections were impending. "We have a new parliament to consider, whose opinions we cannot foretell," Churchill wrote. Public sentiment must be considered, like it or not, fickle though it was, he continued. "These awe-inspiring tides of feeling dominate most people's minds, and independent figures tend to become not only lonely but futile." Churchill knew that a degree of moderation toward Germany was necessary. He also knew that the survival of his government—and his party—depended upon the support of a public which appeared very tough-minded early in 1945. Churchill thus reached the only conclusion on Germany that seemed practical, and one which Roosevelt had insisted upon adopting earlier: delay. Should Germany be partitioned? Should the industry of the Ruhr and Saar be destroyed? On January 4 Churchill wrote Eden that it was "much too soon for us to decide these enormous questions." Eden agreed. In a report to Churchill on February 2 at Malta, he echoed his chief's own sentiments, and those

---

[30] *Ibid.*, 3-17; Stimson and Bundy, *On Active Service,* 586-587.

of Roosevelt: "We would be wise to suspend final decisions until we see what conditions are in Germany." [31]

The Kremlin, meanwhile, had not moderated its objectives for postwar Germany. The Assistant People's Commissar for Foreign Affairs, I. M. Maisky, on January 20 outlined current Soviet aims for Averell Harriman. They included the breaking up of Germany, perhaps by creating an independent state in the Rhineland-Ruhr area and "a Catholic republic" of Bavaria and Württemberg in the south. Germany should be economically de-industrialized. Germany's steel production should be reduced by about 75 per cent. The Soviet Union would hope to strip Germany's heavy industries of machinery and expect other commodities for perhaps a ten year period as reparations. In addition, Harriman reported, Maisky would want German laborers as part of her reparations bill against Germany. "No definite numbers had been agreed upon as a demand but it would run into the millions. He said the Government was more conservative than the Russian people on this point. Later on, but without definite significance, he mentioned two or three millions. . . . He said they had been talking principally about men but some women might be required." The experience, which might last for ten years, would be used "to reeducate the Germans," said Maisky.[32]

The Russians thus remained ready to make definitive and harsh decisions for Germany's future, while the policy of postponement triumphed again at the highest level in London as well as Wash-

---

[31] Churchill, *Triumph and Tragedy,* 350-351; Eden to Churchill, Feb. 2, 1945, *Yalta Papers,* 511-512. A severe British critic of unconditional surrender policy toward Germany has admitted that the British public on the eve of Yalta demanded harsh measures: Grenfell, *Unconditional Surrender,* 116-117.

[32] Memorandum by the Ambassador in the Soviet Union, January 20, 1945, in *Yalta Papers,* 176-178. When this document was published in 1956, the Soviet Union was posing as the patron of German unification. This would seem to explain the denunciation by *Pravda* of the publication. *Pravda* described the *Yalta Papers* as an attempt to "falsify history" and to strengthen "the tottering position" of the Republican administration in Washington. *Pravda* in 1956 described Maisky simply as "one of the former workers of the Peoples Commissariat of Foreign Affairs of the U.S.S.R." and disparaged Harriman's report as "conjectures." (See New York *Times,* January 21, 1956). The Soviet argument was soon echoed in historical writings in the satellite states, according to *Historical Abstracts* (Munich).

ington. Churchill, like Roosevelt, had retreated from the policy agreement he had initialed at Quebec and echoed in Moscow. Amidst fresh memories of German actions under Hitler, constantly augmented by evidence of new atrocities, and with one ally anxious to impose a peace of retribution, the retreat from vengeance could not possibly be complete. To reach no final decision was—under the circumstances—an act of moderation. The policy defaults, by the accidents of history, would leave the way open for more merciful treatment of postwar Germany than even the Western leaders could have foreseen in the winter of 1944-1945, when a new German onslaught in the West reminded all three Allies of their mutual need.

Chapter VI

THE WEAKENING OF NAZI GERMANY

W ARTIME diplomacy can never be conducted in a vacuum. The basic military strategy of one's own armies and those of his enemies must be considered. The military aims of one's allies cannot be ignored. Lines of battle are likely to influence the destiny of the best-considered plans for the postwar treatment of the enemy. Finally, a vigorous and threatening enemy is always the most indispensable ally of a coalition. Germany in the last half of 1944 and the early weeks of 1945 gave new evidence of this, thus helping to slow the disintegration of the "strange alliance" and to shape the character of her own defeat.

President Roosevelt, proposing to Stalin in November, 1944, that a future Big Three meeting be held at the end of January, added that if "the Nazi army or people should disintegrate quickly, we should have to meet earlier." [1] Roosevelt's reservation shows the importance he attached to Germany's future. It revealed at the time his determination that the United States must share in shaping that future. His reservation also documents the optimism with which the Western Allies then viewed the progress of their campaigns against the Third Reich. Both the retreat of German armies and a revolt against Hitler in July, 1944, had prematurely suggested that Germany's collapse was, indeed, near at hand.

THE ATTEMPT TO OVERTHROW HITLER

By the fall of 1944 Germany had failed to capitalize upon its one hope for moderate treatment after World War II. That hope lay in a successful and massive uprising against Hitler, led by

---

[1] Ministry of Foreign Affairs of the U.S.S.R., *Correspondence . . . Chairman of the Council of Ministers of the U.S.S.R. . . . 1941-1945*, II, 169.

Germans who could win the trust of either the Soviet Union or the Western Allies.

The U.S.S.R. had tried to arouse a rebellion without making any specific promises to the Germans. Despite the unconditional surrender formula, Roosevelt, too, was willing in 1944 to appeal to this "other Germany." On May 23, shortly before the D-Day invasion, he proposed to Churchill and Stalin the draft of a propaganda appeal he wanted to make after the landings in France. He would impress upon the German people that their defeat was "inevitable." He would tell them that it was "unintelligent on their part to continue in the war." And, like a latter-day Wilson, Roosevelt would tell the Germans that the Allies did not seek "the total destruction of the people of Germany," but rather "the total destruction of the philosophy of those Germans who have stated that they could subjugate the world." The cleverly-worded appeal was never issued. The British government raised "a definite and positive objection" to it, Roosevelt on May 27 sent word to Stalin; and in fact on May 24 Churchill had declared before the House of Commons that the British Commonwealth would fight on until Germany should surrender unconditionally. On May 26 Stalin himself had already recorded his opposition to the appeal. We are left to speculate about what might have happened if the rising of July 20 against Hitler had, in fact, achieved success.[2]

For years anti-Nazi Germans had longed for some hint from the Western Allies that the overthrow of Hitler might be rewarded, if it were dared. Even with encouragement from outside it would have required great physical courage for Germans to risk rebellion against the totalitarian regime which the Nazis had fastened upon the country. Great moral courage as well as physical courage was needed. It was not easy to be sure that one's obligations to humanity, God, or even the long-range interests of one's country were sufficient to warrant acts which would immediately aid the nations that fought against Germany.

The record of the opposition up to 1944 did not inspire hope or trust in London or Washington, not to mention Moscow. Hap-

2 *Ibid.*, II, 141-144; Gerhard Ritter, *The German Resistance: Carl Goerdeler's Struggle against Tyranny,* R. T. Clark, trans. (New York, 1958), 274.

hazardly organized and hesitant conspirators in 1938 had explained their failure to strike down Hitler by saying they waited for an act of strength by Great Britain in the Munich crisis. Mainly army officers or authoritarian civilians, they failed to understand that the Western democracies necessarily viewed them with suspicion and would not take their talk of an anti-Nazi Resistance movement seriously until they saw successful action against Hitler inside Germany. The same dilemma held back the conspirators and the Western democracies during the war. The German Resistance leaders expected a lot of the West. They hoped to win recognition from the Allies. They also hoped to be allowed to keep some of Hitler's spoils. Some hoped for even more, speaking of the frontier of 1914 in the east.

Not wanting to rise unless they could get an impossible bargain with the Western statesmen, the German Resistance leaders failed to rebel during the years of Hitler's victories. Even when the British government strongly encouraged them in February, 1940, they failed to rise. Endlessly they talked of striking at Hitler, only to be rendered inactive by the pale cast of thought. The Western Powers were thus unable to believe that there was any potentially successful opposition to the Nazis; and there appeared to be no significant movement of a democratic character. The policy of unconditional surrender must be seen against this background. It was the tragic destiny of the German Resistance movement not to rise in strength against the dictator as long as his empire stood unthreatened by military defeat.[3]

The invasion of France on June 6, 1944, moved the anti-Nazi Resistance leaders at last to desperate action. On July 20—captains without an army—they struck at the fanatical tyrant who ruled Germany.

Much of Europe still lay under German occupation on that July 20. Six hundred miles still lay between the Anglo-Saxon

---

[3] The best account of the German Resistance movement is by an honorable and apologetic participant who continues to insist that the Resistance was crippled by the lack of Western encouragement. See Ritter, *The German Resistance*, 40-256. For the aims of the Resistance leaders, see especially 184-201 in Ritter's account. For other literature see the bibliography in the Ritter volume and Walter Schmitthenner, "Neue Literatur zum deutschen Widerstand gegen Hitler," *Geschichte in Wissenschaft und Unterricht*, IX (1958), 189-192.

forces in France and the city of Berlin; six hundred miles also separated the stalemated armies in Italy from the German capital; even the Russians were then four hundred miles from Berlin. But, as in 1918, there were German officers who knew that the conflict could not end well for Germany. They also knew that their Nazi warlord would never admit defeat. His hair grayed, tortoise-shell glasses before his eyes, his shoulders stooped, given to periods of brooding silence and vacant stares, irritable at unpredictable intervals, the Nazi *Führer* remained resolute, his increasing hysteria clarified occasionally by flashes of the old uncanny genius. There was no doubt about it, Hitler had to be killed if Germany were to get peace. In earlier justifications of his overthrow of the Weimar Republic Hitler himself had provided a fitting epitaph: "if a people is led to destruction by its government, rebellion on the part of each and every member . . . is not only a right but a duty."

At about noon on that July 20 Colonel Claus von Stauffenberg heard the roar of the bomb he had planted near Hitler, saw the flying flames, and quickly caught a plane to Berlin; surely the way to successful revolt had now been cleared by one man's courage. But this was cruel illusion. The bomb proved fatal only to von Stauffenberg himself. That night, with the cry, "Long live eternal Germany" on his lips, Stauffenberg fell before an improvised firing squad. The only significant German attempt in a dozen years to overthrow the Nazi regime was crushed. There was not to be another. July 20 proved not only that the Resistance leaders were courageous men but that they had too few supporters. The brutality with which the revolt was put down only intensified the loathing of the Nazi regime among the Allies. The lack of mass action encouraged no faith in German democracy. Both considerations must have encouraged the Allied leaders to formulate and insist upon harsh terms of peace. Perhaps there would have been no Morgenthau Plan in August and September of 1944 if the July revolt had succeeded.[4]

---

[4] Wheeler-Bennett, *Nemesis of Power*, 635-702; Ritter, *The German Resistance*, 274-314; Hans Bernd Gisevius, *To the Bitter End*, Richard and Clara Winston, trans. (Boston, 1947), 536-575. Georges Blond, *The Death of Hitler's Germany*, Frances Frenaye, trans. (New York, 1954), 23, 35,

One Western interpretation of the July revolt was almost in-escapable. On July 21 President Roosevelt sent the following words to Stalin: "We have just received news of the difficulties in Germany and especially at Hitler's headquarters. It is all to the good." [5] The revolt was the first significant evidence (it proved to be premature) that Germany was weakening politically.

REALITY OF DECLINE AND ILLUSION OF STRENGTH

Signs of economic weakness in Hitler's Reich also multiplied in the summer and fall of 1944. Aircraft production reached the highest level of the entire war in September, 1944, but fuel was insufficiently available to keep the planes in the air, thanks to Allied bomber attacks upon the synthetic oil plants and the capture of the Ploesti fields by the Russians in September, 1944. *Luftwaffe* casualties rose rapidly. From 1941 through June, 1944, 31,000 flying personnel were lost; 13,000 more were added in the period June-October, 1944 alone. Allied air forces methodically disrupted railroad marshalling yards and war factories as well as the oil industry, adding to German despondency. The Russian drive into Central-Eastern Europe deprived the Reich of the resources of Russia, Finland, eastern Poland, Rumania, Bulgaria, and parts of Hungary by September, 1944, in spite of the fact that Germany kept 2,000,000 men on the eastern front while deploying only 700,000 in the west. How much the losses of territory in both west and east hurt the German economy can be estimated when it is realized that early in 1944: (1) almost all of Germany's mangan-ese had come from the Nikopol mines of the Ukraine; (2) 23 per cent of the molybdenum of Germany came from the mines of central Finland; (3) 80 per cent of the German needs for nickel were satisfied by the Petsamo mines of Finland; and (4) between

---

40, 53; Alan Bullock, *Hitler: A Study in Tyranny* (New York, 1953), 672-689. On Hitler's personality and entourage in this period see H. R. Trevor-Roper, *The Last Days of Hitler* (New York, 1947), *passim*. See also Karl O. Paetel, "Der 20. Juli 1944 und das Ausland," *Aussenpolitik*, V (1954), 438-448. For Hitler's own justification of rebellion see Franz Neumann, *Behemoth: The Structure and Practice of National Socialism, 1933-1944*, 2nd ed. (London etc., 1944), 64.

[5] Ministry of Foreign Affairs of the U.S.S.R., *Correspondence . . . Chair-man of the Council of Ministers of the U.S.S.R. . . . 1941-1945*, II, 151.

30 and 40 per cent of the entire German bauxite (aluminum ore) production was drawn from France. All this, plus the oil of Rumania, was denied to Germany by late September, 1944. Coal production sank in the last quarter of that year. Tank production slumped seriously during the fall months.[6]

German cultural and social life also suffered from hardships which defensive warfare imposed. Though food and clothing were still plentiful, life became increasingly drab. On August 24 Goebbels issued the following order: "All theaters, music halls, cafes, concerts, and dramatic schools will be closed. Only scientific and technical books, together with a few important political works, will be published. . . . And in order to obtain a maximum output from homefront workers, all government and private business offices will go on a sixty-hour week." On October 18 Hitler called for all men of sixteen to sixty years of age to serve in the armed forces, and decreed the organization of the *Volkssturm* (People's Army) for the youngest and oldest warriors.[7]

Though conditions were bad, hope and fear still helped greatly to hold together the Hitlerian empire. One of the chief sources of hope lay in a major scientific accomplishment of wartime Germany. On October 3, 1942, German rocket scientists (including Wernher von Braun) sent a five-and-a-half-ton missile sixty miles up into space from Peenemunde and down only three miles off target 120 miles distant. Production of the new weapon—soon to be called the "V-2"—began only slowly in 1943, but by 1944 it caused hopes of victory to soar again, not just among Germany's deluded leaders but among the populace as well. For the Germans were told mysteriously of a secret weapon which might enable the Reich to knock Britain out of the war in three months.

The launching of that rocket in a forest on the north-German

---

[6] Pogue, *The Supreme Command*, 246-247; Wilmot, *The Struggle for Europe*, 554-556; Wilhelm Treue and Günther Frede, *Wirtschaft und Politik 1933-1945* (Braunschweig, 1953), 54-64; Arnold and Veronica M. Toynbee eds., *Hitler's Europe* (London, 1954), 186-198; Adolf Galland, *The First and the Last: The Rise and Fall of the German Fighter Forces, 1938-1945* (New York, 1954), *passim*. Percy Ernst Schramm, "Die Treibstoff-Frage von Herbst 1943 bis Juni 1944, nach dem Kriegstagebuch des Wehrmachtführungsstabes," in *Mensch und Staat in Recht und Geschichte: Festschrift für Herbert Kraus* (Kitzengen/Main, 1954), 394-421.

[7] Blond, *The Death of Hitler's Germany*, 79, 158.

plain will mark the beginning of man's flight into worlds beyond his own. The new weapon, we know, was only to play a role in World War II like that of the submarine in the First World War: it prolonged and intensified the fantasy of victory among the German people in a war they could not win.

A crude missile, the V-1, began to fall upon England in June, 1944, and the first V-2 came down on September 8. The British thus became the first civilians to experience space-age warfare. As the rocket campaign continued into the fall it only served to toughen the British attitude toward Germany. It may even have had a subtle effect upon Churchill's attitude toward Germany at Quebec and in his October meeting with Stalin. But in Germany it gave a lift to morale. The V-1 and V-2 weapons were such good Nazi propaganda, in fact, that the United States bomber crews over Germany were called upon to drop special leaflets along with their explosives to counter the effects of the weapon on Germany's war spirit. Text and diagrams were designed to show the Germans that the Allies had full knowledge of the workings of their new "mystery" weapon.[8]

German political propaganda also kept German hope alive. The Germans were told that the "strange alliance" would fall apart. "The time will come," Hitler told his generals once again on August 31, 1944, "when the tension between the Allies becomes so strong that, in spite of everything, the rupture occurs." Again on December 12 Hitler assured his generals: "Never before in history was there a coalition like that of our enemies. . . . Even now these states are at loggerheads." The Ministry of Propaganda played upon the same theme. The various editions of the Nazi central organ, the *Völkischer Beobachter,* and other newspapers preached that the Allied advance would soon be halted, giving time for Germany's "new weapons" to be put in operation; thus Germany could hold out until political conflict among the Allies would increase, as it inevitably would "with the apparent approach of an Allied victory."[9]

---

[8] Walter Dornberger, *V-2*, James Cleugh and Geoffrey Halliday, trans. (New York, 1954), especially 3-17. As a B-17 pilot the author helped drop the American propaganda.

[9] Wilmot, *The Struggle for Europe*, 444-445, 578; Pogue, *The Supreme Command*, 249.

If hope kept the German war morale alive, fear kept it from dying, and German fear fed upon news of the Morgenthau Plan. To the German people the Morgenthau Plan was described as a "satanic plan of annihilation," inspired by the Jews and devised by "cannibals." Berlin Radio proclaimed that: "The Jew Morgenthau sings the same tune as the Jews in the Kremlin." The *Völkischer Beobachter* warned that the Morgenthau Plan would require half the German population to choose between starvation or migrating from Germany "as slave laborers." Even Germans who hated Hitler were horrified by the prospects which the news of the Morgenthau Plan opened before them; to many of these the plan seemed "equal to Hitler's own nihilistic fanatacism." There had been some disposition in Germany to let the West in the front door while keeping the Russian wolf away from the back. This disposition suffered greatly after the news of the Roosevelt-Churchill agreement of September 15. For once the *Völkischer Beobachter* printed the truth when it proclaimed that "the Quebec decision will only serve to redouble German resistance." On into 1945 the *Völkischer Beobachter* continued to make use of the Morgenthau Plan as a morale booster, insisting that it had Roosevelt's full endorsement. What the British, Americans, Bolsheviks, and "international Jews" wanted was clear, Hitler told the German people in his New Year's message. "The complete ripping apart of the German Reich, the uprooting of 15 to 20 million Germans and transport abroad, the enslavement of the rest of our people, the ruination of our German youth, but, above all, the starvation of our masses." [10]

THE "BULGE"

September, 1944, was a month of debate about Allied strategy to defeat Germany as well as the month in which the Morgenthau doctrine became public knowledge. As supplies ran short and Allied soldiers wearied, as Frenchmen celebrated the liberation of Paris and German troops held doggedly to important Channel ports, the advance into Germany slowed and almost stopped.

---

[10] Wilmot, *The Struggle for Europe*, 549-550; Bullock, *Hitler*, 693-694; Pogue, *The Supreme Command*, 342; Paul Schmidt, *Statist auf diplomatischer Bühne 1923-1945* (Bonn, 1950), 571; *Völkischer Beobachter*, Jan. 2, 27, 1945.

General Bernard Montgomery, the chief British commander of ground forces under Eisenhower's command, produced a dramatic plan for finishing off the defeat of the Reich. His proposal: "one powerful full-blooded thrust" should be made to the north across the Rhine and into the heart of Germany." If backed by "the whole of the resources of the Allied Armies," he believed it was likely to achieve decisive results."

But Montgomery was notoriously impulsive and anxious to win new glory for himself and the great Commonwealth he served. Eisenhower, plagued by worry about logistics and extended lines and confident of the power of his reserves, decided to beat Germany a slower but surer way. He would slow the attack and mass his forces all along the Rhine before crossing that mighty river. In December Germany's Ardennes offensive—"the Battle of the Bulge"—would convince the American Joint Chiefs of Staff that Eisenhower's strategic decision had been correct.[11]

Hitler had seized upon the new morale of the German people and the respite in the West to prepare countermeasures against the Allied military advances. By September 25 the Morgenthau Plan was known in general outline in Germany. At the end of that month Hitler revealed to his closest generals his intention to launch a counterattack against the West and to re-take Antwerp, even if it were necessary to weaken the eastern front to carry out the western operation. In 1939-1940 he had fundamentally betrayed the West, of which Germany claimed to be a part, by making a pact with Stalin. Now, at a crucial moment in the war, Hitler prepared to betray the interests of his countrymen once more by striking west. As in 1940, the German forces would drive across the rough terrain of the Ardennes Forest. In October and November plans were pushed for the coming "Battle of the Bulge." Troops were in fact moved westward for this great drive, remarkable skill being demonstrated in keeping the Allies guessing about preparations. Then, early on the morning of December 16, the Germans

---

[11] See Bernard Montgomery, *The Memoirs of Field-Marshal the Viscount Montgomery of Alamein, K. G.* (Cleveland and New York, 1958), 238-257; Bernard Montgomery, *Normandy to the Baltic* (Boston, 1948), 193; Ehrman, *Grand Strategy*, V, 524-529.

struck out of an icy fog that embraced the sharp hills of the Ardennes like a halo.

For a time the *Wehrmacht* seemed to be irresistible. "We shall yet master fate," Hitler told his generals on December 28. The drive engendered great enthusiasm among the German troops "We're smoking American cigarettes and eating American chocolate," one exuberant infantryman wrote home. Eisenhower's concern became so great that he urged the Combined Chiefs of Staff to approve the arming of eight French divisions. A question which had been delayed for months was now settled quickly under the pressure of events; the Combined Chiefs of Staff on December 29 approved Eisenhower's request, just twenty-four hours after it arrived in Washington. In the midst of the crisis Eisenhower also urged London and Washington to persuade the Russians to undertake action on the eastern front to distract the Germans. But the German drive was checked without Soviet help. On January 9 Hitler ordered a general withdrawal. Only three days later did Stalin launch his offensive on the Polish front, though Churchill had hinted strongly at the need for aid on December 24 and again on January 6.

Did the Red Army finally move to aid the Allies? Or to take advantage of the awkward military position in which Germany found herself in the east as a result of Hitler's adventure and to prepare for the diplomatic bargaining that was already scheduled to begin early in February? By the time the Big Three met at Yalta, Eden seemed concerned about the extent of the Russian thrust to the west. But nobody stopped in January and February 1945, to argue out the question of Russian motivations. Instead Churchill informed Stalin on January 17: "On behalf of His Majesty's Government, and from the bottom of my heart, I offer you our thanks and congratulations on the immense assault you have launched upon the Eastern Front." The threat of the *Wehrmacht* in the west made the Americans as well as the British grateful for the Russian drive. Germany's continued military power, even if only used in last desperate gambles, still made it impossible for the Big Three to part company—save at their own peril. "What would have happened if we had quarreled with Russia . . . ?" Churchill has wisely asked in retrospect, as he must have asked himself at the time. "Our hopeful assumptions were soon to be falsified. Still, they were the only ones possible at the time." Hitler saw to that.[12]

THE MILITARY-DIPLOMATIC BALANCE ON THE EVE OF YALTA

The "Battle of the Bulge" had cast deep gloom over the West for a time, though by January 31, on the eve of Yalta, the Anglo-American forces had regained the positions they had held that disastrous morning six weeks before. One can only speculate about the possible effects upon the Yalta bargaining in February if Eisenhower's forces had continued their advance into western Germany unchecked in December and January. When the conference opened in the Crimea the Red Army had pushed to the outskirts of Königsberg in East Prussia and one of Marshall Zhukov's spearheads was halted about fifty miles from Berlin. As the Yalta Conference began, Marshal Stalin confidently—and perhaps pointedly—informed Roosevelt that the Red Army already held the Silesian industrial complex, and he told Churchill on February 4 that the Oder River was no longer an obstacle to the Red Army, since several bridgeheads had already been established and the German defense was not distinguished. At that time British and American troops huddled with frozen feet in the snowy lines which they had just regained after Hitler's December offensive. They were almost completely excluded from German territory when the Yalta discussions occurred. It would be March 24 before the Rhine was crossed; and Eisenhower's forces first got to within fifty miles of Berlin on April 12. The British and American Chiefs of Staff, assembled at Yalta, reckoned that the crossing of the Rhine might fail; that Germany could hardly be defeated before the end of June; and that Hitler might prolong the death agony of his empire

---

[12] Wilmot, *The Struggle for Europe*, 575-631; Pogue, *The Supreme Command*, 359-372; Vigneras, *Rearming the French*, 335; *Yalta Papers*, 498-507, 79; Blond, *The Death of Hitler's Germany*, 95-174; Felix Gilbert, *Hitler Directs His War* (New York, 1950), 174; Stettinius, *Roosevelt and the Russians*, 304; Millis ed., *The Forrestal Diaries*, 21; Churchill, *Triumph and Tragedy*, 402; Ministry of Foreign Affairs of the U.S.S.R., *Correspondence . . . Chairman of the Council of Ministers of the U.S.S.R. . . . 1941-1945*, I, 88, 294-295, 300. Cf. John Ehrman. *Grand Strategy*, VI (London, 1956), 14, 64-69; Montgomery, *Memoirs*, 275-282.

until November, 1945. The timing of the Yalta talks was not favorable to the West. And yet, despite the December setback the Western position was *more* favorable than it had been at any time since 1940. Western military power on the continent of Europe was much greater in February, 1945, than it had been in the fall, and the improvement was an asset in the Yalta bargaining.[13]

Hitler himself took fool's confidence from his recent successes in the west. Believing that he had won bargaining power, he sent out feelers for peace on his own terms at the end of 1944, contacting the British through the German embassies in Sweden, Switzerland and Spain. The collapse of these efforts failed to discourage the Nazi dictator, and of course remained unknown to the German people. The *Völkischer Beobachter* greeted the first news of a Big Three meeting with the prediction that the "Jewish-plutocratic visionary" Allies would make an attractive peace offer to the Germans. The Nazi organ, recalling Wilson's Fourteen Points of 1918, headlined the meeting of "the three great war criminals" and a: "HOPELESS ATTEMPT AT A NEW WILSON SWINDLE." The *Völkischer Beobachter* cautioned the Germans not to forget the war aims of "Morgenthau, Vansittart and the Kremlin Jew, Ilya Ehrenburg." But the same number of the *Völkischer Beobachter* reported new reductions in the German food rations. The *Machtstaat* of 1939-1944 was gradually becoming a power vacuum and the greatest tragedy of it all for Germany was the refusal of her leaders to recognize the fact.[14]

Hitler's great and desperate military spasm of December may have prevented Western armies from reaching Berlin and Vienna ahead of the Red Army in the spring of 1945. Meanwhile, the military events of late 1944 and early 1945 had cast their shadow over the shoulders of the Big Three as they sat at Yalta in February 1945, influencing their view of the future of Germany, of each other, and of Europe as a whole.

---

[13] Churchill, *Triumph and Tragedy*, 348; Leahy, *I Was There*, 293 Deutscher, *Stalin*, 524; *Yalta Papers*, 570-588, 606-607; Sherwood, *Roosevelt and Hopkins*, 851; Ehrman, *Grand Strategy*, VI, 82.
[14] Schmidt, *Statist auf diplomatischer Bühne*, 776; *Völkischer Beobachter* Jan. 27, Feb. 3-7, 1945.

Chapter VII

YALTA: SUBDUED EAST-WEST SHOWDOWN

WHILE the Red Army rolled across the east-German plains and prepared to cross the Oder River, Roosevelt and Churchill travelled to the mid-Mediterranean island of Malta, there to rendezvous on their way to meet Stalin at Yalta in the Crimea. Even before the great chiefs arrived at Malta, a State Department delegation had held consultations there with Anthony Eden and Sir Alexander Cadogan, Under-Secretary for Foreign Affairs for the United Kingdom.

A certain amount of valuable coordination of plans concerning postwar Germany was achieved during the brief stop at Malta. Stettinius informed Eden there that Roosevelt was "disposed to give France" a zone of occupation in Germany, and suggested that a fourth zone might be created out of the southern part of the British zone and the northern part of the United States zone. They agreed to seek Russian approval of this change in the occupation zones. They also agreed that "the French should be integrated into the control machinery," that is, should have membership on the inter-Allied Control Council for Germany.

Eden quietly voiced his concern about the power of the colossal host who would be waiting at Yalta. With "the Russians so close to Berlin," he said, it was "urgently necessary to reach tripartite agreement" on the following points: "(a) that a common political and economic policy in Germany was required, (b) that no individual nation should take action without the agreement of the others, and (c) that the European Advisory Council was the body in which detailed arrangements should be worked out." These were views to which Stettinius could readily subscribe, and he probably did. Eden and Stettinius also agreed to limit, if possible, the westward expansion of Poland at the expense of Germany. Though efforts were made both before and during the Yalta Conference to reassure the Russians that they were not confronted by an Anglo-American bloc, this coordination of strategy was to be reflected in the Yalta discussions.[1]

Meanwhile, during the voyage to Malta, the President had rested and had continued his preparations for the Big Three meeting. By the time he arrived at Malta, and throughout the conferences there and in the Crimea, Roosevelt was mentally alert, though physically not well. James F. Byrnes, who went to Yalta as the Director of the Office of War Mobilization, has suggested that Roosevelt did not make use of the "splendid studies" of the State Department during the voyage to Malta. A better witness has said that the President, "in the privacy of his own quarters," did "a great deal of studying of papers and documents given to him by the State Department and other experts in preparation for the Yalta meeting." Another companion, Admiral Leahy, has written that the President held daily conferences with him on board ship, "at which we talked over the problems that would be faced at the Crimea meeting." Leahy specifically indicated that the President gave consideration to the problem of reparations, discussing with his personal Chief of Staff the possibility of forming a commission to study the problem in order to "avoid the pitfalls that made the World War I reparations actually a burden on America." Upon arriving at Malta, Roosevelt met with Churchill, Eden, and Stettinius, to hear Eden and Stettinius report informally on their discussions of the previous day. Furthermore, before the first meeting of the Big Three at Yalta, State Department officials specifically reviewed for the President the papers which the Department had prepared for his use.[2]

---

[1] Stettinius, *Roosevelt and the Russians*, 30, 35, 67; *Yalta Papers*, 498-514, 546.

[2] James F. Byrnes, *Speaking Frankly* (New York, 1947), 23; Leahy, *I Was There*, 292-293; Stettinius, *Roosevelt and the Russians*, 74; *Yalta Papers*, II, 487, 502. For comments on Roosevelt's health during the Yalta Conference see: Edward J. Flynn, *You're the Boss* (New York, 1947), 188; Averell Harriman's 1951 statement in: *Military Situation in the Far East: Hearings* . . . . 3330; Leahy, *I Was There*, 290; Stettinius, *Roosevelt and the Russians*, 73.

In view of all this, one must conclude that the President of the United States was well prepared for the discussion of German problems when he arrived at Yalta on February 3. From the minutes of that second and last Roosevelt-Churchill-Stalin conference, it is obvious that the President's great friends—the new Behemoth and the old Leviathan—came equally well briefed and equally determined, each in his own way, that the fruits of victory should not be lost in the planning of peace.

POSTPONEMENT AT YALTA

At his staff meeting in the morning of February 4 Roosevelt learned that the Russians wanted the German problem on the agenda of the first political discussions at Yalta. Later that day Marshall Stalin personally revealed his preoccupation with the German problem when he greeted the President before the first plenary session. Roosevelt, commenting upon German destructiveness in the Crimea, said that he was "more bloodthirsty in regard to the Germans" than he had been a year before. Stalin replied that "everyone was more bloodthirsty than they had been a year ago." The Germans, he said, "were savages and seemed to hate with sadistic hatred the creative work of human beings." To this the President agreed.

Roosevelt then tentatively suggested that France might—"out of kindness"—be given a zone of occupation in Germany. Both Stalin and Molotov sharply indicated their reluctance to agree to this. Thus the question of Germany became the first of the great political issues to be discussed at Yalta, intruding into a social call even before the plenary sessions began. It was inevitable that it should; for then, as in 1918 and in 1959, concern over the German problem must have outweighed all other European problems in the minds of Soviet leaders. It was clear that Stalin was still intent upon ruining Germany. Perhaps his stand would have been different if he had held any hope that Germany as a whole might go Communist after the surrender, but Stalin was a complete realist in this matter. A few months before Yalta he had told the Polish leader, Stanislaw Mikolajczyk that Communism would fit Germany like "a saddle fitted a cow." This being the case, there seemed nothing to do in 1945 but butcher the cow.[3]

Stalin reminded his colleagues on February 5, the second day of the conference, that they had informally favored the dismemberment of Germany at Teheran. "Hasn't the time come for a decision?" he asked. "If you think so, let us make one." He reaffirmed his willingness to accept the kind of partition which Churchill had favored informally, the creation of a north-German state, a south-German state including Austria, and an internationalized Ruhr and Saar.

Churchill himself assumed the chief burden of the argument at Yalta against any binding decision to dismember Germany. While agreeing "in principle" to dismemberment, he insisted that he could not commit himself to any definite plan until much additional study of the problem could be undertaken. Churchill then tried to change the subject to the more immediate and less fateful question of French participation in the occupation of Germany. But Stalin stuck tenaciously to the question of partition, proposing that the Allies should state their intention to dismember Germany in the surrender document which Germany would sign. It appeared that a deadlock existed which could not be resolved, but Roosevelt, hitherto a silent observer, sought to moderate between his two obstinate colleagues. As on many similar occasions the President gave the appearance of supporting Stalin, while proposing action which Churchill wanted. He recalled his experiences as a student in Germany some forty years before Yalta, and said that he still thought, as at Teheran, that the dismemberment (or *decentralization*) of Germany into five or seven states "was a good idea." Roosevelt then suggested that the Big Three refer the matter to the secretaries for foreign affairs and ask them to bring in a plan for dismemberment within twenty-four hours. Was the President, then, with Stalin after all? "You mean a plan for the *study* of the question," Churchill suggested. "Yes," replied Roosevelt, "for the study of dismemberment." Thus the shadow of the Anglo-American policy of postponement softly fell over one of the many German problems on which Stalin was anxious to obtain stark clarity.

---

[3] Churchill, *Triumph and Tragedy*, 350; *Yalta Papers*, 566, 570-573; Deutscher, *Stalin*, 537.

The effect was not lost upon the Soviet dictator. To salvage what he could of his original hopes, Stalin proposed that the Big Three commit themselves to the principle of partition, to the creation of a special commission "to work out the details," and to inclusion in the surrender document of a clause calling for dismemberment. Roosevelt again looked for a compromise, saying that Stalin's desire to mention dismemberment in the surrender document was "somewhat my own." Churchill agreed to this, but balked at any attempt to make a binding decision regarding dismemberment. The foreign secretaries were then instructed to study the possibility of including a dismemberment clause among the surrender terms. The first round in the discussion of Germany's future went to the West.[4]

The foreign ministers considered their troublesome assignment on the following morning, February 6. That afternoon, after a luncheon conference between Roosevelt and Churchill, the foreign secretaries reported to the plenary meeting of the Big Three their agreement that the word "dismemberment" should appear in the surrender document, and their inability to agree how definitely it should be phrased. The foreign secretaries were again left to wrangle over the exact wording of the clause and to provide some mechanism for the study of the dismemberment problem. The Russians apparently decided that they had gotten as specific a decision on partition as they would be likely to get at Yalta. When the foreign ministers met again on the morning of February 7 Molotov was the embodiment of conciliation. The task of drafting a clause for the surrender document was delegated to a special Yalta committee, made up of Andrei Vyshinski, Sir Alexander Cadogan, and H. Freeman Matthews. The wording these men developed was included in the protocol of agreements which Stettinius, Molotov, and Eden signed on February 11. The revised clause now read as follows:

> The United Kingdom, the United States of America and the Union of Soviet Socialist Republics shall possess supreme authority with respect to Germany. In the exercise of such authority they will take such steps, including the complete disarmament, demilitarisation and the dismember-

---

[4] *Yalta Papers*, 611-616, 625-628; Byrnes, *Speaking Frankly*, 25-26.

ment of Germany *as they deem requisite for future peace and security.* [Author's italics.]

Five days earlier Molotov had opposed the inclusion of the phrase "as they deem requisite"; its appearance in the protocol could only leave the partition issue as muddled as it had been before Yalta. The Russians could console themselves with the knowledge that the surrender text would include the word dismemberment. But the important fact is that the plans for partition, so boldly discussed at previous informal meetings, were postponed when first considered formally by the Big Three.[5]

At the very beginning of the Yalta Conference the Russians raised the combined questions of reparations and de-industrialization. As it became apparent to them that they might not be able to eliminate German power through permanent partition, they argued all the more fervently and tenaciously—throughout the entire conference—that they be allowed to strengthen their own economy and weaken Germany by a reparations policy which would in large part de-industrialize Germany. With these interrelated policy demands, Molotov connected yet another on February 5: Russian economic gains from Germany should be discussed in connection with the Russian request for long-term credits from the United States. In the language of diplomacy he was saying in effect: give us credits to buy equipment in America or allow us to take the sinews of industry from the Germans. As "dollar diplomacy" had won concessions from Churchill at Quebec, it threatened to win concessions from the West at Yalta.[6]

The Russian interest in reparations was difficult to oppose, for the U.S.S.R. had suffered heavily at the hands of the Germans during the war. Hitler's troops, driven from Soviet soil in 1944, had left in their trail a devastated area which would require years of rebuilding. Aside from the losses of human lives, the Russians had lost to the *Wehrmacht* more than one third of the total prewar supply of horses in the U.S.S.R., and almost one third of the

---

[5] *Yalta Papers,* 655-660, 699-709, 936, 978; Stettinius, *Roosevelt and the Russians,* 138. Feis, *Churchill, Roosevelt, Stalin,* 539, puts the wrong words in italics. Deuerlein, *Die Einheit Deutschlands,* 75-76, rightly emphasizes the fact that no binding decision was reached at Yalta on the dismemberment of Germany.

[6] *Yalta Papers,* 609-610; Sherwood, *Roosevelt and Hopkins,* 853.

cattle (17,000,000 heads). The Germans had wrecked some 1,710 towns, 31,500 industrial enterprises, and about 40,000 miles of permanent railroad right of way. Russian estimates have claimed that the U.S.S.R. suffered direct losses of as high as $128,000,000,000 as a result of the German invasion. The Russians stated at Yalta that "even direct losses . . . had been so large that no reparations could cover their loss." Yet, the British and the Americans put up a stiffer fight on the reparations questions than on the dismemberment issue. The Western statesmen were willing to concede that certain key industries should be eliminated, but the President himself, and the others even more than he, believed that it was impossible to discuss the amount of reparations to be demanded of Germany until "the Allies discovered what was left of Germany after the war." Anglo-American strategy on this question, too, was to seek postponement. The need to preserve Big Three unity meant that verbal compromises were made with the Russians, even though the hard residue of actual concessions to their demands was disappointing.[7]

The Russians presented their scheme for reparations and the de-industrialization of Germany at the plenary meeting of February 5. Stalin, flanked by Molotov on one side and the Deputy Commissar for Foreign Affairs, I. M. Maisky, on the other, opened the discussion. Roosevelt immediately tried to find out whether the Russians planned to use German forced labor as part of their program, a matter about which some of the Americans had grave misgivings. Stalin dodged this issue by pleading unreadiness to discuss it. But the Soviet dictator, not to be sidetracked from his immediate interests, explained that the Russians had worked out a plan for reparations in kind, and he asked Maisky to present it before the assembled diplomats. Maisky delivered his report "in a forceful manner" and it was clear to the Americans that he had "the full support of Stalin and Molotov." He was greatly aided by the fact that the essential element of his proposals had been previously advanced by the Secretary of the Treasury of the United

[7] Karl Brandt, Otto Schiller, and Franz Ahlgrimm, *Management of Agriculture and Food in the German-Occupied and Other Areas of Fortress Europe: A Study in Military Government* (Stanford, 1953), 148; Arnold and Veronica M. Toynbee eds., *Hitler's Europe*, 632-648; *Yalta Papers*, 620; Byrnes, *Speaking Frankly*, 26; Stettinius, *Roosevelt and the Russians*, 41, 230-231.

States and accepted in principle by Roosevelt and Churchill in the Quebec memorandum of September 15.[8]

The Soviet proposals called for two types of reparations: (1) removal of German heavy industry and (2) annual payments in kind from current production. Maisky explained that by "heavy industry" he meant "iron and steel, electrical power and chemical industries." Specialized industries which were useful only for military purposes (such as military aviation and the production of synthetic petroleum) should be "100% removed" from Germany. Furthermore, the Allies should "withdraw" 80 per cent of *all* German heavy industry. Maisky pointedly clarified his terminology: by "withdraw" he meant "to confiscate and carry away physically." The withdrawals were to be accomplished within two years after the end of hostilities. Reparations in kind would be collected from current German production over a period of ten years. Even beyond this period the three Allies would control the German economy. Maintaining British, American, and Russian representatives on the boards of directors of all German enterprises which "could be" utilized for war purposes. Material taken from Germany under the two types of reparations would be divided, said Maisky, in accordance with two priority indices. Both would guarantee the largest share to Russia: "(1) the proportional contribution of any one nation to the winning of the war, (2) the material losses suffered by each nation." The Big Three should create an inter-Allied Reparations Commission, which would meet in Moscow. This commission, according to Maisky's proposal, would be left only to administer the reparations program. Maisky announced that "the total reparations shown in withdrawals and yearly payments in kind which the Soviets required would reach a total of ten billion dollars."

Churchill was the first to speak after Maisky had completed his presentation of the Soviet proposal. Tactfully, the Prime Minister recognized "that the suffering which the Soviet Union had undergone in this war had been greater than any other power." But he recalled the reparations debacle that had followed World War I, and said that he believed the Soviet Union "would get

---

[8] Byrnes, *Speaking Frankly*, 26; Stettinius, *Roosevelt and the Russians*, 130.

nowhere near the sum which Mr. Maisky had mentioned from Germany." He reminded the Soviet delegation that "Belgium, Holland and Norway also had claims against Germany." Finally, he frankly stated that he was "haunted by the specter of a starving Germany, which would present a serious problem for the Allies." "If eighty millions are starving are we to say, 'it serves you right'?" he asked. If not, he added, who would "pay for feeding them?" Referring to Soviet demands for annual payments in kind, Churchill remarked that if one "wished a horse to pull a wagon" one must at least "give it fodder." Stalin agreed, but revealed his feelings and his quick wit in a short retort: "care should be taken to see that the horse did not turn around and kick you."

The President now recalled that the United States had, by loans to Germany, really financed the reparations program of the twenties. "He said that we had lost over ten billion dollars to Germany and that this time we would not repeat our past mistakes." Roosevelt gallantly offered to support Russian claims for reparations, but quickly qualified his gallantry:

> We must think of the future of Germany. We have always been generous through our Red Cross but we can't guarantee the future of Germany. We don't want to kill the people. We want Germany to live but not to have a higher standard of living than that of the U.S.S.R. I envision a Germany that is self-sustaining but not starving. There will be no lending of money. Our objective is seeing that Germany will not starve in helping the Soviet get all it can in manpower and factories and helping the British get all they can in exports to former German markets. Therefore, the time has come to set up a reparations commission.

A reparations commission would mean further study; once again the President thus sought to retain harmony by implementing his policy of postponement. But Maisky had prepared not only an oration but a rebuttal:

> He pointed out that the amount desired by the Soviet Union was equal only to 10% of the present United States budget and equal to about six months' of the British expenditures in the war. The Soviet demands for German reparations equaled about 1½ times the United States budget in peace and about 2½ times the British budget. He said, of course, there was no intention to force Germany into starvation but

147

he pointed out that he did not feel that the Germans had a right to a higher standard of living than that of Central Europe. He said Germany can develop her light industry and agriculture and that since the Germans would have no military expenditures there was no reason why Germany could not give a modest but decent standard of living to her people.

Churchill sought at this point to turn the Russian flank by endorsing Roosevelt's policy of postponement. He approved the idea of a reparations commission, and proposed that such a commission should consider the claims of all the countries which had suffered from German aggression. Even more significantly, he stated that differences which might arise in the commission "must be referred to and settled by the three governments." Churchill's proposal, while immediately postponing the issue, would also make it possible for any one of the Big Three to veto any other's demands in the future reparations commission.

Stalin sought to salvage his reparations dreams by proposing that the Big Three agree at Yalta upon general directives to the reparations commission. He repeated that the three Great Powers should have "first claim on reparations." Stalin added that he saw no need to provide reparations for France, "since she has suffered less than Belgium, Yugoslavia, or Poland." Stalin then suggested that the three foreign secretaries try to work out a set of directives to the proposed reparations commission. Churchill agreed, hoping that "within one month the governments can receive their version." He reminded Stalin that he had "a cabinet and parliament" to consider. But it was decided that the foreign secretaries should discuss the directives and report back their recommendations at Yalta. The session ended after four hours of tactful haggling, with Churchill insisting that only damage inflicted by the Germans should be considered in allocating reparations payments, not the extent of a country's war effort. Churchill urged Stalin to remember the principle of nineteenth-century socialism: to "each according to his needs." [9]

---

[9] Byrnes, *Speaking Frankly*, 26; Stettinius, *Roosevelt and the Russians*, 168; *Yalta Papers*, 620-623, 630-633.

Molotov and Maisky renewed their efforts in a meeting of the foreign secretaries at noon on February 7, but dropped the proposal that 80 per cent of all German heavy industry should be either taken away or destroyed. There was no further talk of de-industrializing Germany at Yalta, though all the discussion of reparations implied a measure of de-industrialization. In a draft proposal Molotov modified Maisky's suggestions as follows: "(a) USSR—10 billion dollars, (b) United Kingdom and U.S.A.—8 billion dollars, (c) All other countries—2 billion dollars." Then Maisky sought to prove that Germany would be economically able to provide reparations in the amount of $20,000,000,000 and still maintain a standard of living "comparable to those prevailing in Central Europe." Once again the Russians met with the frustrating policy of postponement. Eden in his most conciliatory manner insisted that the British must study the Soviet memorandum before he could discuss it further; and Stettinius stated that "he also wished to give a thorough study to the Soviet document." Somewhat testily Molotov replied that he would be ready to continue the discussion "whenever the British and American representatives were prepared." The foreign secretaries generally approved Molotov's proposal to create a commission at Moscow which would "work out a detailed plan for the exaction of reparations from Germany according to principles adopted at the Crimean Conference of the Three Powers." [10]

The reparations struggle was then abated until February 9. By then the Soviet Union had made various concessions to the West. Stalin had partially accepted the American proposals on voting procedure in the future United Nations, and on February 8, in a private meeting, Roosevelt and Stalin had agreed upon the terms whereby Russia would enter the war in the Far East. But the Russians had thus far held firm against making any of the concessions in Poland which the British and Americans thought essential. It seemed necessary for the West to make some concessions at this point. Stettinius on February 9 made at last a gesture in the direction of compromise on the question of reparations. He proposed to the foreign secretaries that they approve the Russian

---

[10] *Yalta Papers*, 702-704, 707-708.

reparations proposals except for the amount to be collected. Tru
to the tactics of postponement, Stettinius suggested that the deter
mination of the total amount should be left to the proposed rep
arations commission in Moscow. Determination of the total shoul
be the first function of the reparations commission. In a furthe
conciliatory move, Stettinius proposed that the reparations com
mission should "take into consideration in its initial studies th
Soviet government's suggested total of twenty billion dollars fo
all forms of reparations." Even this non-binding compromis
clause was too strong for Eden. He insisted that the Prime Min
ister was "strongly against stating a figure in the basic principle
even as a basis." Molotov sharply interjected that the Soviet Unio
was thinking only of its own interests and said that the onl
thing wrong with the amount Maisky had proposed was it
"minimalism." But Eden remained obdurate. The meeting ende
with Molotov and Stettinius agreeing to refer the Russian claim
to the reparations commission as "a basis for discussion," an
Stettinius reported this to the plenary session that afternoon.[11]

Next day at noon the foreign secretaries again returned to th
troublesome topic, and the result was one of the sharpest exchange
of the Yalta Conference. The British were unhappy over th
obvious Russian determination to control Poland, and when Ede
was pressed by Maisky to accept the Russo-American draft in
structions to the reparations commission he stated that he wishe
to submit a re-draft of his own. Furthermore, Eden raised ne
reservations against the Soviet proposals. He insisted that repara
tions should be considered "in connection with the dismembermen
of Germany"; that France be represented on the Moscow repara
tions commission "from the start"; that the question of collectin
reparations in the form of labor be considered by the reparation
commission; and that "it would be inadvisable to name any figur
for deliveries until the Moscow commission had started its work
At this point Molotov's patience snapped. He asked abruptly i
there were any matters on which Eden agreed. Maisky then adde
that Eden's reply was "very disappointing." Its whole spirit, sai
Maisky, was "to take from Germany just as little as possible.

---

11 *Ibid.*, 709, 738, 802-816, 843-844, 859.

Eden denied this, but insisted that the Russians would not be able to get as much as they expected out of Germany.

The Russians thereupon changed their tactics from head-on clash to persuasiveness. "If Mr. Eden had any doubts," said Maisky, "the easiest way out was to accept the formula agreed upon by the Americans and Russians yesterday." In his efforts to win over the obstinate Britisher, Maisky weakened the gains he had already gotten by stating that "the formula did not commit the Allies to the exact figure." But Eden merely took advantage of the apparent frustration of the Russians to raise a new objection: the British wished to limit the collection of reparations to a five year period instead of the ten year period Maisky had proposed. Stettinius now made it clear that he certainly viewed the Russo-American formula as no binding commitment, pointing out that the ten year period was "merely mentioned as a basis for discussion." "Certainly," said Maisky. And he added that the period might actually prove to be five or six years. Eden thereupon asked why, therefore, there was any need to include a time limit in the formula. The tense discussion ended with Eden promising to bring in a British draft that afternoon. Stettinius had left the British and Russians to argue the issue out except for his single conciliatory comment; and that one was more British than Russian in sub-surface character.[12]

Later that day (February 10) Eden submitted the British proposal on reparations. It altered the Russian draft in one significant way: Molotov's draft of February 7 had stated that capital equipment would be taken from Germany "chiefly for the purpose of military and economic disarmament of Germany." Eden's draft considerably restricted the extent and purpose of reparations in capital goods by proposing that they should be taken chiefly to destroy the "war" potential of Germany. Eden's draft would leave the period of collection of annual payments unspecified. It stated no total figure for reparations. Instead, it further revealed British determination to retain a moderately strong Germany after the war. In fixing the total amount of reparations, said Eden, account should be taken of the following considerations: (1) "any arrangements made for

---

[12] *Ibid.*, 774-780.

the dismemberment of Germany," (2) the requirements of the occupying powers, and (3) the need to leave Germany enough industry to pay for imports and to meet the prewar claims of the United Nations against Germany. This of course failed to convince the Russians. Eden in turn refused to concede to their wishes. There matters stood when the next plenary session was held.

The discussion of reparations was "lengthy and at times somewhat heated" during this plenary meeting of February 10. In one more day the conference would end, and the Russians still had almost no satisfaction in their demands concerning Germany. Eden reported that the British still had reservations on the Russian proposals and then Churchill moved his heaviest field piece into position: he had received instructions from his War Cabinet in London "not to mention figures"; that should be left to the reparations commission. Roosevelt indecisively drew up on Churchill's flank, saying that "he was afraid that . . . if any figures were mentioned that the American people would believe that it involved money."

According to the minutes taken at Yalta by H. Freeman Matthews, this was "the only time during the conference that Stalin showed some annoyance." This is verified by Stettinius: "Stalin . . . spoke with great emotion. . . . On several occasions he arose, stepped behind his chair, and spoke from that position, gesturing to emphasize his points. . . . Although he did not orate or even raise his voice, he spoke with intensity." If "the British felt that the Russians should receive no reparations at all," said Stalin, "it would be better to say so frankly." When Churchill denied this, Stalin added that he had heard much talk of reparations for Russia, but noted that no decisions had been reached. He urged the conference to make two decisions in the matter: "(1) that it was agreed in principle that Germany should pay reparations and (2) that the Reparations Commission to sit in Moscow should fix the amount and should take into consideration the American-Soviet proposal that there should be twenty billion dollars of reparations, with fifty per cent to the Soviet Union."

Churchill was unswayed by Stalin's defensive comments. He

then produced the telegram from the War Cabinet and read its instructions not to state a definite figure and the additional comment that "at any rate the figure of twenty billion dollars was too great"; that it was "beyond the capacity of Germany to pay."

Stalin broadly suggested that Churchill had rigged the receipt of the telegram which he had just presented, but at last moderated the Russian claim by adding that the proposed figure of ten billion dollars was simply to be used as "a basis for discussions—it could be reduced or increased by the Commission in Moscow." At this point, to break the deadlock, Hopkins passed a note to Roosevelt, suggesting that the President should say that the whole matter should be referred to the reparations commission, "with the minutes to show the British disagree about any mention of the 10 billion." The President followed this suggestion, but the British continued to oppose the specification of any figure in the instructions to the reparations commission. At this point Stalin gave way—or seemed to give way. He proposed that the Big Three directive should merely instruct the Moscow commission "to consider the amount of reparations." "We bring our figures," Stalin told Churchill, "and you bring yours." Churchill agreed and turned to the President: "How about the United States?" "The answer is simple," the President replied, "Judge Roosevelt approves and the document is accepted." The Big Three then took a timely intermission. It seemed that Churchillian obstinacy had paid off.[13]

But the Russians were not ready to admit defeat after all. At dinner that evening Stalin returned to the matter in conversation with the Prime Minister, emphasizing "the unsatisfactory nature of the reparations question at the conference." The master of the Russians then told Churchill that he "feared to have to go back to the Soviet Union and tell the Soviet people that they were not going to get any reparations because the British were opposed to it." Was this a muted threat or a grim jest? Churchill of course insisted that he hoped Russia would receive "reparations in large quantities." And Churchill finally agreed that instructions to the reparations commission should state that "the Soviet Union and

---

[13] *Ibid.*, 885; 901-903, 909-916, 920; Stettinius, *Roosevelt and the Russians*, 263-267; Sherwood, *Roosevelt and Hopkins*, 861 ff.

the United States believed that the Reparations Commission should take as a basis of discussion the figure of reparations as twenty billion dollars and fifty per cent of these should go to the Soviet Union." [14]

All in all, the reparations decisions at Yalta constituted a thinly disguised defeat for the Russians and a clear-cut defeat for the Morgenthau Plan and the Quebec agreement of September, 1944. Nor was there any compensating assurance to the Russians that they would obtain postwar credits in the United States. By agreeing to Stalin's figure as "a basis for discussion," the Americans had successfully sidetracked the Soviet movement for American aid. Once again the policy of postponement had triumphed, and with it, at least temporarily, the policies of the Department of State and of moderation toward Germany.

Soviet diplomats meanwhile had gotten little satisfaction in the discussion of possible reductions in the territory of Germany. Stalin raised the question of the future of the Ruhr and the Saar in the plenary session of February 5, in connection with his proposal to partition Germany. At Moscow in October Stalin and Churchill had informally agreed that these industrial areas should be separated from Germany and placed under international control, but at Yalta Churchill retreated from his earlier position. He was now uncertain whether they should be "handed over to a country like France," be made independent, remain a part of Germany, or be placed under the trusteeship of the future United Nations. "All this," the Prime Minister said, required careful study, "and the British Government had not yet any fixed ideas on the subject." Roosevelt stated that he had understood that the French did not wish "to annex outright the German territory up to the Rhine." But Stalin assured the Big Three that de Gaulle, during his visit to Moscow, had "made it quite plain that they intended to annex permanently the territory up to the Rhine." Thereupon, Churchill terminated this discussion of a reduction of German territory in the west with the statement that he did not "feel it possible to discuss possible

---

[14] *Yalta Papers*, 921-922, 937, 978-979; Stettinius, *Roosevelt and the Russians*, 274.

frontiers." Another victory for postponement and for the West was thus won.[15]

Discussion of Germany's eastern frontier was much more prolonged, but also ended indefinitely and in a way disappointing to the U.S.S.R. Again, it was Stalin who took the initiative, proposing on February 6 that Poland's future frontier should be extended westward to include the German territory east of the Western Neisse and Oder rivers. (See map, p. 160.) This proposed change would separate not only East Prussia but also a sizable slice of Pomerania (including Stettin) and Silesia (including Breslau) from Germany. Since much of this territory was already controlled by the Red Army and the rest would soon be under its occupation, the British and American statesmen had no strong position from which to argue this issue. Yet, they had decided in advance that any such sweeping proposals should be opposed, since the Soviet proposal would place some eight million Germans under Polish rule or cause them to be uprooted and transferred to the German rump state (or states) which would survive the defeat. The issue was not immediately taken up either by Churchill or by Roosevelt, and the subject was not pursued in this first tentative hearing.

Molotov revived the Soviet suggestion at the plenary meeting on February 7. Churchill's reaction was one of conciliatory opposition. He would "always support the movement of Polish frontiers to the west," he said, but he cautioned against giving the Polish nation more German territory than it could handle. It would be a pity, he said, "to stuff the Polish goose so full of German food that it got indigestion." Anticipating Stalin's suggestion that the Germans could be moved out of the exchange areas, Churchill observed that British public opinion would "be shocked if it were proposed to move large numbers of Germans." To this Marshal Stalin cynically replied that "most Germans in those areas had already run away from the Red Army." The plenary meeting was soon adjourned and the issue was thus postponed for another day.

By February 8 it was obvious that Stalin was intent upon creating a Poland which would be closely linked with the U.S.S.R.

---

[15] *Yalta Papers*, 612-625.

and whose frontiers would extend as far westward as Stalin could put them. Roosevelt, in an attempt to achieve compromise in this problem, agreed on February 8 to recognize the western expansion of Poland's frontier to the Oder River (a territorial change which would affect some 4,500,000 Germans), but the President simultaneously indicated that *"there would appear to be little justification for extending it to the Western Neisse."* Again, the Russians failed to press the issue; all were primarily concerned at the moment about the more immediate problem of creating a government for Poland which both East and West could support.[16]

The problem of Germany's eastern frontier again arose on February 10, when Churchill agreed, as had Roosevelt, to grant German territory east of the Oder to the Poles, if they wanted it. But the Prime Minister indicated that this was as far as he was willing to go. "I have received a telegram from the War Cabinet deprecating any frontier going as far west as the Neiss {sic}," he said. "They feel that the population problem is too large to handle." Roosevelt suggested that the Big Three should consult the future Polish government before making any public statement about the frontier, and he soon added: "I have no right to make an agreement on boundaries at this time. That must be done by the Senate later." Later in the evening the conference approved a British-American draft for a public statement which would simply declare that Poland "must receive substantial accessions of territory in the North and West," and that the final delimitation of the German-Polish frontier should await the Peace Conference."

Molotov made one last effort to salvage success for the Russians, however. Seeing that no specific agreement was to be reached, he proposed that the conference agree to promise Poland the return of "her ancient frontiers in East Prussia and on the Oder." The Russian was then chastised by a flurry of Western wit. Roosevelt impishly asked how long ago these areas had been Polish. Very long ago, Molotov replied, but he added, dead serious, that "they had in fact been Polish." The President then suggested laughingly that on historical grounds Churchill might ask for the return of

---

[16] *Ibid.,* 669, 716-721, 776. The italicized quotation is from Churchill, who emphasizes this point: *Triumph and Tragedy,* 377.

the United States to Great Britain. Churchill took his cue and quipped back that the United States might be "as indigestible for us as it might be for the Poles if they took too much of German territory." Molotov persisted for awhile, but finally Stalin intervened to "withdraw the Soviet amendment" and accept the Anglo-American draft on the German-Polish frontier.[17]

Thus there were no specific decisions at Yalta regarding the future frontiers of Germany. The Russians did not present their demand for Königsberg, as had been expected; and, faced by the combined opposition of Roosevelt and Churchill, they gave up their efforts to define Germany's frontier with Poland. The West and the policy of postponement won out at Yalta in these frontier questions. But it was only a legal vacuum that the Yalta discussions left, and the Soviet leaders probably made no greater effort to fill it because they knew that the power vacuum in eastern Europe was already being filled by the Red Army. They could have their way without the approval of the West.

For two years before the Yalta Conference informal discussions of the treatment of German war leaders and military officers had been held among the Allies, sometimes in a highly frivolous manner. A formal statement, known as the Moscow Declaration, in October, 1943, had (see pp. 43-44 above) threatened dire punishment to the offenders, but there had been no Big Three decision for action since that statement was issued. The Soviet Union had not participated in the work of the War Crimes Commission at London, though it had not opposed it.

Churchill raised the question at Yalta. Stating that the Moscow Declaration was "an egg that he had laid himself," the Prime Minister proposed on February 9 that the Big Three at Yalta draw up a list of the major war criminals, those whose crimes had no specific locus. Churchill first stated that "they should be shot once their identity is established," but he quickly added that they should be "given a judicial trial." Stalin agreed. There was no time at Yalta to draft a list of names such as Churchill had sug-

---

[17] *Yalta Papers*, 897-913, 980. Cf. Wolfgang Wagner, "Eden und die Oder-Neisse-Linie: Die deutsche Ostgrenze in den Jalta-Dokumenten," *Aussenpolitik*, VI (1955), 714-721.

gested, and virtually no more discussion of the matter occurred during the conference. The final agreements, as embraced in the protocol of the conference, simply stated that "the question of major war criminals should be the subject of enquiry by the three foreign secretaries "for report in due course after the close of the Conference." On one more matter moderation seemed to have won out at Yalta, though it was modestly covered by the camisole which postponement provided.[18]

DECISIONS AT YALTA: FRANCE AND FOUR-POWER CONTROL

Partition, de-industrialization, territorial reduction, and the trial of war criminals were all matters which could await the end of hostilities. The occupation of Germany had to be planned in advance of victory. The question of zones of occupation was of more than short-term importance, as events have shown. The post-war de facto partition of Germany rests upon the zonal division, not upon any formal decision of the wartime Allies to dismember Germany. The power-political potentialities of the zonal arrangements were not naively ignored by Roosevelt and others at Yalta, as has been suggested. At the very outset of the discussion Stalin asked whether the Big Three should create one occupation government or "three separate governments for the various parts of Germany." At this same meeting Roosevelt revealed his awareness of the implications of occupation when he remarked that "as he understood it, the permanent treatment of Germany might grow out of the question of the zones of occupation, although the two were not directly connected." [19] Not because they ignored the realities of power politics, but specifically because they acknowledged them, Roosevelt and Churchill attached great importance to plans for the joint occupation of Germany under an inter-Allied Control Council in Berlin.

One matter was easy to decide, because the preliminary negotiations had been thorough and the decision had been virtually determined in advance: approval was given at Yalta to the Anglo-

---

18 *Yalta Papers*, 849-850, 938, 979.
19 *Ibid.*, 612.

American zonal arrangement which had been tentatively approved at Quebec. Britain should occupy the northwestern zone of Germany, promising the United States control over a Bremen enclave and transportation-communication facilities to the United States zone in the south.

With this done, determination of the part France should play in the occupation of Germany became the major remaining occupation issue at Yalta. Its discussion brought out very fully Churchill's concern over the balance of power in Europe, and Russian fear that a Western bloc of anti-Soviet states might be in the making. The issue was twofold: (1) was France to have a zone of occupation? and (2) was France to be given membership on the inter-Allied Control Council for Germany as a whole? The first of these questions proved to be the easier to answer in the affirmative, though the U.S.S.R. would have given a negative answer to both questions. On both questions Roosevelt seemingly overcame a personal antipathy toward contemporary France to cast his vote against Stalin. The result was a positive victory for the West which was even more impressive than the victories which had been won through the negative policy of postponement.

Churchill was the first of the Big Three to state categorically that France should be given a zone of occupation, though Roosevelt had himself tentatively suggested it to Stalin on February 4. At Malta Stettinius had suggested to Eden that a zone for France might be carved out of the British and American zones, but it was Churchill, not Roosevelt who made the suggestion at Yalta that the French territory should "come out of the British and possibly the American zones." He especially emphasized the fact that the zone for France "would not in any way affect the proposed Soviet zone." Churchill, afraid that American troops would soon return home or go to the Far East after the defeat of Germany, wanted French forces to be on the Rhine with his own when that time came.

Stalin first balked at the idea, suggesting that to grant France a zone would create "a precedent for other states." Warily, he asked if a French zone of occupation would not call for four-power integrated control of Germany instead of the tripartite Allied Control Council which had been proposed before the trip to Yalta. Churchill readily agreed that if the French were given a zone

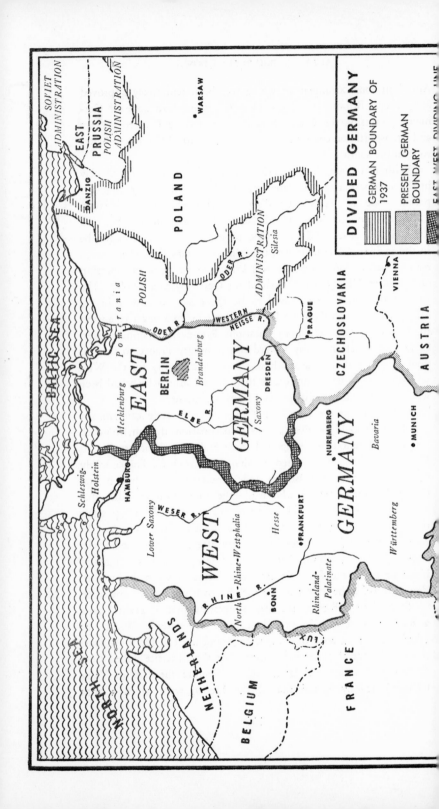

"they would, of course, participate in the control machinery." When Stalin quibbled at this, Churchill made a strong and lengthy statement, insisting that the decision involved "the whole question of the future role of France in Europe." He stated that "he personally felt that France should play a very important role." Roosevelt's comment that the United States would probably not keep troops in Europe more than two years strengthened Churchill's determination and made his argument seem all the more reasonable. It may have caused Stalin to weaken. But the President's next comments strengthened Stalin. Roosevelt approved giving France a zone of occupation, but he questioned the desirability of admitting France to the Allied Control Council. Stalin, overlooking his own conduct in 1939-1941, argued that France had "opened the gate to the enemy" in 1940 and had "contributed little to this war." At this, Churchill—ever so tactfully—reminded the Soviet leader that "every nation had had their difficulties in the beginning of the war and had made mistakes." Stalin then agreed that France could be "given a zone within the British and American zones," and with that the first question concerning France was settled at Yalta. (See map, p. 160.)[20]

In the same breath, Stalin indicated that a long fight lay ahead before the second question could be answered: "I am still against France taking part in the control machinery," he stated in his calm, deliberate fashion. This was a tone of voice Hopkins knew, and he passed Roosevelt a note which read as follows: "1. France is on the European Advisory Committee now. That is only body considering German affairs now. 2. Promise a zone. Postpone decision about Control Commission." Roosevelt at this point suggested postponement of the discussion of control machinery, and agreed with Stalin that France should not take part in the Control Council. But Eden and Churchill "fought like tigers for France," as Harry Hopkins noted, and a complete impasse resulted. Finally, either Stalin or Molotov broke the immediate deadlock temporarily by proposing that the relationship of France to the control machinery in Germany should be considered by the foreign ministers. It

[20] *Ibid.*, 616-618, 628-629; Stettinius, *Roosevelt and the Russians*, 63.

appeared that the policy of postponement might work for the Russians as well as for the West.[21]

But Soviet persistence in trying to clarify the situation prevented a Soviet victory through postponement. Molotov raised the issue again on February 7, urging upon the foreign secretaries a statement which would commit them to excluding France from the Control Council. Again he encountered opposition from Eden. Instead of having his way, Molotov only provoked his opponent to take an even stronger position. Eden now insisted that postponement was not enough, that the Yalta Conference itself should assign France a place on the Control Commission for Germany. Molotov then conveniently found himself in agreement with Stettinius that the whole problem of French participation in the control machinery should be submitted to the European Advisory Commission, in which France already was represented.

When this deadlock was reported to the Big Three at the plenary session on February 7, Churchill again—though certainly out of consideration of Britain's self-interest—proved himself a friend of France:

> If the French were given a zone without participation they would cause endless trouble. If we were strict in our zones, they might be lenient in theirs and vice versa. He felt that it was of the utmost importance that there should be uniformity in the treatment of Germany by the three or four Allies. He repeated that he felt the Control Commission for Germany would be a subordinate instrument as was the case in Italy, although we recognized that the German Commission would have more important tasks. He said he wished to make it clear that he did not consider that French participation in the Control Commission would give them any right to attend a conference such as this one, at least for the time being. He said he must state frankly that he found the arguments on the subject somewhat futile since it was obvious that France would accept no zone unless they were given participation in the Control Commission and he for one thought that they were right. He felt it was no good to refer the question to the European Advisory Commission which was a weaker body and particularly as France

---

21 *Yalta Papers*, 618-619, 629-633, 701-710, 718-719; Sherwood, *Roosevelt and Hopkins*, 858.

was represented on the Commission and only a deadlock could result with the French and British on one side and the Russians and Americans on the other.

Roosevelt continued to try to by-pass this issue, and suggested that it would be better to postpone the matter "for two or three weeks instead of two or three days," as Churchill proposed; and it was Roosevelt who broke the immediate impasse by suggesting a discussion of the problem of Poland.

But the President himself eventually settled this issue in favor of France. Probably Roosevelt genuinely meant it when, early in the conference, he remarked that he would be "just as satisfied if the French are not in on the control machinery." Possibly because of Soviet intransigence in the Polish problem, possibly because of the strong advice of Hopkins, Harriman, and Byrnes, Roosevelt was won over to French participation. The President abruptly changed his stand in the plenary meeting of February 10. He simply stated that he had "changed his mind." He now agreed with Churchill that it would be impossible to give the French a zone of occupation "unless they were members of the Control Commission." The President's words seemed to have a magical effect upon the Russians, who ceased their opposition with all the suddenness of Roosevelt's shift in position. As Stettinius relates: "The Marshall replied to the President's announcement with just two words: 'I agree'." [22]

Thus it was that France began her frustrating efforts to climb back to Great Power status at the expense of her ancient enemy and with the support of Britain and the United States. Within a few months de Gaulle would show his appreciation to the West by following a German policy which caused no end of grief for his patrons.

In retrospect, it appears that the most important decision on Germany which was made at Yalta was one which had been prepared long in advance and which was little discussed there, except as France was involved. That was the decision to approve the plans for the zonal division of Germany and for an inter-Allied

---

[22] *Yalta Papers,* 629, 899-900, 936-937, 978. See also Byrnes, *Speaking Frankly,* 25; Sherwood, *Roosevelt and Hopkins,* 858-859; Leahy, *I Was There,* 301-302.

Control Council, meeting in Berlin. These were the plans that had been prepared in the European Advisory Commission in 1944. The Russians on February 6 approved the Control Council and occupation zone plans, including the provision that an inter-Allied governing authority—later called the *Kommandatura*—should be established under the Control Council for Germany "to direct jointly the administration of the 'Greater Berlin' Area."

Still no provision was made for western transportation facilities into Berlin. Though the military authorities reviewed the E.A.C. proposals, they suggested no amendments. The United States Joint Chiefs of Staff, meeting at Yalta on February 7, simply approved the following statement: " . . . there are no reasons from a military viewpoint why the Draft Protocol of European Advisory Commission relative to Zones of Occupation in Germany and Administration of Greater Berlin should not be approved."

Thus was laid the foundation for the political disunity of postwar Germany and for seemingly endless Cold War crises. Did the military leaders not forsee the difficulties that would soon arise? Did they fail to act out of concern lest they offend Russian sensitivities at Yalta? Or because they did not wish to commit themselves to holding transport facilities which might be in worse condition than others at the end of hostilities? Overshadowing these questions, and related to them, it would seem, is a bigger one: Why did the Russians agree to permit Western forces a share of Berlin at all? In "Cold War" terms, both sides made mistakes. In explaining these mistakes it is well to remember that the Grand Alliance of World War II was still functioning in February, 1945, though it was slowly beginning to be loosened by the tensions of approaching victory. The Big Three, like the European Advisory Commission, expected some free movement of both Germans and occupation forces from zone to zone, as Lord Strang has recalled. It was not expected that the zones should be "sealed off from one another," and it seemed to the E.A.C.—and apparently to everyone else—that "any necessary arrangements for transit could be made on a military basis by the Commanders-in-Chief when the time came." This is, in fact, what happened in 1945.[23]

---

[23] *Yalta Papers*, 118n, 121, 688; Strang, *Home and Abroad*, 215-216.

THE YALTA BALANCE ON GERMANY

Basic issues concerning Germany remained unresolved by the Yalta Conference. But a number of decisions were reached without debate. Some of these matters of common agreement were summarized in a press report of February 12. This public proclamation embraced certain decisions on which there was such general agreement that they required little or no discussion at Yalta; it included other statements which camouflaged the extent of the Soviet retreat on German matters at Yalta. In it the Big Three announced:

> It is our inflexible purpose to destroy German militarism and Nazism and to ensure that Germany will never again be able to disturb the peace of the world. We are determined to disarm and disband all German armed forces; break up for all time the German General Staff that has repeatedly contrived the resurgence of German militarism; remove or destroy all German military equipment; eliminate or control all German industry that could be used for military production; bring all war criminals to just and swift punishment and exact reparation in kind for the destruction wrought by the Germans; wipe out the Nazi Party, Nazi laws, organizations and institutions, remove all Nazi and militarist influences from public office and from the cultural and economic life of the German people; and take in harmony such other measures in Germany as may be necessary to the future peace and safety of the world. It is not our purpose to destroy the people of Germany, but only when Nazism and militarism have been extirpated will there be hope for a decent life for Germans, and a place for them in the comity of nations.

In a restrained bid for German action to shorten the war, the Big Three proclaimed that: "The German people, as well as the German soldiers, must realize that the sooner they give up and surrender, by groups or as individuals, the sooner their present agony will be over." [24]

The proclamation of February 12 masked the vast indecision of the great Allies in questions concerning Germany. They could not

---

[24] *Yalta Papers*, 969-971; United States Department of State, *The Axis in Defeat: A Collection of Documents on American Policy toward Germany and Japan* (Washington, n.d.), 8-9.

agree and as long as Germany fought on they could not afford to disagree. Even the decisions on zones of occupation reflected the ambiguity of the situation. Would Germany be administered as a unit by uniform control and through uniform policies? The creation of an inter-Allied Control Council in Berlin, deep within the Soviet Zone of occupation, suggested that there would be one Germany and one German policy, implemented by all the occupation forces. But the documents approved at Yalta also provided for separate control of the occupation forces in each of the zones of Germany.

The ambiguity reflected not carelessness but a dilemma, and the dilemma was not a passing one. The prospects of Germany's early collapse had brought the Western statesmen face to face at last with the greatest European dilemma of the last four decades: how can the threat of German power be eliminated from Europe without leaving Soviet power dominant throughout the Continent?

Roosevelt was no conscious advocate of the balance of power concept, but, like other American statesmen since Wilson, he supported a principle which was but a corollary to the balance of power concept: that it was not in the interest of the United States for any one state in Europe to dominate the whole. Churchill, on the other hand, consciously followed a balance of power policy in his negotiations with the Russians concerning the future of Germany. Thus it came about that the net balance on German questions at Yalta revealed beneath the verbiage of conciliation toward Russia the hard rock of Anglo-American solidarity and moderation toward Germany. The Russians failed to win full satisfaction on a single one of the demands they raised at Yalta concerning Germany's future.

The credits and debits of Yalta concerning the German problem read as follows: Stalin demanded a decision to dismember Germany; Churchill and Roosevelt postponed any specific plans, though they agreed in principle to the possibility of dismemberment. Stalin demanded a decision to de-industrialize Germany and rebuild the U.S.S.R. with German equipment; the President and the Prime Minister refused to agree to de-industrialization and postponed consideration of reparations. The Russians hoped that the western boundary of Poland might be drawn by Big Three agreement at the Neisse River and that the Ruhr and the Saar would be separated from Germany; Roosevelt and Churchill both opposed these Russian demands. The single set of demands concerning Germany which were met fully at Yalta were those concerning France which Roosevelt and Churchill advanced there: France was to have a zone of occupation and to participate in the integrated administration of Germany through the Control Council.

The material regeneration of Germany was not desired at Yalta by any of the participants, nor could it possibly have been planned there. Even the permanent destruction of Germany was avoided by Roosevelt and Churchill only at the risk of alienating their Kremlin ally. This situation, so unfavorable for Germany, was of Germany's own creation. Adolf Hitler had sought to conquer Europe while posing as its saviour against Bolshevism.[25] Hitler himself had offered Europe its choice of mistresses: Nazism or Bolshevism. But he had shown the opportunistic motivation of his ideology by outlawing his own nation within the Western community. In February, 1945, it seemed certain that Europe would soon be rid of the ruthless and insatiable mistress which Hitler had forced upon it: Germany's hegemonial period in European history was almost over, having been desperate in character but brief in duration. Was the second mistress which Hitler had offered to be the only choice left after the debauchery into which Hitler had led Europe? This was the verdict of the Nazi *Völkischer Beobachter*, which headlined the Yalta communique as the "DEATH SENTENCE FOR EUROPE," and insisted that conference unity had been preserved only by the surrender of Roosevelt and Churchill to every demand Stalin raised.[26]

Ultimately a combination of American and British military and economic power would broaden the choices facing Europe, but only after it became unmistakeably clear that Stalin thought in terms of the same two crude alternatives which Hitler had presented. In February, 1945, this was not fully apparent, and Hitler's Germany still held the Big Three together as it had made them

---

[25] Paul Kluke, "Nationalsozialistische Europäideologie," *Vierteljahrshefte für Zeitgeschichte*, III (1955), 240-275.
[26] *Völkischer Beobachter*, Feb. 13-16, 1945.

"strange allies" in the first place. "We separated in the Crimea," Churchill has recalled, "not only as Allies but as friends facing a still mighty foe with whom all our armies were struggling in fierce and ceaseless battle." [27]

The Yalta negotiators had done an essential job of "papering over the cracks" in an alliance which could not be sacrificed until victory was won. They tacitly acknowledged the existence of a "dilemma over Germany." If we are tempted to censure them for failure to solve it, it is only fair to remember that by 1959 fourteen years of relatively peaceful conditions in the "Cold War" had not provided a solution either.

[27] Churchill, *Triumph and Tragedy*, 510.

Chapter VIII

TRIUMPH AND TRAGEDY

THE pessimistic forebodings of William Morris, a nineteenth century British socialist, may well become the collective epitaph of those who lived mature lives through World War II and its sequel, the Cold War: "Men fight, and lose the battle, and the thing they fought for comes about in spite of their defeat, and, when it comes, turns out not to be what they meant, and other men have to fight for what they meant under another name."

Few men saw this as early as did Winston Churchill. Writing to Stalin in the spring of 1945, he forecast a bleak future for the world if the trends of Soviet policy in Poland and Yugoslavia continued: "There is not much comfort," Churchill wrote, "in looking into a future where you and the countries you dominate, plus the Communist parties in many other States, are all drawn up on one side, and those who rally to the English-speaking nations and their Associates or Dominions are on the other. It is quite obvious that their quarrels will tear the world to pieces and that all of us leading men on either side who had anything to do with that would be shamed before history." [1]

The triumph over Germany was turning sour even as it was being accomplished. Germany in victory had been a unifying factor in East-West relations. Germany in defeat became a yawning chasm between East and West. The mere possibility of German surrender in March, 1945, was enough to provoke a brief crisis in the relations between the Anglo-American statesmen and their Russian ally.

---

[1] Llewellyn Woodward, "Some Reflections on British Policy, 1939-45," *International Affairs*, XXXI (1955), 290; Ministry of Foreign Affairs of the U.S.S.R., *Correspondence . . . Chairman of the Council of Ministers of the U.S.S.R. . . . 1941-1945*, I, 343-344.

THE COLLAPSE OF GERMANY

In March, 1945, almost every German, including Hitler, concluded that Germany could not win the war. On March 8 the commander of the Nazi S. S. forces in Italy sought to arrange a surrender of German forces in the south with Allen Dulles, chief of United States intelligence operations in Switzerland. Dulles made it clear that the Allies would permit only unconditional surrender; yet the S. S. commander, Karl Wolff, met again on March 19 with one British and one American general from the Anglo-American command in Italy. On March 21 Anthony Eden advised the British Ambassador in Moscow to tell the Russians of these developments, knowing that they would suspect some kind of "deal" if they should learn of them in some other way. But the Russians refused to take even voluntary notification in good spirit. Molotov on March 22 handed the British Ambassador a formal message which mercilessly rebuked the British and the Americans for negotiating "behind the backs of the Soviet Union, which is bearing the brunt of the war against Germany." Molotov informed the British and the Americans that the Soviet government saw in the surrender negotiations no mere misunderstanding, "but something worse." Stalin soon informed Roosevelt that he knew negotiations were underway whereby the Germans in Italy would be offered special "peace terms" for agreeing "to open the front to the Anglo-American troops and let them move fast"—obviously into Central-Eastern Europe.

General Eisenhower, upon learning of the Russian protest, advised Churchill that he was prepared, "without asking anybody's opinion," to accept the purely military surrender of German forces of any size at any time they might choose to surrender unconditionally. But special efforts were made to coordinate the British and American responses to the suspicious denunciations of the Western Allies, and to soothe Soviet sensitivities. Churchill advised Eden on March 25—the day after Western armies crossed the Rhine—that he could understand Russian fear of secret and separate negotiations: German surrender in the west would allow Anglo-American forces to reach "the Elbe, or even Berlin, before the Bear." Therefore, he informed Eden, the Russians should be "in from the start" on

170

any German surrender negotiations on the western front. But this same comment to Eden showed that the Prime Minister fully reciprocated Soviet suspicions and hostility: "They are claiming to have everything yielded to them at every point, and give nothing in return except their military pressure, which has never yet been exerted except in their own interest. They ought to be made to feel that we also have our point of view."

In Washington, too, the Russian suspicions and protests aroused strong emotions and called forth a blunt American rejoinder. General George C. Marshall drafted the message which on April 5 Roosevelt sent Stalin as his own, seven days before his death. Roosevelt protested against Stalin's insinuations and the lack of confidence they revealed. The President attributed the Soviet misinformation to the Germans, suggesting that Nazi efforts to create discord among the Allies seemed at last to be meeting with success. Roosevelt stated that it would be "one of the great tragedies of history" if, on the eve of certain victory, lack of faith "should prejudice the entire undertaking after the colossal losses of life, material, and treasure involved." Stalin's reply seethed with distrust and boasted tactlessly that the Red Army was winning the war while the West pulled its punches against Germany. Roosevelt sought to minimize the frictions that had arisen in an effort to restore a cooperative spirit, but on April 12 the President added, in his last message to Churchill on the subject: "We must be firm however, and our course thus far is correct." That night Franklin Roosevelt was dead.[2]

Roosevelt had returned from Yalta in good spirits. "The President has come home in the pink of condition—hasn't looked better in a year," his personal secretary wrote on February 28. "The long journey homeward has given him a chance for much-needed rest and relaxation." But the toll of work and disharmony that his position made inevitable soon caused new worry about the President's health.

---

[2] The Berne surrender episode is documented in some detail in Churchill, *Triumph and Tragedy*, 440-454; see also Ministry of Foreign Affairs of the U.S.S.R., *Correspondence . . . Chairman of the Council of Ministers of the U.S.S.R. . . . 1941-1945*, I, 311-320; II, 198-204; Byrnes, *Speaking Frankly*, 56-57.

What is to be said here of this man's role in history may be said briefly. It is too much to expect Germans to see anything good in Roosevelt's statesmanship, for it would require much distortion of the facts to make him appear in the war years as a friend of a powerful Germany. The President must be judged as a statesman by other observers and in a context of a vast number of complicated considerations. One conclusion will probably stand the test of time: frustrating as it was to his experts, Roosevelt's policy of postponement of German questions until after the war was a wise act of statesmanship. Compared with his two famous contemporaries, Roosevelt will probably emerge in history—for all his faults—as the greatest of the three. Both Churchill and Stalin may have been more conscious—more narrowly conscious— of their responsibilities to their own people. But Roosevelt demonstrated a sense of world responsibility and a sense of proportion that neither of the others possessed. His greatest political weakness was probably his disinclination to make unpleasant decisions, and even this was a virtue in his treatment of German questions.

The President was not lacking in short-run considerations of power which usually pass in political vocabulary for "realism." The changes in his views on the treatment of Germany show this. But there was about him an infinitely more profound "realism," which was derived from a longer vision of the future than either Churchill or Stalin demonstrated. If he clung firmly to his troublesome Soviet ally it was not out of naive unwillingness to see his faults. It was because he had soberly considered the alternatives. It is often said that the President "had a hunch" that he could get along with Stalin, or that he "thought" he could, or that he "hoped" he could. None of these things were quite true; Roosevelt was "determined" to get along with Stalin, as he himself informed the Soviet master in the midst of a dispute at Yalta. The entire Western World is still reaping the moral rewards of the determination he showed, and they are moral rewards which have carried material power with them.

Even in terms of short-run power, there was triumph in Roosevelt's tragedy. He left the United States with more actual influence in world affairs than it has ever possessed—either before or since—a fact that is not often admitted. It should be remembered amidst lamentations over the "lost peace," and soberly considered in all attempts to explain the loss.

Roosevelt was denied the full flavor of both the sweet and the bitter fruits of victory, though he had foretasted the bad before the good could be gathered. F. D. R. was allowed neither to experience nor to analyze the total dessication of wartime unity; Stalin could have explained it intelligibly only by self-indictment; Churchill was left to clarify what happened in the spring of 1945: "The destruction of German military power had brought with it a fundamental change in the relations between Communist Russia and the Western democracies. They had lost their common enemy, which was almost the sole bond of union." [3]

Even before they could quarrel over the spoils of triple victories, the selfish national passions and anxieties of "the strange allies" were aroused by the death rattle of their once mighty and still terrible opponent. Western suspicions of Russia, aroused in March, had already affected Anglo-American military strategy, and thus the future of Germany, when Harry S. Truman succeeded Roosevelt in the White House. Eisenhower on April 7 ordered British units under Field-Marshal Bernard Montgomery to push northeastward to Lübeck and Wismar on the Baltic. The Supreme Commander made it clear that the move was designed to forestall Soviet occupation of Schleswig-Holstein, Russian control over the Kiel Canal, and Russian access to the Atlantic Ocean. Eisenhower threw an American army corps into the advance and the combined forces reached the strategic prize on the Baltic on May 2, just twelve hours ahead of the Russians. [4] Had Berlin and Vienna been within easy reach of the Anglo-American armies, Eisenhower would undoubted-

---

[3] Churchill, *Triumph and Tragedy*, 456. Among the more intelligent negative evaluations of F. D. R. are: John C. Campbell, "Negotiations with the Soviets: Some Lessons of the War Period." *Foreign Affairs*, XXXIV (Jan. 1946), 305-319; Raymond J. Sontag, "Reflections on the Yalta Papers," *Foreign Affairs*, XXXIII (July, 1955), 615-623; and see Ministry of Foreign Affairs of the U.S.S.R., *Correspondence . . . Chairman of the Council of Ministers of the U.S.S.R. . . . 1941-1945*, II, 188, for the following note from Roosevelt to Stalin: "I am determined that there shall be no breach between ourselves and the Soviet Union," written in the midst of the unresolved haggling at Yalta about Poland's future.

[4] Pogue, *The Supreme Command*, 446; Montgomery, *Normandy to the Baltic*, 340-345; Montgomery, *Memoirs*, 297-298.

ly have seized those cities too. But Eisenhower and the Joint Chiefs of Staff put other military objectives ahead of Berlin in March and early April and in mid-April Eisenhower advised General Marshall that it would be "foolish" to try a race for Berlin "in view of the relative position of the Russians and ourselves." At about the same time, Churchill himself admitted that the Western Allies were not in a good position to outrace the Red Army to the German capital. Nevertheless, Churchill and Eden would have been happy to see United States troops push on to Prague; it would "do the Russians much good" to face American power in Czechoslovakia, Eden asserted.[5]

From all this, it is plain that the previous agreement upon zones of occupation in Germany in no way limited the military advances in April and May, 1945, as has been suggested by critics of Western strategy. In fact American troops occupied a good bit of the Russian zone (much of Saxony and Thuringia), the French zone, and possibly as much as two-thirds of the British zone of occupation, besides the one designed for American control. Eisenhower's forces were not pulled out of the Soviet zone until Western armies were allowed to enter Austria and access to Berlin was guaranteed by the Russians.[6]

Meanwhile, one more German attempt had been made to make a favorable peace with the Western powers and to play them against the Russians. Heinrich Himmler on April 24 had sought through Count Folke Bernadotte of the Swedish Red Cross to arrange a meeting with Eisenhower. Churchill and Truman quickly agreed on April 25 to send word that Germany must surrender to the three great Allies simultaneously. Himmler won only denunciation by

---

[5] Pogue, *The Supreme Command*, 445; Churchill, *Triumph and Tragedy*, 515, 539; Ehrman, *Grand Strategy*, VI, 131-149. On September 13, 1944, meeting with Roosevelt at Quebec, Churchill had informed the British War Cabinet: "The idea of our going to Vienna, if the war lasts long enough and if other people do not get there first, is fully accepted here." Quoted by Feis, *Churchill, Roosevelt, Stalin*, from Churchill, *Triumph and Tragedy*, 155. See also Feis, *Churchill, Roosevelt, Stalin*, 608-609.

[6] Churchill, *Triumph and Tragedy*, 456, 516; Ministry of Foreign Affairs of the U.S.S.R., *Correspondence . . . Chairman of the Council of Ministers of the U.S.S.R. . . . 1941-1945*, I, 365-367; II, 245-248; Holborn, *American Military Government*, 47; Clay, *Decision in Germany*, 22-27; Harry S. Truman, *Memoirs by Harry S. Truman*, Vol. I: *Year of Decisions* (Garden City, 1955), 212-218, 297-308; Strang, *Home and Abroad*, 216.

Hitler for his efforts.[7]

Adolf Hitler, lost in Wagnerian fantasies, remained to the end the damnation of his chosen people. If Germany lost the war, he told his Armaments Minister, Albert Speer, on March 15, the German people had "no right to live." It was only because Speer and others sabotaged the *Führer's* "scorched earth" orders that the Russian occupation authorities found any industry to remove when the Allied armies occupied the Nazi Reich. Deploring the failure of the German people to be worthy of his grandiose ambitions for them, Hitler concluded in April that suicide was the only way out of his own dilemma. The Nazi leader took his own life in mid-afternoon on April 30, as Russian shells fell into the courtyard of the Reichs Chancellory. Heinz Linge, Hitler's valet, later related that he personally "carried his body out of the bunker and then helped to pour gasoline over it." Linge's testimony, given in 1955 after he was returned from the U.S.S.R. as a prisoner of war, verified what was already virtually a certain interpretation of Hitler's personal fate. On May 7 a makeshift government under Admiral Karl Dönitz surrendered to Eisenhower. Russian insistence upon a repetition of the ceremony on May 9 in Berlin provided additional evidence of the creeping dissolution of Allied unity in the moment of victory. The price of Hitler's folly had been staggering: 1,650,000 German soldiers killed in action, 2,000,000 more as prisoners at the end of the war, and 1,600,000 missing. Worse yet, a nation of some 66,000,000 survivors remained to pay the penalty which Hitler escaped by death.[8]

Virtually all of Germany was already under Russian or Western occupation when the two surrender ceremonies were staged. There

---

[7] Truman, *Memoirs*, I, 88-94, 99-100, 106, 202. See Feis, *Churchill, Roosevelt, Stalin*, 612-616 for a brief account of the steps leading to the surrender of Germany. See also Felix Kersten, *The Kersten Memoirs, 1940-1945*, Constantine Fitzgibbon and James Oliver, trans. (London, 1956), 272-273; Folke Bernadotte, *The Curtain Falls: Last Days of the Third Reich*, Eric Lewenhaupt, trans. (New York, 1945), 89-93, 105-117; Ministry of Foreign Affairs of the U.S.S.R., *Correspondence . . . Chairman of the Council of Ministers of the U.S.S.R. . . . 1941-1945*, I, 333-336; II, 222-223, and 298-299n.

[8] Montgomery, *Memoirs*, 299-310; Ehrman, *Grand Strategy*, VI, 113-163; Julian Bach, *America's Germany: An Account of the Occupation* (New York, 1946), 12-13; *Time*, LXVI (Oct. 17, 1955), 35; H.R. Trevor-Roper, "The 'Mystery' of Hitler's Death," *Commentary*, XXII (July, 1956), 1-12.

followed years of great hardship for the German people. Germany reentered the bicycle age; she experienced a *Stummel* era, during which her economy was geared to the wild fluctuations of cigarette and other black market commodity prices; a period in which German *Fräuleins* sold their super-race indoctrination for K-rations, stockings, and chocolate bars. What the Americans won with favors and smiles the Russians took by force: rape and plunder accompanied the occupation of Silesia and other eastern areas. In Silesia the Red Army quickly made room for the Poles, who in May, 1945, initiated a mass movement of Germans to the west. Paul Löbe, President of the Reichstag in the Weimar era and a recent inmate of Nazi concentration camps, went to Berlin at the end of June to protest and seek relief. Though there had been no Big Three decision concerning the future of Silesia, Löbe was assured by Wilhelm Pieck, the German Communist leader who had recently returned from Moscow, that the expulsion of Germans and Polish control of Silesia had been approved at Yalta and were legal developments which could not be avoided. Simultaneously, the Russian-backed Poles began removing coal from the Silesian mines, though no reparations agreements had as yet been reached. In central Germany, even in areas where the Red Army had slightly overreached its zone of occupation, the Russians ignored American arguments and dismantled equipment for removal to the U.S.S.R. as reparations.[9]

POLICIES FOR GERMANY

The slow collapse of Hitler's Reich in March and April, 1945, accentuated the need for high-level policy decisions on future Big Three policy in Germany, and the character of the collapse inevitably conditioned those decisions.

Western discussions of policy toward Germany in the spring and summer of 1945 were a curious blend of determination to preserve Big Three unity, growing distrust and opposition to Soviet objectives and methods, and determination to make the German people feel their defeat. The world learned after 1945 how trouble-

---

[9] Koppel S. Pinson, *Modern Germany: Its History and Civilization* (New York, 1954), 535; Paul Löbe, *Der Weg war lang: Lebenserinnerungen von Paul Löbe*, 2nd ed. (Berlin, 1954), 249-254; Byrnes, *Speaking Frankly*, 82-83.

some for East and West alike the dissolution of Big Three unity could be. For the West the unity of the Great Powers seemed in 1945 to offer the only means of restraining unilateral Soviet actions in the heart of Europe, while at the same time holding down Germany. The desire to maintain this unity was reflected in the quick Anglo-American rejection of Heinrich Himmler's offer to surrender to the West only; and it was also reflected in the policy directive for the occupation of Germany which was formulated in Washington in March and April, 1945, and which became notorious as "JCS 1067."

Viewed at close range, this policy directive appeared to be a compromise between the views of the Treasury Department and those of the State and War Departments, with Morgenthau's concepts forming the dominant theme. Viewed against the background of the Yalta Conference, as it must be viewed, JCS 1067 may appear as part of the search for an occupation policy upon which integrated inter-Allied control of Germany—and peacetime Big Three unity—could be founded. Its terms struck a compromise between the relatively moderate aims of Britain and the harsh demands of the U.S.S.R. It is interesting and perhaps significant that it was formulated just when Soviet suspicions and protests over surrender discussions in Switzerland were causing grave concern in Washington, and at a time when the Joint Chiefs of Staff had to assume that Hitler might hold out for six more months.[10]

The basic policy directive for the occupation of Germany, evolving since the autumn of 1944, was reconsidered in the light of the Yalta Conference. On February 28, 1945—the very day that Bill Hassett noted in his diary that the President had come home "in the pink of condition"—Franklin Roosevelt seemed to turn his back on the Morgenthau Plan in planning for postwar Germany. On that day he instructed the Secretary of State to carry through the understandings of the Yalta Conference. The State Department either prematurely thought Morgenthau's influence over the German question was broken, or grasped at what seemed an opportunity to win a decision before Morgenthau could swing into action again. By March 10 the State Department, ignoring the various drafts of

---

[10] Truman, *Memoirs*, I, 17.

JCS 1067, produced its own directive for the military occupation of Germany and put it before the President. State Department officers consulted neither the Treasury Department nor War Department officials, apparently because they knew that each would object to different parts of their own program.

The State Department memorandum of March 10 bore little resemblance to the previous interdepartmental drafts of an occupation directive. It provided for the integrated treatment of Germany by a Control Council which could override the commanders of the separate zones. It did not provide for the destruction of a large portion of Germany's heavy industry, and instead called upon the Allies to maintain "a minimum standard of living for the German people." It urged that Germany be made to begin "paying her own way as soon as possible." It made no provision for dismemberment. These features were sure to rally the Treasury Department against the directive if it found out about it. And this was inevitable. The document itself called for the creation of a new interdepartmental committee to coordinate the planning of various agencies for policies in Germany. Apparently the State Department hoped by getting the President to approve its principles to leave the new committee little to do but implement them. If this in fact was State Department theory it was naive. The tactics were entirely too primitive.

And yet for a while it looked as though they had succeeded. The President returned the document of March 10 with his approval, two days after receiving it. The committee that the State Department had asked for was created on March 15. It was called the Informal Policy Committee on Germany. Assistant Secretary of State William L. Clayton served as chairman of this committee. Other members were John J. McCloy, Assistant Secretary of War; Harry Dexter White, Morgenthau's Special Assistant; H. W. Fowler, representing the Enemy Branch of the Foreign Economic Administration; and Ralph A. Bard, Under-Secretary of the Navy.

Apparently White lost no time in briefing his chief on these disturbing developments. On March 20 Morgenthau called a meeting of his own in his office. He and White discussed the unexpected turn in events with John J. McCloy and General Hilldring of the War Department. The State Department paper ran so far counter to the President's desires, said Morgenthau, that he could not understand how Roosevelt could have approved it. McCloy indicated that Stimson also disliked the new directive, but reminded Morgenthau that Stimson had also disapproved of the harsh Quebec agreement of September, 1944. With the Treasury and War Departments both opposed, Roosevelt decided to withdraw his approval of the State Department directive of March 10. It had lasted only a few days as officially approved United States policy for Germany.

To fill the vacuum the President—his health deteriorating—on March 22 called representatives of the three disharmonious departments to his office. At the end of this meeting a new memorandum was drafted, a three-page amalgam of three divergent viewpoints. President Roosevelt approved this directive the next day. It was in general principles a rough draft of the ultimate directive known as JCS 1067/6. The memorandum advocated softer measures than those Morgenthau had wanted and harsher ones than the State Department had thought wise. It favored "decentralization" of the political structure and the economy of Germany, not dismemberment or sweeping de-industrialization. The Treasury officials—and apparently the War Department, too—viewed it as a nest of many eggs from which they could pick the ones that promised to hatch what they wanted. Henry L. Stimson described it in a diary entry of March 29 as "a fairly good paper." Though this memorandum was presented before the European Advisory Commission on April 4, it was never much discussed there. But in Washington the Informal Policy Committee in April used it and papers prepared by the Foreign Economic Administration to prepare JCS 1067, the proposed military government directive to Eisenhower. Meeting in Morgenthau's office for plenary sessions, the Informal Policy Committee was very strongly influenced by the Secretary of the Treasury.[11]

---

[11] The foregoing is based upon correspondence with participants and upon: Dorn, "The Debate over American Occupation Policy," *loc. cit.*, 495-501; Truman, *Memoirs*, I, 16; State Department, *Postwar Foreign Policy Preparation*, 370; Stimson and Bundy, *On Active Service*, 582; copy, Memorandum for the President, March 10, 1945; and original, Joseph C. Grew to the President, March 23, 1945, with attached White House note of approval initialed by F. D. R. (Historical Division, Department of State); Foreign Economic Administration, *A Program for German Economic and Industrial Disarmament*, I, 48-61.

General Lucius Clay has stated that he "knew nothing" of this policy directive even when he left Washington in April, 1945, to begin service as Deputy Military Governor of the American zone under Eisenhower. At that time members of the Informal Policy Committee were still locked in controversy about its clauses, and the death of the President an April 12 caused new uncertainties about the directive. On April 26 McCloy reported to President Truman on the work of the committee, emphasizing the twin need for positive measures in Germany and a "practical relationship" with Russia. Truman consulted with the Joint Chiefs of Staff and approved the slightly amended version of the directive on May 10. Both the War Department and the State Department were pleased that it was designated as a short-term directive for the initial period after Germany's surrender. Dorn credits McCloy for the provisional character of the directive, but others, too, wanted it this way. "It was my hope at the time that, if we could not stop it then, we could at least secure a technical ground for re-opening the issue," one of the State Department experts remembers.

Immediately after Truman approved the directive it was issued to General Eisenhower. The directive soon became notorious under the Joint Chiefs of Staff file number—JCS 1067/6—as a symbol of the harshness of early post-surrender policy in Germany. It was treated as a top secret directive; General Clay has recalled that "for some months we were carrying out a policy whose existence we could not even admit." Behind the scenes the directive was presented simultaneously to the British and the Russians in the hope of obtaining agreement upon a uniform policy for all of Germany, and General Eisenhower was instructed to seek joint acceptance of it in the inter-Allied Control Council for Germany.[12]

Thus JCS 1067 had to be, as McCloy's comment suggests, harsh enough to win Russian support and yet moderate enough to prevent total chaos in Central Europe. It did not incorporate outright the Morgenthau Plan, as Morgenthau himself and others have asserted.[13] In fact it ignored the essence of Morgenthau's proposal, the deliber-

12 Truman, *Memoirs*, I, 101-102, 104-105; State Department, *Postwar Foreign Policy Preparation*, 370; Clay, *Decision in Germany*, 7, 16; Holborn, *American Military Government*, 41-47.

13 New York *Post*, Nov. 24, 1947.

ate destruction of Germany's heavy industry. It was a much more negative policy statement than the State Department wanted, but above all it was a *temporary* program for the treatment of Germany "in the initial post-defeat period"; it was not, the Joint Chiefs of Staff informed Eisenhower, "an ultimate statement of policies of this Government concerning the treatment of Germany in the post-war world." The directive anticipated that disagreements might arise in the Control Council; while instructing Eisenhower to carry out the policies agreed upon there, the Joint Chiefs of Staff instructed him to act in accordance with the provisions of JCS 1067 "in the absence of such agreed policies."

JCS 1067/6 informed Eisenhower that he should work toward the following goals: (1) moderate decentralization of Germany (the word dismemberment was not mentioned); (2) inter-zonal trade; (3) separation of Austria from Germany proper; (4) the "elimination of Nazism and militarism in all their forms," a provision which was expanded to embrace the purging of Nazi personnel, ideas, and institutions from the German judiciary, bureaucracy, and educational system; (5) the apprehension of war criminals; (6) the "eventual reconstruction of German political life on a democratic basis"; (7) collection of reparations and relief for countries which had been devastated by German forces during the war; and (8) "the industrial disarmament and demilitarization of Germany." But amidst the negative provisions one or two key positive statements appeared that could be stretched far in interpretation—and were. Economic controls were to be exercised "to assure the production and maintenance of goods and services required to prevent starvation" and such "disease and unrest" as would endanger the occupation forces. Furthermore, JCS 1067/6 provided in a back-handed way for outside aid to the Germans in decreeing that imports should be "strictly limited." The German standard of living was not to be maintained at a level higher than that in "any one of the neighboring United Nations." On the one hand the document provided that no measures were to be taken "to maintain or strengthen the German economy"; on the other, it specifically advised the American zonal commander that he should "maximize agricultural output," and authorized him to re-settle

"Germans and others" on large-landed estates and public lands.[14]

When the directive was finally formulated and issued to Eisenhower, Anglo-American forces were already deep in Germany; in fact the surrender of Germany was achieved three days before Truman finally approved JCS 1067/6. As they went into Germany, American troops were given mimeographed sheets of advice which breathed the spirit of JCS 1067/6:

> You are entering Germany, not as a liberator but as a victor.
>
> Do not keep smiling. Never offer a cigarette to a visitor whom you do not know well, nor offer him your hand. The Germans will respect you as long as they see in you a successor to Hitler, who never offered them his hand.
>
> Forget the American habit of meeting everyone in an open way. Distrust everybody who has given you no proof of his honesty.
>
> Always wear a uniform, never wear civilian clothes.
>
> Never give way. Anything that is granted as a favor will be regarded by the German as his right, and he will subsequently demand twice as much. He thinks fair play is cowardice.
>
> The only way to get along with the Germans is to make them respect you, to make them feel the hand of the master.[15]

These instructions were not authored by Morgenthau nor by anyone else in the Treasury Department, nor were they devised in Moscow; they came from the pen of a noted emigrant German novelist in America, Emil Ludwig.

THE ABANDONMENT OF FORMAL PLANS FOR DISMEMBERMENT

If the desire for Big Three unity still impelled Roosevelt to make concessions to Russia, suspicions of Soviet policies in Central Europe increasingly affected policy formulation in Washington and especially in London. The interaction was revealed when Churchill, in the midst of the dispute over the surrender negotiations in Switz-

---

[14] JCS 1067/6 as formulated in April, 1945, is reproduced in Department of State, *The Axis in Defeat*, 40-59.

[15] Friedrich and associates, *American Experience in Military Government*, 233. Quoted by permission of the publisher, Rinehart and Co., Inc.

erland, commented on March 24: "I hardly like to consider dismembering Germany until my doubts about Russia's intentions have been cleared away." [16]

On this particular matter Churchill did not have long to wait, for Soviet intentions soon coincided with his own fundamental desires. At Yalta the Big Three had created a special committee under the chairmanship of Anthony Eden to study "procedure for the dismemberment of Germany," but this committee received no instructions from the governments it represented. When it met on March 7 to review its powers, its members concluded that they were not positively instructed to partition Germany. Soon the Soviet representative, F. T. Gusev, was reminded from Moscow that the Yalta decisions did not regard partition as obligatory, but only as one means of preventing future German aggression "if other means proved insufficient." Roosevelt on April 6—true to the end of his life to the strategy he had adopted in 1941—in commenting on the report of the London meeting, stated: "I think our attitude should be one of study and postponement of final decision." This view was communicated to Winant on April 10. Thus the committee held only two formal meetings and never discussed even the merits of partition, much less specific plans for it.

The policy of postponement thus won yet another victory on the eve of Roosevelt's death, and in the next month Stalin himself publicly proclaimed a profound change of mind in the whole matter: On May 9, one day after the German surrender terms were signed with the Russians, Stalin proclaimed that "the Soviet Union . . . does not intend either to dismember or to destroy Germany." When Hopkins asked Stalin later in May why he had changed his attitude, Stalin replied that "his recommendation had been turned down at Yalta." Hopkins sought to reassure Stalin that Truman was "inclined towards dismemberment and in any event was for the detachment of the Saar, Ruhr and west bank of the Rhine under international control." Stalin replied that he "did not regard the lopping off [of] parts of Germany as dismemberment." While it is possible that Hopkins on May 28 may have been right about Truman's views, the President would not favor the partition of

---

[16] Churchill, *Triumph and Tragedy*, 443.

Germany or even the separation of the Rhineland from Germany when he met Stalin at Potsdam in July. Never since has it been the avowed policy of any of the victors to make permanent the de facto partition of Germany which has developed as a consequence of the Cold War and the zonal arrangements of 1945.[17]

The immediate zonal problems in the spring of 1945 were not created by the Soviet Union but by France. The government of Charles de Gaulle put to a first test the ability of the Western Powers to cooperate among themselves. The month of April was marked by strong insistence by the French that they be allowed to use their troops only in the zone of occupation in Germany which they had been promised. Since the zone had not yet been delimited this could only be interpreted as pressure upon the Allies to make good their promise of a zone. In the European Advisory Commission the nationalistic perversity of the French severely strained the patience of the American negotiators. René Massigli, representing the government of General de Gaulle, insisted repeatedly that France must control a sector of occupation in Berlin as well as a large part of the Rhine area, including Hesse-Cassel, Hesse-Nassau, Baden, Württemberg, the Saar, the Palatinate, and the Rhine Province. The British agreed with alacrity to separate the last three areas from the zone they had been assigned, for they were anxious to reduce their liabilities in Germany. The United States insisted, however, that the creation of a French zone should not be allowed to break direct transportation and communication between the American zone in the south and the North Sea ports.

Complications were also introduced by the Soviet Union. Insisting that the French sector in Berlin must be carved from the previously allotted British and American sectors, the Russians would not agree to the French zone in western Germany until agreement was reached on Berlin on their terms. After weeks of negotiations, in and outside the European Advisory Commission, the negotiators agreed upon the creation of a French zone and a French sector in

---

[17] Mosely, "Dismemberment of Germany," *loc. cit.*, 493-498; memorandum by Bohlen, May 28, 1945, on conversation of Hopkins with Stalin, May 28, 1945, No. 26, Potsdam Papers, galleys. Cf. Nos. 330, 331, Potsdam Papers, galleys. As this book went to press the Department of State still had not published the records of the Potsdam Papers. I used the galleys, and it is these that are always cited in this book.

Berlin. The French zone in western Germany looked like a geographical hour glass—or a tightly corseted lady's waist. The upper torso was taken from the western part of the zone Britain had been assigned. Getting the lower torso for France required a highly artificial division of the states of Baden and Württemberg. Parts of these states were left under American occupation as originally assigned, while western sections of both were turned over to the French. (See map, p. 160.) The French were formally presented with a map and an agreement designating their proposed zone on May 2, but final action was delayed while the Russians argued over Berlin. They eventually had their way. Final agreement was reached in London on July 26 while the Big Three met at Potsdam.[18]

WAR CRIMINALS

Greater harmony prevailed in 1945 between Moscow and the West on the question of treatment of German war criminals than on most German issues. In this matter Stalin seems to have been content to leave the initiative to the West. Thus, whatever the merits or demerits of the war crimes trials after World War II in the long run, they cannot be accounted for as a Bolshevik invention. The 1945 decisions on these as on other matters must be measured against the background of outrage which the Nazis had inspired through their barbaric practices against their own fellow Germans and the conquered peoples of Europe.

On the day Roosevelt died the question of war criminals was discussed by the British War Cabinet. Samuel J. Rosenman, the President's assistant in war crimes questions, was informed on April 23, just before returning to the United States, that the War Cabinet *unanimously* opposed a judicial trial of Hitler and "a number of arch-criminals associated with him." The War Cabinet proposed instead that "execution without trial is the preferable course." They would simply be shot. According to Truman, Churchill himself told Rosenman that he fully agreed with this

---

[18] Mosely, "The Occupation of Germany," *loc. cit.*, 600-601; Clay, *Decision in Germany*, 13; Vigneras, *Rearming the French*, 342-344; Potsdam Papers, galleys, documents Nos. 407-411 and especially Assistant Secretary of War McCloy to Assistant Secretary of State Dunn, July 17, 1945, No. 1028; report of agreement by E.A.C., July 26, 1945, No. 1032; and No. 1033.

decision of the War Cabinet. In view of the high moral position Churchill had taken at Teheran on this question there is much irony in this. Truman was unmoved by the suggestion. In asking Rosenman to continue his work on war criminal questions, the President on April 30 flatly stated that the United States was "opposed to such a policy." Rosenman was authorized to negotiate with representatives of the Soviet Union, Britain, and France "for the purpose of obtaining agreement as to the method, procedures and tribunals for trying the war criminals of this war." He was specifically instructed to "insist upon a fair method of trial, but one which will be as short and expeditious as possible."

On May 2 President Truman designated Associate Justice Robert H. Jackson of the Supreme Court of the United States as United States Chief of Counsel in preparing and prosecuting the charges which would be lodged against the as yet un-named European war criminals. Next day, at Truman's request, Rosenman discussed the troublesome question of war criminals at San Francisco with Edward R. Stettinius, then Secretary of State, and with Eden and Molotov. When Rosenman informed the British and Soviet foreign secretaries that the United States was opposed to the summary treatment of the top war criminals, Eden indicated that the British War Cabinet had also changed its position on the matter. (Many of the leading Nazis had by then committed suicide, and others were likely to do so.) On May 6 Rosenman was able to advise Truman that the representatives of France, Britain, and Russia seemed to be prepared to accept the American proposals, which he summarized as follows: setting up an international military tribunal of one representative of each power; a trial rather than summary disposition of the major criminals; and a committee of four chiefs of counsel, one from each of the Great Powers, including France.

On June 6, Robert H. Jackson submitted a report to the President which summarized at length the principles that had been evolved in discussions in Washington and Europe during April and May, principles which should underlie American policy toward the Axis war criminals. These called for swift prosecution and fair hearings of those suspected of atrocities and other war crimes. "To free them without a trial would mock the dead and make cynics of the living," Jackson asserted. Who should be accused? The list would include members of the German General Staff, political leaders, and persons in "the financial, industrial and economic life of Germany who by all civilized standards are provable to be common criminals." Jackson also proposed that organizations allied or associated with the Nazi Party, especially the Gestapo and the S. S. Corps, should be branded as criminal. Jackson added words of caution:

> It is not, of course, suggested that a person should be judged a criminal merely because he voted for certain candidates or maintained political affiliations in the sense that we in America support political parties. The organizations which we will accuse have no resemblance to our political parties.
>
> The groundwork of our case must be factually authentic and constitute a well-documented history of what we are convinced was a grand, concerted pattern to incite and commit aggressions and barbarities which have shocked the world.
>
> . . . We must establish incredible events by credible evidence.[19]

REPARATIONS DEADLOCK

Meanwhile, the Western Powers had sought in vain to persuade Stalin that France should be represented in the Moscow Reparations Commission, authorized at Yalta. Stalin became completely defensive in this matter, and the question of French participation proved to be only the first of a great many deadlocks that frustrated the members of the Reparations Commission in their efforts to determine the amount and methods of German reparations payments. Stalin, obviously upset, on May 27 told Harry Hopkins during his last visit to Moscow that Western efforts to place France on the Reparations Commission "looked like an attempt to humiliate the Russians."

By this time many other sources of friction had developed between Russia and the West, all of which conditioned the work of

---

[19] See Department of State, *Report of Robert H. Jackson, United States Representative to the International Conference on Military Trials*, 18-419; Sidney S. Alderman in Raymond Dennett and Joseph E. Johnson eds., *Negotiating with the Russians* (Boston, 1951), 31-98.

the Reparations Commission. Stalin frankly revealed his grievances to Hopkins on May 27. Argentina had been invited to participate in the founding conference of the United Nations at San Francisco, though it had not declared war against Germany prior to the Yalta-imposed deadline of March 1; the United States had persisted in its interference with Soviet policy in Poland; on this point Stalin warned that the Russians "should not be regarded as fools," and added ominously that "their patience has limits"; Lend-Lease aid had been abruptly terminated after the end of hostilities in Europe, and Stalin warned that it was "a fundamental mistake" to try to bring political pressure against Russia in that manner; and finally, directly pertinent to the questions of peace with Germany, Stalin reminded Hopkins that the U.S.S.R. had laid claim to one third of the German naval and merchant fleets, but had received no vessels at all from the Western Powers, which had received the surrender of the German fleet; he warned Hopkins that "it would be very unpleasant" if the Russian request were refused.[20]

The fundamental East-West conflicts of purposes in Germany that gradually emerged in 1945 were first revealed at the policy level in the Reparations Commission. Directly after the Yalta Conference, Stettinius persuaded Roosevelt to name Dr. Isador Lubin of the Bureau of Labor Statistics as the head of the United States delegation to the Reparations Commission, and Roosevelt on March 12 actually appointed Lubin to the position. President Truman revised this decision, however. Believing that the assignment demanded "someone who could be as tough as Molotov," Truman named Edwin W. Pauley, prominent Democratic Party oil magnate, as Ambassador and head of the American delegation; Lubin went to Moscow as Minister and as Pauley's deputy on the Reparations Commission. On May 18 Truman approved a policy directive to Pauley, stating the official American policy on reparations. This memorandum, like JCS 1067, was drafted by the President's Informal Policy Committee on Germany. It reflected to some extent the views of the Department of State. It also bore the marks of

---

[20] Sherwood, *Roosevelt and Hopkins*, 893-895; Truman, *Memoirs*, I, 228-229; Mosely, "The Occupation of Germany," *loc. cit.*, 603. See also Roosevelt to Stalin, March 29, 1945, in Churchill, *Triumph and Tragedy*, 743-745; and 418-503, *passim*.

the Morgenthau-Quebec concepts. And Pauley's instructions also were much influenced by the recommendations of the Foreign Economic Administration. These were harsh, but not nearly as ruthless as the Treasury Department would have liked. The F.E.A. cautioned that Germany should be left enough industry to support a minimum standard of living. It warned that in removing productive facilities care should be taken not to make Germany into "a relief burden for the rest of the world." While favoring removal of existing plant equipment over the exaction of reparations from current production, F.E.A. advised that the United States should "encourage the maintenance of industries in the 'safe' category in order to prevent excessive unrest." Yet, the F.E.A. also recommended the "permanent detachment" of the Ruhr and Rhineland from Germany as a way to obtain reparations and as a guarantee against future German aggression.

With advice from several quarters, Pauley sought chiefly at Moscow to achieve the following aims: (1) agreement upon the removal from Germany of "that part of her industry which would enable her again to make war"; (2) agreement upon the division of German industrial equipment which was to be removed; and (3) establishment of "a just and proper burden of reparation" which would leave Germany "a minimum subsistence standard of living without sustained outside relief." Pauley was specifically instructed to oppose any reparations plan which the United States would be forced to finance by "sustained relief to the German people." [21]

These American goals were very general, and the Americans in the Moscow commission devoted more time during the meetings of June to questioning the specific Soviet demands than to formulating specific proposals of their own. Pauley repeatedly requested from I. M. Maisky, the Soviet representative on the Reparations Commission, data which would rationally support Soviet demands

---

[21] Secretary of State ad interim to Pauley, July 2, 1945, No. 363, Potsdam Papers, galleys; Truman, *Memoirs*, I, 106, 308, 309; Stettinius, *Roosevelt and the Russians*, 289; Leahy, *I Was There*, 149; Ratchford and Ross, *Berlin Reparations Assignment*, 41; State Department, *The Axis in Defeat*, 103-106; State Department, *Postwar Foreign Policy Preparation*, 371; Foreign Economic Administration, *A Program for German Economic and Industrial Disarmament*, I, x; II, 411-421, 426, 435-443, for papers of March 28, March 30, and April 15, 1945.

for reparations in the amount of ten billion dollars. Maisky never supplied the justification and Pauley never accepted his figure. The Department of State believed that a total of $12 to $14 billion would be more appropriate than $20 billion as an overall figure. At Moscow Pauley resorted to a homely metaphor to make his point with Maisky: "You want a plan which will give lots of milk. We both expect that the cow will lose both horns and will get mighty thin. We want to be sure that the small amount of fodder required will be paid for with some of the milk. Last time [after 1918] we put up the fodder." [22]

Once again Soviet pressure for definite concessions in Germany was blocked. The immediate result was failure of the Reparations Commission to achieve agreement. But a by-product of this failure was the prevention of Russian victories on these issues. This was not positive victory for the West or for moderation toward Germany, but it was a negative victory for both; for agreement upon Soviet aims and an exploitative policy toward Germany were avoided, at least for the time being.

Surely this was not what the Russians had looked forward to through the bitter fighting of World War II. And so this chapter can be ended as it was begun; by June, 1945, Stalin, too, might well have been saying with William Morris: "Men fight, and lose the battle, and the thing they fought for comes about in spite of their defeat. . . . "

Stalin was getting no agreement in the Reparations Commission. But he was taking reparations anyway, to the chagrin of both Truman and Churchill. By mid-summer there were many things that needed to be discussed among the heads of governments. Many of them concerned Germany. And so the two friends-come-protagonists of the Old World agreed to sit down in July with their new and relatively untried partner from Missouri at a round table in Potsdam, just outside Berlin. There, near the parade

---

22 Byrnes, *Speaking Frankly*, 81-82; Ratchford and Ross, *Berlin Reparations Assignment*, 41-48; Truman, *Memoirs*, I, 310-311; Pauley to Secretary of State, June 19, 1945, No. 356, Potsdam Papers, galleys; Pauley to Maisky, July 13, 1945, No. 376, Potsdam Papers, galleys. See also Nos. 362, 364, 366, 367, 370, 374, 375, and 376 *inter alia*, Potsdam Papers, galleys.

grounds where Frederick William I had drilled an army to build a state, the architects of world peace would commemorate the destruction of German militarism. This done, they would look around to find what more there was to cement their alliance, and find, alas, only a Japanese Empire which was itself but a few weeks away from unconditional surrender.

Chapter IX

THE POTSDAM STALEMATE

THE Potsdam Conference began its work on July 16 and finished on August 2, 1945. Stalin refused at Potsdam to commit himself to the limitations in Europe which the British and the Americans desired him to acknowledge. As a result, Western military forces were to be maintained in Europe for many years to come. The Potsdam Conference was thus both a manifestation of the beginnings of the Cold War and a chapter in its intensification. Amidst the niceties of diplomacy, it registered the determination of the Soviet Union to establish its hegemony over as much of Central Europe as possible and the determination of the West to oppose this wherever Western armies were at hand.

In many parts of Europe the West had no armies, and discussion near the seat of Frederick the Great's court of these areas would verify the eighteenth century Prussian's precept that "negotiations without weapons are like music without instruments." But Western armies had taken considerably more of Germany than Stalin's, and retained control over 53 per cent of it. The Soviet leader found it impossible, therefore, to secure approval of the aims for Germany he had cherished since 1941. The conference as a whole thus represented a great stalemate. For those who participated in it, the last wartime Big Three conference made starkly apparent the existence of an East-West dilemma over Germany.

PREPARATIONS FOR THE CONFERENCE

On May 6, worried about Soviet policies in Europe, Winston Churchill suggested to President Truman that a Big Three meeting should be held "as soon as possible." "I feel," Churchill wrote, "we must most earnestly consider our attitude toward the Soviets and show them how much we have to offer and withhold." The Prime Minister was most immediately concerned about the fate of Poland, but Soviet power in Germany contributed to his worries. "I fear terrible things have happened during the Russian advance through Germany to the Elbe," Churchill advised his Foreign Secretary on May 4. He specifically indicated to Eden that he no longer wished to respect the zonal division of Germany which his own Cabinet colleagues had drafted and which he himself had persuaded President Roosevelt to accept at Quebec and Yalta. Churchill also reiterated his opposition to Russian reparations demands in Germany, warning Eden that they alone would "enable her to prolong the occupation almost indefinitely." The sweep of Soviet power westward and the inability of Britain to stand against the changing tide of history convinced Churchill that outstanding questions in Europe must be settled before the United States armies in Europe were weakened. "It is to this early and speedy show-down and settlement with Russia that we must now turn our hopes," he wrote.

To this Churchill added on May 5 that the showdown should be staged "at some point in Germany which is under American and British control and affords reasonable accommodations." In this Churchill was not to have his way. The accommodations which Stalin ultimately offered at Potsdam were adequate, and once again the Russian leader determined the location of the Big Three meeting.[1]

During the weeks before the conference the Prime Minister both publicly and privately, indirectly and directly, advised Stalin of his misgivings about Soviet policy. In his address to the British people upon the occasion of the German surrender, Churchill cautioned that his people had yet "to make sure that the simple and honourable purposes for which we entered the war are not brushed aside or overlooked in the months following our success." On May 12 Churchill strongly warned Truman about the danger of Communist technique and Russian power in Europe, especially when in the near future the British and American armies would "have melted" and the French had not yet formed armies on any major

---

[1] Churchill, *Triumph and Tragedy*, 501-503; Truman, *Memoirs*, I, 263.

scale. Then, in a phrase that would soon become well known, Churchill warned of the Russians: "An iron curtain is drawn down upon their front. We do not know what is going on behind." The Prime Minister concluded that the issue of "a settlement with Russia before our strength is gone seems to me to dwarf all others." Three weeks before the Potsdam Conference began, on June 23, the Prime Minister directly though tactfully informed Stalin of his concern, again playing upon the "iron curtain" theme: "A Russianized frontier running from Lübeck through Eisenach to Trieste and down to Albania is a matter which requires a very great deal of argument conducted between good friends. These are just the things we have to talk over together at our meeting, which is not long now." [2]

In Washington the new President had been urged by Averell Harriman in mid-May to arrange for a conference before July. Harriman described the problem of relations with Russia as "the number one problem affecting the future of the world" and warned that "at the present moment we were getting farther and farther apart." In the United States as in Britain, the eve of the conference provided evidence of a tougher policy toward Russia and opened the way for an eventual policy of moderation toward Germany. President Truman shared Churchill's anxieties about the future of Soviet policy in Europe after the armies were reduced. He had opposed the Morgenthau Plan while still a member of the Senate, and had "come to feel even more strongly about it" since he became President. While admitting that Germany must be disarmed and occupied under the inter-Allied Control Council, Truman opposed the de-industrialization of Germany. Knowing this, and seeing that the President was relying far more upon the State Department for advice than had Roosevelt in 1944, Henry Morgenthau provoked a cabinet crisis with the President on the eve of Truman's departure for Potsdam. Truman has told the story of the incident in his memoirs:

> When he found out I was going to Potsdam in July, Secretary Morgenthau came in to ask if he could go with me. I told him I thought the Secretary of the Treasury was badly

---

[2] Churchill, *Triumph and Tragedy*, 548, 561; Churchill to Truman, May 12, 1945, No. 6, Potsdam Papers, galleys.

needed in the United States—much more so than in Potsdam. He replied that it was necessary for him to go and that if he could not, he would have to quit.

"All right," I replied, "if that is the way you feel, I'll accept your resignation right now." And I did. That was the end of the conversation and the end of the Morgenthau Plan.

Morgenthau formally resigned as Secretary of the Treasury on July 5. Five days earlier, in order to obtain a Secretary of State who had held public elective office and to assuage James Byrnes for his failure to obtain the Vice Presidency in 1944, Truman named Byrnes to succeed Edward R. Stettinius as Secretary of State. This was no reflection on the policies Stettinius had developed. But the break with Morgenthau provided a significant demonstration—to Russians as well as to Britons and Americans—that the Quebec agreement of 1944 no longer guided the President of the United States in his formulation of policies for defeated Germany.[3]

The new President thoroughly briefed himself on the problems which were sure to arise at Potsdam. The very inadequacy of his knowledge of foreign affairs soon became an asset in the eyes of State Department experts, for Truman relied much more thoroughly upon their advice than had Roosevelt. On July 3, in one of his characteristic letters to "Mama and Mary," Truman wrote that he was prepared for the "chore" that lay ahead: "I have a brief case all filled up with information on past conferences and suggestions on what I'm to do and say." During the ocean crossing, the President engaged in daily conferences with Secretary of State Byrnes and Admiral Leahy, priming himself for the approaching negotiations. Byrnes himself, meanwhile, was thoroughly briefed by his State Department aides during the trip to Europe.

Thus, on the eve of the Potsdam Conference, the two Western leaders prepared to play as strong a hand in European affairs as conditions then allowed, and both were determined to check the spread of Russian power in Europe. It mattered relatively little that Churchill's days at the conference were numbered, for the Labor

---

[3] Truman, *Memoirs*, I, 22-23, 235-236, 326-327; Truman to Churchill, May 14, 1945, No. 9, Potsdam Papers, galleys. The passage from Mr. Truman's memoirs is quoted by permission of the holder of the copyright, Time, Inc.

Party leaders who would succeed him there were men of like views on foreign policy for Germany. Ernest Bevin, the successor to Eden as British Foreign Secretary, was if anything more wary of Russia than Churchill himself, and Clement Attlee, the new Prime Minister, in a quieter way was just as firm in his dealings with the Russians at Potsdam. Both Attlee and Bevin since 1943 had won an intimate knowledge of German problems as "most active members" of the British ministerial committee which had advised Churchill, Eden, and Strang in the E.A.C. on armistice and postwar problems. Only the advantages of hindsight and a strong element of egotism allowed Churchill the luxury of contending in his memoirs that the conference would have ended differently if he had only been allowed to remain at the helm he had tended so well during the war years. The British general elections, which in July ousted Churchill's Conservative Party from the government altogether, for the first time in some fifteen years, probably altered the outcome of the Potsdam talks in no particular whatsoever.[4]

Changing British personalities failed to change the basic factors in the power relationships of Europe which then prevailed. Factors which favored Russia must be measured against the Western determination to check the spread of Soviet power. Stalin, alone among the original Big Three of the war, remained throughout the Potsdam Conference. He was still the Stalin of previous conferences: he "knew exactly what he wanted to say and what he wanted to obtain," Truman has recalled. His very presence at Potsdam after a recent heart attack symbolized the tenacity with which the Russians at Potsdam sought to harvest the fruits of their victories in Central Europe. The symbolism was especially striking for those who remembered that the death of a Russian empress in 1762 had saved Frederick the Great's Prussia from sure defeat in the Seven Years War. But Russia's greatest asset in the Potsdam discussions of the future of Germany was the presence of the Red Army in Central Europe, not that of the leader of the Russians at the conference table.

Stalin's bargaining power in Europe was enhanced by Anglo-American obligations in the Far East. The evidence at hand suggests

---

[4] *Ibid.*, 331, 335; Byrnes, *Speaking Frankly*, 67; Strang, *Home and Abroad*, 203; Leahy, *I Was there*, 388-390.

that Truman and his staff welcomed Russia into the Pacific War, and yet were concerned about the possible results of Soviet intervention. They were convinced that the U.S.S.R. would enter the war against Japan, whether encouraged to do so or not. They may have been accepting gracefully what had earlier been eagerly sought but what was no longer needed. They probably hoped to disperse Russian power to the east, for the prospect of sending Anglo-American forces to the Pacific and leaving the Red Army almost alone in Europe was not a happy one. In any case, on July 24—seven days after they knew that an A-bomb had been successfully tested, and the very day on which Truman told Stalin of it—the Anglo-American Combined Chiefs of Staff at Potsdam recommended and Truman and Churchill agreed that they should encourage Russian entrance into the war against Japan, even if it were necessary to provide the Soviet Union with supplies. Truman has written that his "most urgent" reason for going to Potsdam was to secure Russian participation in the Pacific War.[5]

Whether out of eagerness for Soviet help or anxiety about Soviet power, any decision to use either diplomacy or military forces to push back Soviet power in Europe was out of the question as long as the war against Japan continued. Once again, therefore, the desires of the West could not be fully reflected in Western diplomacy. To press for specific commitments which would check or, in some cases, retract Soviet expansion, and to prevent the settlement of the future of Germany on Soviet terms, these were the major elements in the policy of the British and American statesmen at Potsdam.[6]

---

[5] Truman, *Memoirs,* I, 322-323, 364, 380, 411; and United States Department of Defense, "The Entry of the Soviet Union into the War against Japan: Military Plans, 1941-1945," (mimeographed report released to the press on Oct. 19, 1955), 90-91. Churchill, *Triumph and Tragedy,* 639, argues that the Americans at Potsdam did not want Soviet aid in the war against Japan. See also Leahy, *I Was There,* 397, 415-418, 420, 422, 424. For a scholarly discussion of the Yalta agreements concerning Soviet entry into the Pacific war see: George A. Lensen, "Yalta and the Far East," in John L. Snell and others, *The Meaning of Yalta,* 127-166. See also Ernest R. May, "The United States, the Soviet Union, and the Far Eastern War, 1941-1945," *Pacific Historical Review,* XXIV (1955), 153-174; Louis Morton, "The Decision to Use the Atom Bomb," *Foreign Affairs,* XXXV (Jan., 1957), 334-353; Ehrman, *Grand Strategy,* VI, 275-309.

[6] Churchill, *Triumph and Tragedy,* 671-672, 674; Byrnes, *Speaking Frankly,* 79; Churchill to Truman, May 12, 1945, No. 6, Potsdam Papers, galleys; Truman to Churchill, May 14, 1945, No. 9, *ibid.*

POLITICAL DECISIONS CONCERNING GERMANY

German problems were among the most troublesome and important that arose during the Potsdam Conference, as each delegation acknowledged at the very first meeting of the Big Three on July 17. The first two points in the agenda which Stalin proposed concerned the defeated Reich: (1) the division of the German merchant fleet and navy; (2) reparations. Truman likewise emphasized the importance of German issues, suggesting at the first plenary meeting on July 17 that the three leaders should discuss the integral control of Germany during the initial period of occupation. Truman insisted that the Control Council "should begin to function at once," and that Germany must be treated as a single economic unit.[7]

Next day, acknowledging the total powerlessness of Germany, the Big Three began their serious discussion of German matters with the question: "What is meant by Germany?" It is indicative of the gulf that had come between the wartime Allies that they disagreed over even this basic question. Churchill posed the question; and Truman agreed with the Prime Minister that they should talk about the future of Germany in terms of the Germany of 1937, that is, a Germany that included the Ruhr, the Rhine, and the area east of the Oder-Neisse "line." Stalin insisted that the Big Three should talk of what Germany "has become after the war," merely four occupied zones minus territory in the east and Austria. In defining the basis of discussion at Potsdam, Truman had his way; the Germany of 1937 was taken as a "starting point" for discussions. But, as the following days were to show, the three debaters could never ignore the realities of the Germany of 1945.[8]

President Truman on July 17 had submitted to the Big Three a proposed statement of political and economic principles—approximately those of JCS 1067/6—which would guide the occupation authorities in their integrated control of Germany. These were referred to the foreign secretaries for consideration and revision. Eden reported the revised statement of political principles to the

---

[7] Churchill, *Triumph and Tragedy*, 647; Truman, *Memoirs*, I, 344-345; Byrnes, *Speaking Frankly*, 79; minutes by Llewellyn E. Thompson, Jr., and Ben V. Cohen, 1st plenary meeting, July 17, 1945, Potsdam Papers, galleys.

[8] Churchill, *Triumph and Tragedy*, 651; Truman, *Memoirs*, I, 352-353; Leahy, *I Was There*, 399; minutes, 2nd plenary meeting, July 18, 1945, Potsdam Papers, galleys.

Big Three at their third meeting on July 19. Subject to final revision, this statement of political principles, which was essentially the same as the draft Truman had presented two days earlier, was approved by the Big Three after very little discussion.[9]

The major objective of the United States was accepted among the Potsdam political principles for the occupation of Germany: though Germany was, "for the time being," to be allowed to have no central government, so far as "practicable" the Allies would provide "uniformity of treatment of the German population throughout Germany." But another principle stated that Allied administration "should be directed towards the decentralization of the political structure and the development of local responsibility." The ability of the Allies to pursue diverse policies in their separate zones of occupation was protected by this and by the ambiguity of the remaining principles. Negative provisions testified in part to the hostility of the West toward Germany, but marked even more closely the determination of the U.S.S.R. to render Germany permanently powerless. Thus Germany was to be disarmed and demilitarized. The German people were to be convinced that they had suffered total military defeat, and that they themselves bore the blame for their condition. The Nazi Party and "all Nazi institutions were to be destroyed; all Nazi racial laws were to be abolished. All members of the Nazi Party except "nominal participants in its activities" were to be removed from public and "semi-public" offices and from responsible positions in private organizations. German education was to be closely controlled and used to foster democratic ideas. And German war criminals were to be "brought to judgment."

These negative principles were less harshly stated than had been anticipated in 1944, or even in the spring of 1945 in some Washington circles. Nazis were to be removed from office, not necessarily arrested; education was to be controlled, not suspended until it could be completely altered. And positive principles mingled

---

[9] Truman, *Memoirs*, I, 345, 355; Leahy, *I Was There*, 401; and cf. the Briefing Book papers of June 27 and June 29, 1945, No. 327, Potsdam Papers, galleys, with United States proposal of July 16 as submitted by Truman on July 17, 1945, No. 848, *ibid.*; Protocol of the Proceedings of the Conference, Aug. 1, 1945, *ibid.*

with the negative planks in the Potsdam platform for the occupation of Germany. The Potsdam agreement stated that it was the purpose of the Allies to prepare for "the eventual reconstruction of German political life on a democratic basis and for eventual peaceful cooperation in international life by Germany." This implied a unified Germany, and represented a major step toward moderation since the Yalta days, five months earlier, when Stalin had proposed the permanent partition of Germany.

Admiral Leahy has asserted that Truman planned during the Atlantic trip to say at Potsdam that "the separation of Germany into separate sovereign states would be advantageous to future peace and security, and that a southern German state, with its capital in Vienna, should be formed composed of Austria, Bavaria, Württemberg, Baden, and Hungary." According to the Leahy memoirs the President would also propose that the Ruhr and Saar should be placed under the temporary control of the United States, Britain, France, and the U.S.S.R., as a step toward eventual "independence and sovereignty as a separate state." But in fact the British and Americans at Potsdam showed no interest in the Soviet proposal for a share in the control of the Ruhr through four-power control, and Truman has stated in his memoirs: "My aim was a unified Germany with a centralized government in Berlin. In the case of Austria, I hoped for a unified country with its own government in Vienna."

The seeming contradiction of the Leahy "agenda" for Potsdam and Truman's recollections is not difficult to resolve when it is realized that the "agenda" in Leahy's memoirs was recalled from memory, and that Leahy's memory was not always reliable. It is misleading to conclude, as Alfred Grosser has done, that Truman favored the dismemberment of Germany. Even in Leahy's "agenda" it was not proposed that Truman would agree at Potsdam to partition of Germany. Instead, the "agenda" specifically stated that "Germany be not partitioned along the lines of the zones of occupation," and called instead for the creation of a Council of Foreign Ministers for the post-Potsdam study of the problem. The foreign ministers would "report to their governments a recommendation *as to the* dismemberment of Germany." (Author's italics.) This

200

would seem to have envisioned a report either for or against partition. And before leaving this troublesome question it is well to report that the records of the Potsdam Conference in the Department of State reveal no discussion of dismemberment of Germany at Potsdam, whatever might have been put into Truman's shipboard agenda for the conference. They also show equally conclusively that the U.S.S.R. sought four-power control of a separated Ruhr-Rhineland area and that the United States and British delegations resisted these Soviet demands.

The Potsdam agreements looked forward to the political recovery of Germany. In order to begin the democratic reorganization of Germany the Big Three authorized and encouraged what the Soviets had already fostered in their zone, the reappearance of political parties "throughout Germany." At Potsdam they also proclaimed that the parties should enjoy "rights of assembly and public discussion." Furthermore, the Potsdam agreement provided that local self-government should be "restored throughout Germany on democratic principles" as rapidly as security considerations would permit.[10]

---

[10] Leahy, *I Was There,* 388-390; Truman, *Memoirs,* I, 306; State Department, *The Axis in Defeat,* 11-13; Potsdam Papers, galleys, minutes of 10th meeting of foreign ministers, July 30, 1945; and cf. the following materials in the Potsdam Papers, galleys: memorandum by the Joint Strategic Survey of the Joint Chiefs of Staff, passed on to Leahy on June 26, No. 332; Briefing Book Paper on Policy toward Germany in the Initial Control Period, June 27 with supplement of June 29, 1945, No. 327; Briefing Book Paper of June 29, 1945, opposing the partition of Germany, No. 331; Briefing Book Paper of June 29, 1945, opposing the separation of the Ruhr or the left bank of the Rhine "either by internationalization or by other means," No. 398; paper on the Ruhr, June 27, 1945, warning that an extension of Soviet power "into the heart of Western Europe through the device of trusteeship would manifestly be open to grave doubt," No. 399; and Nos. 400, 401, 404, 1022, 1023, 1024, 1025, 1026, 1027.
A United States "working paper" (No. 1021) which *did* propose international control over a separate Ruhr and Rhineland was inscribed by Truman (n.d.) as follows: "Not presented, but discussed [.] Decided they should remain in Germany [.]" This document was either authored by the Foreign Economic Administration or reflected its thinking on this matter. The F.E.A. recommended in April, 1945, the "permanent detachment" of the Ruhr and Rhineland from Germany, and this may be what Leahy remembered. See Federal Economic Administration, *A Program for German Economic and Industrial Disarmament,* II, 435-443. Cf. *ibid.,* I, 33, 327-331; II, 517, 645-660.

THE ODER-NEISSE LINE

Early in the conference the Big Three reached agreement upon political principles for the occupation of Germany. But what was "Germany"? Hours of discussion were devoted at Potsdam to the question of Germany's eastern frontier, and in the end no definitive agreement was reached.

On one aspect of the problem, agreement "in principle" was quickly obtained. During the plenary meeting on July 23, Stalin reminded the conferees of the long-known Russian desire to annex the port and the area surrounding the city of Königsberg in East Prussia. Since the existing Russian seaports on the Baltic Sea froze over during parts of each winter, the U.S.S.R. "felt it was necessary to have at least one ice-free port at the expense of Germany." Furthermore, said Stalin, "the Russians had suffered so much at the hands of Germany that they were anxious to have some piece of German territory as some small satisfaction to tens of millions of Soviet citizens." Both Truman and Churchill agreed to support the Russian claim to the Königsberg area in the eventual peace conference, "subject to expert examination of the actual frontier." [11]

Both of the Western leaders reacted differently to another Soviet demand in this area. To compensate Poland for the loss of extensive eastern territories to the U.S.S.R., Stalin was determined to secure land from the eastern provinces of Germany (eastern Pomerania, West Prussia, parts of East Prussia, and Silesia) for the Russian-influenced provisional government of Poland. The Poles themselves, Communists and non-Communists alike, demanded that all German territory east of the "Odra" (Oder) and the Western "Nisa" (Neisse)—including Stettin—should be included in the new Poland. Both the American and the British leaders—and especially the Americans—thought that this would place too many Germans under Polish rule, or send them into exile. While the British were prepared to see Poland win all the east-Oder territory, the State Department actually recommended in Briefing Book papers for Truman's use at Potsdam that Germany be allowed to keep some territory east of the Oder. In an exchange of views

---

[11] State Department, *The Axis in Defeat*, 17; Truman, *Memoirs*, I, 378; Department of State minutes, 7th plenary meeting, July 23, 1945, Potsdam Papers, galleys.

on the eve of the conference a representative of the British Foreign Office let the State Department know that at Potsdam Great Britain would oppose the cession of the Western Neisse to Poland "here and now." To do so, he stated, "might be regarded as a sign of weakness and provoke other excessive demands elsewhere." [12]

On the eve of the Potsdam Conference the U.S.S.R. sought to arrange a *fait accompli* by transferring administration of the German lands east of the Oder and Western Neisse to Poland. At the Conference Stalin worked to win approval of this. No other Soviet demand was pushed more consistently or more vigorously than this from the beginning of the conference to the end. Stalin raised the demand on July 18. Referred to the foreign ministers, the problem led to endless wrangling during the next several days. On July 20, keeping a vigilant eye on Potsdam, Polish President Boleslaw Bierut and Prime Minister Osóbka-Morawski sent identical notes to Truman, Churchill, and Stalin, warning that: "The Polish Nation would consider any other solution [than that of the Western Neisse] as harmful and injurious."

The foreign ministers, unable to reach any agreement, on July 21 submitted the troublesome question back to the Big Three. Truman protested on this day that the unilateral Soviet action had not been authorized by the Yalta agreement, and he reminded Stalin that the Big Three had agreed to accept the Germany of 1937 as a "point of departure" in their discussions. Truman refused to recognize the transfer of German territory to Poland, and suggested that a general revision of all the German zones of occupation should be arranged if Poland was to occupy so much eastern German territory. Seeking to make bargaining capital out of Anglo-American control of the industrial areas of western Germany, both Truman and the British suggestively warned Stalin that Polish

---

[12] For a careful discussion of this problem through the Yalta Conference see Charles F. Delzell, "Russian Power in Central-Eastern Europe," in Snell and others, *The Meaning of Yalta*, 75-126. For the period between Yalta and Potsdam see Wiskemann, *Germany's Eastern Neighbours*, 86-98; Herbert Kraus, *Die-Oder-Neisse-Linie: Eine völkerrechtliche Studie* (Cologne, 1954). See also the following materials in the Potsdam Papers, galleys: Briefing Book papers of June 29, June 30, July 4, 1945 (Nos. 509, 510, and 513); Polish Deputy Foreign Minister Modzelewski to Ambassador Harriman, July 10, 1945, No. 517; memorandum by the Chief of the Division of Eastern European Affairs (Elbridge Durbrow) on a conversation with George Middleton of the British Embassy, July 13, 1945, No. 518.

control over the eastern provinces might adversely affect action on Soviet reparations demands. Stalin sensitively retorted that the U.S.S.R. was not worried about reparations, and "would, if necessary, renounce them."

Stalin held out a subtle threat of additional advances to the west if the Western leaders did not reach agreement on the line of the Western Neisse and the Oder. "The western frontier is open and the Soviet Union is not bound," said Stalin. "You are not?" Truman asked. "No," Stalin replied. Subsequently he returned to this guarded threat, saying the frontier remained "open and no discussions are binding on us." Stalin argued that the German provinces of the east were only German "on paper," and that "for all practical purposes they were actually Polish territories since there was no German population." Truman and Churchill both challenged Stalin's contention that all the Germans had fled the provinces. Both Truman and Churchill strongly suggested that the West had as much right to give France the Ruhr as Russia had to convey eastern Germany to the Poles. Stalin thereupon reiterated his absurd contention that "no single German remained in the territory to be given Poland." Churchill remained adamant, emphasizing that the British government could "never admit" that so much eastern German territory overrun in the war had become Polish. The Prime Minister pointed out that separation of this territory from Germany alienated one fourth of the arable land of the Germany of 1937, and that this would have to be considered in assessing the reparations obligations of Germany. The Prime Minister complained that a German rump state whose economy was thus amputated would simultaneously be forced to accommodate some eight million additional inhabitants because of the influx of refugees—"bringing their mouths with them"—from the eastern provinces. Stalin answered that it was better to make trouble for the Germans than for the Poles; but Truman bluntly reminded him that it was better still not "to create difficulties for the Allies."

Clearly, a deadlock had been reached. Truman re-stated his original position as the session of July 21 drew to a close:

> It seemed to me that nothing remained to be said except to repeat in all frankness where I stood: I could not agree to the separation of the eastern part of Germany.

Stalin, too, apparently had decided there was nothing to be gained by continuing this discussion.

"Are we through?" he asked abruptly.

Churchill suggested that we were hardly through but that we should turn now to more agreeable things.

I announced that the conference had apparently reached an impasse on this matter and that the session was adjourned.[13]

Next day the Big Three returned to the dispute over the German-Polish frontier. After the arguments of the day before had been repeated, Stalin showed his iron fist. He stated frankly that the situation in the east was not the result of Polish action, but that "circumstances and the Russians were to blame." Stalin pointed out that the Yalta agreement had called for definition of the German-Polish frontier after consultation with the Polish leaders, whereupon the Big Three decided to invite leaders of the new Polish government to Potsdam. Their desires would be heard in an effort to arrive at "some kind of practical solution . . . which could last until the matter was finally settled at the peace conference." [14]

The representatives of the Polish provisional government, led by President Boleslaw Bierut, arrived in Potsdam on July 24, but they remained impervious to Churchill's pleas that they be reasonable. To Churchill's reminder that Britain had entered the war to help Poland in 1939, Bierut answered that Britain should now show more understanding for Poland. Churchill assured Bierut that he favored "ample compensation" for the Poles for their eastern losses to the U.S.S.R., but warned him that they were "wrong to ask for so much." "We are not going to support your request for the western frontier," he told the Poles. "We were talking about

---

[13] Truman, *Memoirs*, I, 366-371; Byrnes, *Speaking Frankly*, 79-81; Churchill, *Triumph and Tragedy*, 654-658; Leahy, *I Was There*, 406-407; Bierut and Osóbka-Morawski to Truman, July 20, 1945, No. 1146, Potsdam Papers, galleys, and the following materials in the same collection: Department of State minutes, 1st and 5th plenary meetings, July 18 and 21, 1945; No. 1144 for memorandum by British Delegation of July 18, 1945; No. 1145 for Soviet proposal of July 20, 1945. The passage from Mr. Truman's memoirs is quoted by permission of Time, Inc.

[14] Churchill, *Triumph and Tragedy*, 658-616; Truman, *Memoirs*, I, 372-373; Leahy, *I Was There*, 407-408; minutes of 6th and 7th plenary meetings, July 22-23, 1945, Potsdam Papers, galleys.

the Oder Line but now you are asking for more. . . . You are showing too great appetites." According to an informed Polish-born commentator, the Poles at Potsdam thought Churchill's "defense of Germany" was based on his realization that it was "an integral part of the defense of the British Isles." "My appeal came to nothing," Churchill later recalled.

Meanwhile, the conversations between the Polish leaders and the Big Three foreign secretaries on the afternoon of July 24 had ended on the same note. Such opposites as Mikolajczyk and Bierut unanimously insisted that Poland's western border should be established along the Oder and the Western Neisse rivers, as Stalin had proposed. They reminded the Western foreign secretaries that even with the desired annexations of German territory, Poland would be smaller than before the war, because of the loss of the eastern third of prewar Poland to the U.S.S.R. Foreign Minister W. Rzymowski described the proposed frontier as "an ancient boundary of a state which was the cradle of the Polish nation." When Churchill met for the last time as a member of the Big Three on July 25, the conference was still no closer to an agreement than before the visit of the Polish leaders to Potsdam.[15]

Three days later, on July 28, Clement Attlee and the new British Foreign Secretary, Ernest Bevin, arrived from London to continue the conference. That evening the new British spokesmen met with Truman, Byrnes, and other American representatives, and reassured them that British policy remained unaltered on the Polish boundary proposals: "Mr. Bevin immediately and forcefully presented his strong opposition to those boundaries," Byrnes later wrote in his memoirs. But Churchill himself had indicated his willingness to grant the German area east of the Oder River and the Eastern Neisse to the Poles, as had Roosevelt at Yalta. In an effort to break the deadlock on this issue, Byrnes on July 29 suggested in a meeting with Molotov that the United States might make a concession on the Polish frontier in the West if the Russians would

---

[15] Churchill, *Triumph and Tragedy*, 661-667; Leahy, *I Was There*, 421, 423. Byrnes, *Speaking Frankly*, 80; Truman, *Memoirs*, I, 388; Rozek, *Allied Wartime Diplomacy*, 405-408, is not very full on the Polish frontier problem at Potsdam. Mikolajczyk's minutes of the meeting of July 24, 1945, are to be included in Potsdam Papers as an appendix. Cf. Mikolajczyk memorandum for Harriman, July 24, 1945, No. 1149, Potsdam Papers, galleys.

relent somewhat in their reparations demands. Byrnes indicated his readiness to approve Polish "administration" of the area east of the Eastern Neisse River. Molotov objected that this was insufficient. But Truman informed him that this was "a very large concession on our part," and urged Molotov to lay the proposal before Stalin. That same night, it now appears, Stalin himself asked Bierut if the Poles might not "agree to certain concessions, e.g. the line of the Queis [Kwisa] instead of the Lausitzer [Western] Neisse." This would have set the German-Polish boundary between the Western and the Eastern Neisse rivers, and the Poles seem to have agreed to make the concession. It never was presented to the conference, however.[16]

Tired of haggling, Byrnes on July 30 provoked a showdown on the boundary question and that of reparations, which was also still outstanding. He made a three-way proposal to Molotov, linking German reparations, the admission of Soviet satellite states as members of the United Nations, and the German-Polish boundary. Byrnes said he was prepared "as a concession to meet the Soviet desire" to approve provisionally the Polish "administration" of the areas east of the Oder and Western Neisse line; but he did not commit the United States to support this arrangement at the future peace conference. In a subsequent meeting on July 30 Byrnes told Molotov that the United States would agree only to a "package deal" on all three proposals. Then or on July 31 he added that he and President Truman would "leave for the United States the next day."

When the plenary session opened on July 31, Stalin protested against the Byrnes "ultimatum," insisting that it linked unrelated subjects. Byrnes agreed that it did, but pointed out that the issues had been discussed for weeks, and that they were presented together in hope of finding an agreement. "The U. S. Delegation was not willing to accept one without the others," said Byrnes.

After bargaining an agreement was reached on August 1. Pend-

---

[16] Truman, *Memoirs*, I, 395, 400-401; Byrnes, *Speaking Frankly*, 79; minutes of meeting at Truman's quarters, July 29, 1945, Potsdam Papers, galleys; diary entry in Mikolajczyk Papers, July 29, 1945, not published by Rozek, *Allied Wartime Diplomacy*, 410, but to be included as an appendix in the Potsdam Papers of the Department of State.

ing the final decision of a future peace conference, Poland was to administer the German territories east of the Oder and Western Neisse rivers. At the last minute the Russians again tried to rescue a definitive legal victory for their claims by demanding that only Polish and Russian experts should determine exactly the future German-Polish frontier. But on this matter the West held firm, insisting that experts of other nations should also participate in the future determination of the boundary.[17]

Meanwhile, a number of other German matters had been discussed with no more unanimity than was achieved on the Oder-Neisse line.

THE GERMAN FLEET

Stalin lost no time after arriving at Potsdam in pressing one of his favorite subjects upon the conference, the Soviet demand for one third of the remains of the German Navy and merchant fleet. Truman did not argue against the principle involved in this demand, but he was strongly advised by the Joint Chiefs of Staff on July 17 to insist that the captured German vessels first should be used in transporting American troops for wartime operations before they were shared. Even after Truman proposed the adjournment of the first day's plenary session, Stalin bitterly returned to the subject, asking, "Why does Churchill refuse to give Russia her share of the German fleet?" The Prime Minister dodged the question, suggesting that the fleet should be destroyed. Weapons of war were horrible things, Churchill observed. But Stalin insisted: "Let's divide it. If Mr. Churchill wishes, he can sink his share."

When the first separate meeting of the foreign ministers was held on July 18 Molotov revived the discussion of the German fleet, but was stalled by Byrnes and Eden. Eden promised that the fleet would not be sunk until its disposition could be discussed. Again during the evening of July 18, when Stalin and Churchill dined with

---

[17] Byrnes, *Speaking Frankly*, 85; Leahy, *I Was There*, 421-423; Truman, *Memoirs*, I, 404-406, 409; Rozek, *Allied Wartime Diplomacy*, 410-411, which quotes the agreement from Mikolajczyk's private files; and see especially the United States proposal of July 29, 1945 (Nos. 1152 and 1153) and minutes of Byrnes-Molotov meeting of July 30, 1945, Potsdam Papers, galleys; United States memorandum on the foreign ministers' meeting of July 30, 1945, *ibid.*; minutes of plenary meetings, July 19, 31, and Aug. 1, 1945, *ibid.*; Protocol of the Proceedings of the Conference, Aug. 1, 1945, *ibid.*

only their translators, Stalin pressed for delivery of Russia's share of the German ships. This time Churchill, by his own admission, "did not dissent." Next day the Soviet Union presented its proposal in writing and demanded that delivery should "begin August 1 and shall be completed by November 1, 1945." Churchill and Truman both indicated that they would approve "a three-way division of the German merchant and naval fleets," but Truman suggested that the division should take place only after the cessation of hostilities in the Pacific. The British tried for a time to secure one fourth of the German merchant fleet for countries other than the Big Three powers, and in any case refused to accept the Russian timetable for deliveries. Truman on July 19 proposed that the ships Russia should gain ought to be counted as reparations, but he succeeded only in delaying decisions by introducing this idea. Stalin on July 19 said that he would give up his demand for immediate delivery of the captured German vessels if the Big Three could agree upon the principle that the U.S.S.R. should receive one third of them. Churchill stated that even this should wait until the end of the conference, and Truman agreed. The Western leaders gave their definite approval of Stalin's demand for one third of the German vessels only after Stalin had slightly moderated his demands for reparations.[18]

The intensity with which Stalin pushed his demand for an equal share of the German fleet is interesting evidence of the sensitivity in 1945 of the Soviet leaders to questions of prestige. It also suggests that the U.S.S.R. was even then determined to embark upon a period of naval growth such as it did in fact achieve after 1945.

REPARATIONS

East and West divided as sharply at Potsdam over German reparations as over the German-Polish frontier. As at Yalta, I. M. Maisky presented the Soviet reparations demands at the beginning

---

[18] Churchill, *Triumph and Tragedy*, 635; Truman, *Memoirs*, I, 349-350, 354-357; Joint Chiefs of Staff to the President, July 17, 1945, No. 1005, Potsdam Papers, galleys; minutes, 1st plenary meeting, July 17, 1945, *ibid.*; minutes of the meetings of the foreign ministers, July 18 and 19, 1945, *ibid.*; proposal by the Soviet delegation, July 19, 1945, No. 1007, *ibid.*; proposal by British delegation, July 30 (apparently), 1945, No. 1014, *ibid.*; minutes of 11th meeting of foreign ministers, Aug. 1, 1945, *ibid.*

of the conference. He continued to insist as he had in February that Soviet reparations must total ten billion dollars in value. Molotov and Stalin likewise advanced these demands with great vigor. Not content with the potentialities of the Soviet zone's resources, they demanded a large share of the industry of the British, American and French zones of occupation. Churchill and Truman, pressing equally hard to limit the reparations payments which Russia would exact from Germany, pointed critically to the withdrawals the Red Army had already carried out. Molotov's only compromise in the early discussions was to agree to reduce the Soviet claim from ten to nine billion dollars. The result was a deadlock which remained unbroken until the last moments of the conference.[19]

The United States delegation at Potsdam showed great concern over the question of reparations, greater than on any other issue that arose in discussions of German problems. Truman and Byrnes went to Potsdam convinced that they could not prevent or even limit the Russian seizure of reparations from the eastern zone of occupation, and they were advised to approve the removal of some capital equipment from western Germany to aid European recovery. But they were determined to restrict Soviet withdrawals from the western zones of Germany, and were very much intent upon treating Germany as a unit. The costs of any imports into Germany must be met, they argued, before reparations could be exacted by any power.

Truman was especially eager to use German coal as reparations. On June 24 the President had expressed to Churchill his concern about the economic crisis in Europe:

> The coal famine which threatens Europe this coming winter has impressed me with the great urgency of directing our military authorities in Germany to exert every effort to increase German coal production and to furnish for export the whole quantity over and above minimum German needs.
>
> From all the reports which reach me, I believe that without immediate concentration on the production of German coal we will have turmoil and unrest in the very areas of

---

[19] Byrnes, *Speaking Frankly*, 83.

western Europe on which the whole stability of the continent depends.

Truman proposed, therefore, that Churchill instruct Field-Marshal Montgomery, commander of the British zone, and that he himself instruct Eisenhower, "to take all steps necessary to achieve the following objectives":

> To make available for export from Germany out of the production of the coal mines in western Germany, a minimum of 10 million tons of coal during 1945, and a further 15 million tons by the end of April 1946 . . . subordinate only to requirements necessary to ensure the safety, security, health, maintenance and operation of the occupying forces and the speedy redeployment of the Allied Forces from Germany . . . .

While the Big Three were assembled at Potsdam, instructions to this effect were issued to the commanders of the British, French, and United States zones of occupation in Germany. A desire to rehabilitate Europe thus indirectly helped to prepare the way for an eventual economic comeback by Germany.[20]

But Truman and Churchill realized that industrial western Germany, if its production was to be revived, must obtain food supplies and raw materials from the provinces which lay under Soviet occupation. Current production in the industrial centers of western Germany was not sufficient to pay for eastern farm produce. This explains why the Anglo-American representatives were anxious to treat Germany as a unit in reparations questions. If this should fail, some other way must be found to get East German food. The only alternative was for the Western Powers to feed the western Germans from Anglo-American warehouses. For the British, barely able in 1945 to feed themselves, this was out of the question.[21]

Stalin at Potsdam was reluctant to promise food deliveries to the western zones of Germany, but he demanded a share in the current coal and steel production of the western zones as well as capital equipment. The Americans at Potsdam were determined, as Pauley had been in the Moscow Reparations Commission, that "there could

[20] Potsdam Papers, galleys, No. 420, for Truman to Churchill, June 24, 1945; Nos. 329, 417-434; Truman, *Memoirs*, I, 496-497.
[21] Truman, *Memoirs*, I, 311; Churchill, *Triumph and Tragedy*, 671.

be no reparations from current output until Germany exported enough goods to pay for essential imports." Both Truman and Churchill were prepared to compromise in return for Soviet concessions. On July 25, during his last meeting as a member of the Big Three, Churchill told Stalin: "We will send coal from the Ruhr to Poland or anywhere else providing we get in exchange food for the miners who produce it." Since Stalin wanted western German industrial output without giving east German food in exchange for it, tempers ran high during this plenary session. When Churchill finally announced that he had finished his last speech of that session and would return to Britain next day for the election results, Stalin sardonically quipped: "What a pity." Churchill's optimistic rejoinder, "I hope to be back," was not to be justified, and the dispute over reparations was continued by his successor, Clement Attlee, when Attlee returned to the conference on July 28 as Prime Minister. In the end there was absolutely no provision in the Potsdam agreement for Soviet collection of reparations from the current industrial production of western Germany.[22]

Negotiations between the Russians and the Anglo-American representatives over reparations in capital equipment continued throughout the conference. By July 26 it was apparent that the U.S.S.R. was not going to participate in a common program of reparations for Germany on a whole, but would act unilaterally in its own zone. The United States delegation then altered its objectives. The argument for treatment of Germany as a whole in reparations questions was temporarily dropped. Instead, the United States group at Potsdam decided to agree to Russian reparations from the western zones of occupation in exchange for foodstuffs and raw materials from the Soviet zone of occupation. Strongly advised to do so by Pauley, Truman held out against the Soviet desire for agreement upon specific tonnages to be removed as reparations from western Germany. What was contemplated by the British and Americans was so much less than Russian expectations, Pauley advised on July 28, that Byrnes should mention only

22 Churchill, *Triumph and Tragedy*, 671; Truman, *Memoirs*, I, 389; Byrnes, *Speaking Frankly*, 83-84; State Department, *The Axis in Defeat*, 15-16; Protocol of the Proceedings of the Conference, Aug. 1, 1945, in Potsdam Papers, galleys.

percentages of a total which as yet was undefined.

The United States delegation at Potsdam estimated that 55-60 per cent of the industry which was "deemed unnecessary for a peace economy" of Germany was located in western Germany, and that 40-45 per cent was in eastern Germany. On the assumption that the U.S.S.R. should receive half of the total *surplus* German industrial equipment (not half the total of German industry as a whole), Byrnes finally agreed that the U.S.S.R. might obtain 10 per cent of the *surplus* capital equipment of western Germany. Thus, while the Russians strove with great vigor to establish a specific figure in dollars or tons for their reparations exactions, the Western statesmen insisted that percentages of an undefined total must be sufficient. This was a Potsdam variation of an old United States technique in such questions: the policy of postponement was again put to use, reluctantly, after the U.S.S.R. refused to accept the American proposals to treat Germany as an economic unit. The Russians must have found the proposal less than satisfying, since their gains would depend upon the decisions of the commission that would eventually report how much industry was needed and how much was surplus.[23]

Attlee and Bevin on July 28 agreed to the American percentage plan for reparations, and on July 29 Byrnes made his proposal of concessions on Poland's western frontier in return for Soviet concessions on reparations. That day Molotov suggested a compromise: the Soviet Union would settle for two billion dollars (or five to six million tons) in capital equipment from the Ruhr. Byrnes refused as before to agree to any absolute value of reparations; Molotov insisted, on the other hand, that "a percentage figure would be meaningless." Thus the stalemate continued.[24]

Finally, on July 30 Byrnes broke the immediate impasse on reparations with his three-way ultimatum, linking reparations, the German-Polish frontier, and proposed admissions to the United Nations. Molotov again suggested that four-power control over the Ruhr should be arranged as part of the reparations agreement,

---

[23] Byrnes, *Speaking Frankly,* 83-84; Pauley to Secretary of State, July 28, 1945, No. 491, Potsdam Papers, galleys; No. 942, enclosure 2, *ibid.*

[24] Byrnes, *Speaking Frankly,* 84; Truman, *Memoirs,* I, 400-401; minutes of meeting at Truman's quarters, July 29, 1945, Potsdam Papers, galleys.

but Bevin said this could not be decided "without the French." Stalin on August 1 protested strongly against the Byrnes tactics, but soon began to bargain. The Soviet leader eventually accepted the principle that Soviet reparations exactions from western Germany must be stated in percentages, but haggled over the exact percentages. Considerable time was consumed in reconciling a difference in the bargaining positions of 3 per cent. Finally, a two-fold agreement was reached which, by its very nature, provided the prologue for a long postwar stalemate. The U.S.S.R. should get:

(A) 15 per cent of such usable and complete industrial capital equipment . . . as is *unnecessary* for the German peace economy and should be removed from the western zones of Germany, *in exchange for* an equivalent value of food, coal, potash, zinc, timber, clay products, petroleum products, and such other commodities as may be agreed upon.

(B) 10 per cent of such industrial capital equipment as is *unnecessary* for German peace economy and should be removed from the western zones, to be transferred to the Soviet Government on reparations account without payment or exchange of any kind in return. [Author's italics.] [25]

Thus, at a time when no one knew how much German industry would be declared to be *unnecessary,* and when it was uncertain how much should be removed in order to prevent future acts of aggression, the U.S.S.R. reluctantly agreed that it should receive no more than 25 per cent of an uncertain West German surplus. The scope of Stalin's disappointment in the reparations issue at Potsdam can be readily imagined if one remembers that only five months earlier he had asked for the withdrawal of 80 per cent of *all* German heavy industry. The postwar East-West dispute on this matter was probably inevitable; for even at Potsdam it was Truman's intention "to make it possible for Germany to develop

---

[25] State Department, *The Axis in Defeat,* 15-16; James F. Byrnes, *All in One Lifetime* (New York, 1958), 301-302; Byrnes, *Speaking Frankly,* 85; Truman, *Memoirs,* I, 404-405; Leahy, *I Was There,* 423; and see especially Clayton to Byrnes, July 29, 1945, No. 947, Potsdam Papers, galleys; Pauley to Byrnes, July 30, 1945, No. 956, *ibid.;* Nos. 953-955, 961, 963, and 980, *ibid.;* minutes of Byrnes-Molotov meeting of July 30, 1945, *ibid.;* minutes of 12th plenary meeting of Aug. 1, 1945, *ibid.;* Protocol of the Proceedings of the Conference, Aug. 1, 1945, *ibid.*

into a decent nation and to take her place in the civilized world," while Stalin's mind was set upon rendering the ruthless invader of Russia innocuous and using its economic power to rebuild the Soviet economy.[26]

ECONOMIC PRINCIPLES FOR THE OCCUPATION

Only after the reparations agreement was reached on August 1 were the economic principles for the treatment of defeated Germany finally approved. Truman presented a draft statement of economic principles during the first plenary meeting at Potsdam, but the Big Three deferred consideration of these principles until after the political aims could be tentatively approved. Meanwhile, a special Economic Sub-Committee was created to formulate a draft of economic principles. It was in this committee that I. M. Maisky, as the Soviet representative, argued that the Ruhr should be separated from the British zone proper and jointly administered by the Russians, British, and Americans. The Soviet claim was understandable, for Churchill had told Stalin as recently as October, 1944, that he favored the internationalization of the Ruhr. But dramatic changes had occurred since October, 1944, and Maisky was unable to convince the British and American representatives that the Ruhr should be shared with Russia. Molotov then carried the Soviet argument to Byrnes, complaining that the Economic Sub-Committee "had not done so well." But Byrnes resisted Molotov's demands and on August 1—at least for the time being—Molotov abandoned his effort to obtain a voice for Russia in the occupation of the Ruhr. The chief industrial prize of Europe had been captured by the Western armies, as Silesia had been captured by the Russians. In both cases, the military realities determined the outcome of the diplomatic skirmishes at Potsdam.[27]

The philosophy that lay behind Soviet reparations demands also guided Russian thoughts about the economic principles for the occupation: "There is still a good deal of fat left in Germany,"

---

[26] Truman, *Memoirs*, I, 411. The 1945-1947 phase of the dispute over reparations is recounted in detail in Ratchford and Ross, *Berlin Reparations Assignment*, 49-198.

[27] Truman, *Memoirs*, I, 406; Byrnes, *Speaking Frankly*, 85; and see Nos. 398, 399, 400, 401, 404, 1021, 1022, 1023, 1024, 1025, 1026 and 1027 of the Potsdam Papers, galleys.

Stalin commented sarcastically when Churchill asked him how the Germans were to meet their economic obligations.[28] Because of the harshness of Soviet thinking and because the West, too, was determined to curb the possibility of future German aggression, the economic principles which were accepted seem harsh in retrospect. They must be compared with the proposals that had been discussed in 1944 if the march of moderation toward Germany is to be fully appreciated. The production of all arms and implements of war was forbidden, of course. No aircraft or sea-going ships were to be produced in postwar Germany. Manufacture of "metals, chemicals, machinery and other items that are directly necessary to a war economy" were to be "rigidly controlled and restricted to Germany's approved post-war peacetime needs." Productive capacity which exceeded "peacetime needs" was to be withdrawn or destroyed. Only a faint trace of the Morgenthau Plan is to be seen in the Potsdam economic agreement on Germany: the agreement provided that "primary emphasis" in the reorganization of the German economy was to be given "to the development of agriculture and peaceful domestic industries." Stalin had already been indirectly informed on July 27 that these "peaceful domestic industries" included the powerful coal industry, the foundation of Germany's steel industry.[29]

The compromise nature of the Potsdam principles was clearly revealed in contradictory articles. The statement on Allied economic controls reflected the divergent views of the victors: its first clause embodied Soviet demands and its second and third revealed the Western intention to prevent the destruction of the German economy:

> Allied controls shall be imposed upon the German economy but only to the extent necessary:
>
> (a) To carry out programs of industrial disarmament and demilitarization, of reparations, and of approved exports and imports.
>
> (b) To assure the production and maintenance of goods and services required to meet the needs of the occupying forces and displaced persons in Germany and essential to

---

28 Churchill, *Triumph and Tragedy,* 671.
29 Truman, *Memoirs,* I, 497-498.

maintain in Germany average living standards not exceeding the average of the standards of living of European countries. (European countries means all European countries excluding the United Kingdom and the Union of Soviet Socialist Republics.)

(c) To ensure in the manner determined by the Control Council the equitable distribution of essential commodities between the several zones so as to produce a balanced economy throughout Germany and reduce the need for imports.

The Anglo-American attempt to restrain unilateral Soviet action in Germany and to preserve the economic unity of the country was reflected in the provision—soon freely violated—for common Allied economic policies in Germany, specifically for wages, prices, imports and exports, currency, tariffs, central taxation, transportation, mining and industrial production, and reparations. And the clearest statement of the positive aims of the West in the economic reorganization of the defeated state was contained in articles seventeen and nineteen of the Potsdam principles:

17. Measures shall be promptly taken:
(a) To effect essential repair of transport;
(b) To enlarge coal production;
(c) To maximize agricultural output; and
(d) To effect emergency repair of housing and essential utilities.

19. Payment of reparations should leave enough resources to enable the German people to subsist without external assistance. In working out the economic balance of Germany the necessary means must be provided to pay for imports approved by the Control Council in Germany.[30]

On the whole, the economic principles were as contradictory as the provisions of JCS 1067/6, from which they were in part derived. They lent themselves to the most diverse interpretations. Thus they, like the reparations formula, led to endless recriminations between Russia and the West after Potsdam.

WAR CRIMINALS

The question of punishment of Nazi war criminals caused little dispute among the Potsdam negotiators, and was decided much as

---

[30] State Department, *The Axis in Defeat*, 13-15.

American leaders wished it to be. The legal basis for international prosecution of war criminals had been well laid before the Potsdam Conference began. The Soviet Union had on June 14 given its approval to the United States proposals, subject to technical revisions of no great significance. By mid-summer, 1945, all of the Allied governments agreed fully with Justice Jackson's central aim: "to punish acts which have been regarded as criminal since the time of Cain and have been so written in every civilized code." In late June an international conference began in London to prepare for the trials which all had now agreed should be held. This discussion in London among four-power legal experts continued in July and into August while the Big Three met at Potsdam. The principal problem encountered in these "conference sessions" was that of reconciling the American view of court procedures—largely supported by French and British experts—with the Soviet system of legal proceedings. On July 18 Justice Jackson invited the representatives to fly to Nuremberg to inspect the facilities for such a trial which the United States offered for the use of the international tribunal. All went but the Russians.[31]

Eleven days after the Potsdam Conference had begun, Judge Rosenman arrived at Potsdam on July 27 to work with President Truman in the war criminal negotiations. By August 1 agreement was reached upon general procedures. No list of the persons to be tried had as yet been accepted, though Stalin and Molotov pressed hard at Potsdam for the announcement of names. Stalin especially wished to make certain that German industrialists—he specifically named Krupp—were included. He quite rightly argued that public opinion in the Allied countries desired that all the Nazi leaders should be punished. The Americans opposed the naming of specific individuals at that time, and it was Stalin himself who finally proposed the compromise formula which broke the deadlock on this

---

[31] The minutes of the London conferences are given with other documents in Department of State, *Report of Robert H. Jackson, United States Representative to the International Conference on Military Trials*, 18-419. See also the report by the Associate Counsel for the United States, Sidney S. Alderman, "Negotiating on War Crimes Prosecutions, 1945," in Raymond Dennett and Joseph E. Johnson eds., *Negotiating with the Russians* (Boston, 1951), 31-98.

question at Potsdam: the first list of war criminals would be published by September 1.[32]

No detailed statement on war criminals was included in the Potsdam agreement. Prosecution of war criminals was to be provided by the newly established International Military Tribunal, agreed upon in the London Conference on August 8. The Potsdam agreement merely provided that "the trial of those major criminals should begin at the earliest possible date." In general, however, the Big Three at Potsdam found little disagreement with the crimes trial principles of the United States as these were discussed there.[33]

POTSDAM IN PERSPECTIVE

The Potsdam Conference, like other Big Three meetings, ended on a friendly note, though the final cordialities were briefer and dryer than before. At about midnight on August 1-2 Truman expressed the hope that "the Three" might next meet in Washington. "God willing," was Stalin's cryptic reply.

"Frustration was the fate of this final Conference of 'the Three'," Winston Churchill wrote of Potsdam some seven years after he returned to England in July, 1945.[34] At the end of the conference it seemed that the Russians and the French had the greatest reason to feel frustrated about Germany. The possibility of a revived Reich caused the greatest of concern to the Soviet Union. Stalin was determined that the Great Patriotic War should be a "war to end wars," at least to end wars of Germany against the U.S.S.R. And Stalin was determined to make the German people pay for the reconstruction and expansion of the Soviet economy. Yet, at Potsdam the Big Three agreed to the gradual political revival of Germany, and to the control (and therefore preservation, not destruction) of much of German industry.

The integrated administration of the zones of occupation as

---

[32] Truman, *Memoirs*, I, 109-110, 282-284, 312-313, 394, 407-408; Leahy, *I Was There*, 424; Nos. 1016, 1017, 1018 and minutes of pertinent meetings, Potsdam Papers, galleys.

[33] State Department, *The Axis in Defeat*, 17. For the London Agreement and Charter of August 8, 1945, see Department of State, *Report of Robert H. Jackson, United States Representative to the International Conference on Military Trials*, 420-428.

[34] Churchill, *Triumph and Tragedy*, 608; minutes, plenary meeting of Aug. 1, 1945, Potsdam Papers, galleys.

provided at Potsdam would mean, if actually accomplished, the preservation of German political unity and the prevention of Sovietization, even in the Russian zone. While the Soviet Union's right to Königsberg was acknowledged, definitive agreement upon the Soviet-sponsored Oder-Neisse line was held back by Truman and Attlee. They refused to consider Russian desires to separate the Ruhr and the Rhine from Germany and to win a voice in an internationalized province there. An attempt was made to regularize the transfer of Germans from Poland, Czechoslovakia, and Hungary to Germany proper, a transfer which was already in progress under terrible conditions; much was required of the Russians if the flow of those displaced persons was to be slowed and made more humane. The principle of the use of Germans as forced labor in partial payment of reparations, a principle previously favored by Stalin, was not discussed at Potsdam. "By and large," Admiral Leahy has recalled, "the major points in the American plan for political and economic policies to govern the control of Germany during the occupation period were incorporated in the Potsdam report. It was perhaps the President's greatest success."

The French were more openly displeased with the results than were the Russians, and it is instructive to remember why the French objected. In accepting the main points of the Potsdam agreement, reached without its participation, the French government on August 7 made one major reservation: "it could not assent a priori to the apparent intention to revive for a certain period a central German government." The French were thus the last to give up the fight for partition of Germany by international agreement. By September 14 Paris was protesting its official concern over, *"la premiere manifestation d'une renaissance du Reich."* The absence of the French from Potsdam and their wary and vengeful spirit in 1945 meant that another occupation power besides the Soviet Union tended to follow its own harsh whims in Germany, and to ignore or oppose Anglo-American efforts to maintain a unified administration of the defeated state.[35]

---

[35] Leahy, *I Was There*, 427; Alfred Grosser, *The Colossus Again: Western Germany from Defeat to Rearmament*, Richard Rees, trans. (New York, 1955), 33. See also Beate Ruhm von Oppen ed., *Documents on Germany under Occupation, 1945-1954* (London etc., 1955), 67.

It must be emphasized that the Potsdam agreement was not a peace treaty for Germany. It was partly an agreement about occupation practices and partly the outline of tentative provisions for a treaty. In both respects, harsh though it was, it was no worse than the German nation in 1945 had every reason to expect. For the Big Three in 1945 were not dealing with a Bonn Republic in which the West has come to place its hopes. The Germany that had followed Adolf Hitler until after he deserted his own cause deserved no better future than that which her enemies had tried amidst disagreements and uncertainties to plan for her between 1941-1945.

Something far less harsh than Hitler had taught Germans to expect in defeat was tentatively determined upon at Potsdam in 1945. That it was no harsher was due neither to the moral merits of the Germany of World War II nor to the mercy of the victors. The Potsdam moderation—such as it was—resided partly in positive provisions and partly in a continued postponement of decisions that would most unfavorably have affected Germany's future. Earlier the policy of postponement had been required to retain the unity of a warring coalition of mutually wary Allies. After 1945 postponement of some crucial issues gradually became permanent. Out of it came the two German states that emerged in 1949. Wartime postponement was slowly transformed into the postwar dilemma over Germany between a wary Soviet Union and a rightly suspicious West.

Chapter X

BERLIN AND THE GREATER DILEMMA: AN EPILOGUE FOR THE READERS OF THE COLD WAR ERA

FOR four years the war had made comrades of the people of Russia, the British Commonwealth, and the United States, and they could say in the ancient truths of Isaiah: "They helped every one his neighbor; and every one said to his brother, Be of good courage." Now Germany was crushed. No one wanted to remember Hitler's near-prophetic bombast: "We may be destroyed, but if we are, we shall drag a world with us—a world in flames." But, already a few people in the West were beginning to ask in Isaiah's aggrieved accents of consternation and anger: "Who raised up the righteous man from the east, called him to his foot, gave the nations before him, and made him rule over kings?" [1]

Harry Truman, returning in 1945 from Potsdam by way of Plymouth Sound, on August 2 cogently and unknowingly described to King George VI the basic problem of world affairs since 1945: "He could see Stalin wanted to keep what he already had, but he had too much for U. S. & U. K. liking," King George recorded. On a more optimistic note, Truman told the British monarch that the meetings of the newly created Council of Foreign Ministers would secure "concessions from Russia." And the President had brought from Potsdam another conviction which would prolong his efforts to win "concessions from Russia": "He was horrified at the devastation of Berlin by our combined bombing. He could see that

---

[1] Isaiah, XLI, 2, 6; Hermann Rauschning, *The Voice of Destruction* (New York, 1940), 5.

the Big Powers would have to combine for all time to prevent another war." [2]

SCHISM IN GERMANY, 1945-1948

Berlin, 1945 stimulus to the renewed search for Big Three unity, became by 1948 the arch symbol and center of the breakdown of the wartime alliance. But it became the scene of an East-West test of nerves in 1948 only after five meetings of the Council of Foreign Ministers failed to resolve the main dilemmas over Germany that were left over from the Potsdam Conference and new ones that arose before 1945 ended.[3]

Chief among the old dilemmas between 1945 and 1947 were the related problems of reparations and de-industrialization. Consistently and interminably Molotov argued that the Soviet Union must be conceded $10 billion in reparations from Germany; consistently and vainly Byrnes (and then his successor, George C. Marshall) and Bevin sought "concessions from Russia" in this matter. And by the end of 1945 a new dilemma had arisen to plague these tedious and unfruitful meetings: the Soviet Union—secure in its control over East Germany and thus able to block the unification of Germany except on its own terms—became the most impatient and public champion of the quick political unification of Germany. The Soviet strategy on this question that emerged between 1945 and 1947 was thus two-fold, and has changed very little in basic character since that time: while posing before the German public as the patron of a reunified Germany, the U.S.S.R. has effectively prevented unification. It is usually said that the Soviet Union in 1945 abandoned its policy of dismemberment for Germany. This is only half true, for the new lip service to unity was only a partial departure from the policies of 1941-1945. The U.S.S.R. remained determined to preserve the zonal partition of Germany unless an eastern-oriented Germany could somehow be unified under Soviet influence. As General Clay pointed out,

---

[2] Wheeler-Bennett, *King George VI*, 644.

[3] On these meetings see Deuerlein, *Die Einheit Deutschlands*, 110-129; Peter Calvocoressi and others, *Survey of International Affairs, 1947-1948* (London etc., 1952), 228-236, 238-241; United States Department of State, *A Decade of American Foreign Policy, 1941-49: Basic Documents* (1950), especially 568-573; Byrnes, *All in One Lifetime*, 313-391 *passim*.

Moscow showed an acute awareness that a unified Germany might bring the West into "direct touch with the people of Poland and Czechoslovakia." [4]

The Western Powers, meanwhile, had slowly shifted their attitude toward German unity. The French continued through December, 1947, to resist any early move toward German unification under a central government,[5] but the United States and Great Britain worked constantly after 1945 for economic unity as a first step toward eventual political reunification. Obstructed in this by the Soviet Union and France, Great Britain and the United States in the autumn of 1946 took the first steps toward Germany's reunion, agreeing to merge their two zones into a single economic unit. And speaking at Stuttgart on September 6, 1946, Secretary of State Byrnes promised much more: "The American people want to return the government of Germany to the German people," said Byrnes. His last words, immediately published in German, brought a new lift to German hearts: *"Das amerikanische Volk will dem deutschen Volk helfen, seinen Weg zurückzufinden zu einem ehrenvollen Platz unter den freien und friedliebenden Nationen der Welt."* [6] This was more than the language of mercy; it was the language of the Cold War, dramatic evidence that Germany was being sought after as a potential ally by the West as well as by the Soviet Union.

While statesmen and propagandists talked of German reunification, military government authorities in Germany wrestled with serious economic problems. Some were bequeathed by the military operations of the war. Others were created by the division of Germany into zones, by the reparations policies of the victors, by the removal of Nazis from key positions in industry, and by attempts to carry through economic reforms in Germany. Economic reforms were pushed farthest in the Russian zone, where a gradual policy of Sovietization of agriculture and industry was begun in 1945-1946. Meanwhile, memories of the aggressive use of German

---

[4] Lucius D. Clay, *Germany and the Fight for Freedom* (Cambridge, Mass., 1950), 18; Ratchford and Ross, *Berlin Reparations Assignment*, 49-198.

[5] Cf. W. Friedmann, *The Allied Military Government of Germany* (London, 1947), 27-30; Zink, *The United States in Germany, 1944-1955*, 116-120.

[6] Deuerlein, *Die Einheit Deutschlands*, 282-288; Oppen, *Documents on Germany under the Occupation*, 152-160; Byrnes, *All in One Lifetime*, 367-369.

economic power in the past caused the Great Powers to persist as late as the spring of 1946 in their plans to restrict German industry. In March the Allied Control Council in Berlin decided to restrict German industrial production to about 55 per cent of the level of 1936. (About 20 per cent of German industry had already been destroyed by bombardment in World War II.)[7]

This decision did not ease the deadlock over reparations between East and West. The Western Powers insisted that the Soviet Union was already taking too much from Germany and was not supplying East German commodities to the West German zones. In 1946 the United States temporarily halted the dismantling of West German factories for shipment to Russia. The Russians, unable to win large reparations through de-industrialization, sought with greater vigor to gain a part in the control of the Ruhr industrial area. They failed, and thus an often discussed wartime goal for the future of Germany—four-power control over the Rhineland—was discarded.

In only one sure way, removals from the current production of its own zone of occupation, could the Soviet Union win significant reparations from Germany, and it made full use of its exploitative position in 1945-1946. To get even more, the U.S.S.R. in 1947, favored an increase in the level of German production. In the same year the United States inaugurated the Marshall Plan for economic aid to Europe, as a means of combatting the spread of Communism. Since Germany was considered an essential factor in European economic recovery, the West—against French reluctance—determined that the German level of industry should be raised. With East and West agreed on this, the Foreign Ministers at their London Conference in December, 1947, allowed Germany to increase her production of steel from seven million tons, allowed in March, 1946, to eleven million tons per year. Though a few more West German plants were dismantled as late as 1949 for removal as reparations, the agreement of December, 1947, scrapped the last remnants of Morgenthau-type thinking about Germany's economic future. One of the most vigorously supported wartime

[7] Martin, *All Honorable Men*, 59, 89-90, 176, 236, 299; Zink, *The United States in Germany, 1944-1955*, 251-303; United States Department of State, *United States Economic Policy toward Germany* (n.d. [1949]), 133-139.

proposals for the treatment of postwar Germany, de-industrialization, gave way in 1948 as both East and West increased industrial output in their respective zones of Germany.

The spring of 1948 brought a currency reform in West Germany and in the western sectors of Berlin. This reform marked the beginning of West German economic recovery. Expansion of the machine tool inventory under Hitler had left a solid if rusty basis for recovery beneath the rubble of 1945; the currency reform, hard work by the German people, and some $3,500,000,000 in American aid to Germany under the Marshall Plan provided the main additional elements in the so-called "miracle" of industrial growth after 1948 in West Germany.[8]

DIVISION OF GERMANY, 1948-1949

By the spring of 1949 all but three major elements of the harsh wartime plans for postwar Germany had been publicly repudiated by the victors. Germany remained demilitarized. In the west France had not won the Rhineland but she temporarily held the Saar territory, and showed a strong determination to keep it. In the east, a puppet regime in Poland closely guarded the Oder-Neisse line for Stalin's security and Poland's own national gain.

But one of the most drastic wartime proposals which was now publicly repudiated appeared in 1948-1949 to come true. Since Potsdam, while talking of German unity, East and West had hardened the zonal division into dismemberment. By 1948 separate states were emerging in East and West Germany.

Even before the Potsdam Conference the Soviet Union had begun to create an East German puppet state. On April 30, 1945, the day Hitler committed suicide in a Berlin bunker, a Soviet military airplane flew to the Berlin suburbs bearing Walter Ulbricht and nine other German Communists who had spent the war years in Russia. Their mission was to organize Germany politically for the Soviet Union. They were to work in close conjunction with

---

[8] See Joseph M. Jones, *The Fifteen Weeks* (New York, 1955); H. B. Price, *The Marshall Plan and Its Meaning* (Ithaca, 1955); William C. Mallalieu, "The Origin of the Marshall Plan: A Study in Policy Formation and National Leadership," *Political Science Quarterly*, LXXIII (1958), 486, 493-494; Zink, *The United States in Germany, 1944-1955*, 262-263.

the Red Army. Ulbricht, fifty-one years old, notorious for his devotion to Stalinism and for his colorless and humorless personality,
early in May, 1945, defined the broad tasks that lay before his
colleagues: "It's quite clear—it's got to look democratic, but we
must have everything in our control," he told them. Their first
task, said Ulbricht, was to get Berlin well in hand: "About a month
from now we must count on the arrival of the Western Allies, and
by that time the local administrations must be functioning in their
districts unchallenged." Thus Ulbricht explained to his Communist
cadre what Eisenhower could only guess at in May and June, 1945,
as his troops were denied admittance to their allotted sectors of
occupation in Berlin. In an off-hand remark to Harry Hopkins on
May 28 Stalin masked the policy of infiltration. While admitting
casually that "there were a few communists scattered through the
administration in secondary positions," Stalin stated that the top
posts in the Soviet-occupied areas were being filled with Centrists
and Social Democrats.

Achieving control in East Germany as a whole was to be both
slow and subtle at first. Wilhelm Pieck, returning from Moscow
early in June, 1945, reemphasized the need for democratic appear-
ances, and a large measure of democratic freedom was in fact
allowed East Germans at first. But by the fall of 1945 it became
obvious that the anti-Communist Social Democratic Party (S.P.D.)
was growing much more rapidly than the Communist Party. Thereupon, a forced merger of the two parties was rigged in the Soviet
zone of occupation. A former Social Democrat, Otto Grotewohl,
was installed as one of the leaders of the new fusion party, the
"Socialist Unity Party" (S.E.D.). Communist-dominated, this party
was put to its only genuine test of popularity in free elections held
in Berlin and the provinces of the Soviet zone in October, 1946. In
the provincial elections the S.E.D. won 46 per cent of the votes,
but in Berlin it got a little less than 20 per cent. When the elections
in Berlin fell due in 1948 the Soviet occupation authorities refused
to allow them.[9]

---

[9] Leonhard, *Child of the Revolution*, 292-303; Einsiedel, *I Joined the
Russians*, 247-270; Oppen, *Documents on Germany under Occupation*, 121-125;
Bohlen memorandum of May 28, 1945, on conversation of Hopkins with
Stalin, May 28, 1945, No. 26, Potsdam Papers, galleys.

The year 1948 marked a new tenseness in relations between East and West. From Germany, General Clay cabled Washington in March that war could "come with dramatic suddenness," judging from the behavior of "every Soviet individual with whom we have official relations." [10] The year 1948 marked in the Soviet zone of occupation an abandonment of the attempt to build a Soviet-style state slowly and in a "special way," intrinsically German. Instead, in this year of Tito's challenge to Stalin, more open and direct Sovietization was instituted in East Germany. As part of the price of power the S.E.D. leaders publicly recognized the Oder-Neisse line as a permanent frontier between Poland and Germany, though this meant renouncing an area of 47,000 square miles, 24 per cent of the prewar territory (1937) of Germany. The area thus renounced was slightly larger than the Soviet zone of occupation itself; it was larger than Scotland and Wales combined, and larger than the American state of Pennsylvania. As if to leave no doubt about the loyalties of the dominant party in the Soviet zone, the chairman of the S.E.D. would publicly state in years to come that the chief factor in evaluating every member was "his attitude toward the Soviet Union." This was also the test of leadership in the other parties that were allowed in East Germany. In all of them, Germans who had spent the war years in Russia played leading roles. All of the bourgeois parties were discriminated against in favor of the S.E.D. A youth movement, a single national trade union, and other "mass organizations" were similarly used as instruments of Soviet policy in the Russian zone of occupation.

All these elements were given a designated share in the creation of a central government for East Germany in 1948-1949. The "German Democratic Republic" (D.D.R.) formally came into existence in October, 1949. This regime has been supported by the Soviet Union as the true government for Germany as a whole. It has not allowed free elections, but stages Nazi-like plebiscites instead. In these the voter simply votes "yes" or "no" for an entire slate of candidates, fixed for him by the S.E.D. bosses. Great pressure is exerted upon the electorate to go to the polls. Thus in the elections of 1950, 1954, and 1957, almost 100 per cent of

---

[10] Westerfield, *Foreign Policy and Party Politics*, 286.

the voters were said to have cast their ballots, and of these almost 100 per cent were said to have cast votes for the S.E.D.-dominated "National Front" of parties and mass organizations. The 1954 and 1958 elections brought no surprises. Thus, while Wilhelm Pieck has remained the President of the East German regime since 1949, Otto Grotewohl has remained its Prime Minister, and Walter Ulbricht—head of the S.E.D.—has remained its boss, subservient first to Stalin, then to Malenkov, and lately to Nikita Khrushchev.[11]

Many experts insist that the S.E.D. regime would win no more than 10 per cent of the votes in a free election. It would probably do better than this. But the determination with which Soviet and East German spokesmen have resisted Western demands for free all-German elections suggests that they themselves realize that the Pieck-Grotewohl-Ulbricht regime would win no majority even among the seventeen million East Germans. The regime has pushed with steady vigor for socialization of the East German economy, and by 1958 only 26 per cent of the national product was accounted for by privately owned elements of the economy. Though industrial production has been doubled, until 1953 a very large portion of that production was transported to the Soviet Union in reparations. The total value of reparations may have amounted to as much as $12 billion.[12] These facts and the dictatorial political and cultural features of the "German Democratic Republic" account for the constant departures of its citizens for West Germany. Between September 1, 1949, and January 1, 1959, 2,188,435 persons from East Germany sought a better life in West Germany. The largest number fleeing in a single year—331,390—was reached

---

[11] On the evolution of the East German regime see Leonhard, *Child of the Revolution,* 328-329; Peter Calvocoressi and others, *Survey of International Affairs, 1949-1950* (London etc., 1953), 187-196, 210-214, 231-232, 241-243; Oppen, *Documents on Germany under the Occupation,* 282-283, 290-291, 394-395, 420-433, 497-500; Wiskemann, *Germany's Eastern Neighbours,* 113-295; and most especially: Georges Castellan and others, *D.D.R.-Allemagne de l'Est* (Paris, 1955), 94-96, 106, 128-139 and *passim;* Carola Stern, *Portraet einer bolschewistischen Partei: Entwicklung, Funktion und Situation der SED* (Cologne, 1957), *passim;* and the following articles: Melvin Croan and Carl J. Friedrich, "The East German Regime and Soviet Policy in Germany," *Journal of Politics,* XX (1958), 44-63; Helmut Bohn, "Die patriotische Karte in der sowjetischen Deutschland-Politik," *Ost-Probleme,* VII (Sept. 23, Oct. 7, and Oct. 21, 1955), 1446-1457, 1531-1541, 1606-1614.

[12] New York *Times,* Dec. 7, 1958.

in 1953, the year of the East German rising. But the migration continues: in 1958 204,092 came to the West, and the number of teachers, professors, doctors, and students among the emigres then reached the highest levels since 1953. Politicians have also fled. One of the most ironical of the recent departures was that of the deputy chief of Soviet Germany's espionage system, Siegfried Dombrowski, whose presence in West Germany was announced on January 22, 1959.[13]

The features of this East German state, reviewed here, must be remembered at all times in current discussion of the German problem. Its system of social security is one of the few features that can be found in its favor. The existence of this state, ruled from the Pankow district of Berlin, is one of the greatest obstacles to the reunification of Germany. It seems impossible for the East German state (D.D.R.) to cooperate with Western Germany, and it is not easy for Western Germany to compromise at all with Pankow. Nor is it wise for Washington to compromise with Moscow in any way that will offer the leaders of East Germany any guaranteed future in a unified Germany.

But the D.D.R. is only one of the two German states. The other, encompassing 52 per cent of prewar (1937) Germany, is not only a bigger area, but, in Soviet eyes, a far bigger political obstacle to unification than is East Germany. Fifty-four million strong, West Germans possess all the things that Stalin hoped during World War II to deny postwar Germany: economic power easily convertible into military thrust in an age of missiles and nuclear weapons, a strong central government, and powerful allies.

The Bonn Republic and the Pankow regime were created almost simultaneously and as separate responses to the Cold War. By 1948 the attempt at four-power control in Germany had failed. The aims of the wartime allies were impossibly divergent, and in the Control Council each could cast a veto against any proposed policy. More fundamentally still, the "Cold War" in Germany had developed as part of a global crisis; disputes in Germany were

---

13 This and the statistics on refugees are from *The Bulletin*, Jan. 27, 1959, a weekly paper issued by the Press and Information Office of the German Federal Republic.

intensified by seizures of power by Communists in Hungary, Czechoslovakia and elsewhere, and by the American-led countermeasures such as the Truman Doctrine and the Marshall Plan. Tired of the long debate with the Russians over German policies, and determined to achieve the economic recovery of Germany, the Western Powers on June 4, 1948, encouraged West Germans to create what soon became the German Federal Republic. Its constitution ("Basic Law") was completed by a representative assembly of Germans on May 8, 1949, and the first elections to a national parliament were held on August 14, 1949. They gave the largest representation (31.0 per cent of the votes) to the Christian Democratic Union (C.D.U.) and thus made its leader, Konrad Adenauer, the Chancellor of the "German Federal Republic." Theodor Heuss became the first President of the Bonn Republic. The Social Democratic Party won 29.2 per cent of the votes and became the leading opposition party.[14]

As in East Germany, the next decade of political developments brought no major changes in leadership in the Federal Republic. Until 1959 Heuss and Adenauer, men of the oldest generation of Germans, still guided the West German state, their position strengthened by free elections in 1953 and 1957. Under their regime political liberty has been combined with very strong—even paternal—political leadership and stability. One remembers with a start that by 1959 Adenauer had already served longer as German Chancellor than any man since Bismarck except for Adolf Hitler—and Otto Grotewohl. It has been aptly said that Adenauer "brought to his new role in foreign affairs the same qualities that distinguished Bismarck's approach to diplomacy: passion for the task, a feeling of responsibility, and a sense of proportion." [15] Adenauer had emerged as the outstanding statesman of the Western alliance,

---

[14] On the origins and evolution of the Federal Republic see Oppen, *Documents on Germany under Occupation, passim,* and the following: Edgar Alexander, *Adenauer and the New Germany: The Chancellor of the Vanquished* (New York, 1957); Fritz R. Allemann, *Bonn ist nicht Weimar* (Cologne, 1955); Alfred Grosser, *The Colossus Again* and his more recent work (the most up to date account available as this is written): *La Démocratie de Bonn, 1949-1957* (Paris, 1958); Richard Hiscocks, *Democracy in Western Germany* (London, 1957); and John Ford Golay, *The Founding of the Federal Republic of Germany* (Chicago, 1958).

[15] Gordon A. Craig, *From Bismarck to Adenauer: Aspects of German Statecraft* (Baltimore, 1958), 131, 147-148; Alexander, *Adenauer and the New Germany,* 138.

partly because of his own qualities and partly because the constitutional structure of the Bonn Republic guarantees much more
stability than did the Republic that fell to Nazism in 1933. A
Constitutional Court provides one of the many guarantees that
the Bonn Republic can not easily be overthrown.[16]

During the ten years of operation of the Federal Republic the
multi-party system that troubled the Weimar Republic has gradually
developed toward a two-party system. The C.D.U., with 31.0 per
cent of the votes in 1949 raised its share to 45.2 per cent in 1953
and to 50.2 per cent in 1957. In the provincial elections of July 6,
1958, in North-Rhine-Westphalia, both the S.P.D. and Adenauer's
C.D.U. received more votes than they had gotten in the elections of
1954, and between them they captured 90 per cent of the total
(76 per cent in 1954). In the elections of September 26, 1958,
in Schleswig-Holstein the two parties emerged with 80 per cent
of the votes (65.4 per cent in 1954). In elections in Bavaria on
November 23, 1958, the two parties won 76.5 per cent of the votes
(66 per cent in 1954). On the same day, 79 per cent of the voters
in Hesse cast ballots for the two large parties (67 per cent in
1954). In none of these 1958 elections did any other party win
as much as 10 per cent of the vote. This is reassuring to those
who hope for a democratic future in Germany, for the two large
parties are the most reliably democratic in the Federal Republic.[17]

The Social Democrats have emerged as the party of the opposition in West Germany, and have been completely free to de-
nounce the domestic and the foreign policies of the Adenauer
regime. They have done this almost constantly. Many S.P.D.
leaders were born east of the Iron Curtain and the party has insisted
that Adenauer did not work with sufficient vigor for reunification
and that he also looked too exclusively to the West for a solution to
the problem. But the S.P.D. is also basically a pro-West party for
all its talk about the neutralization of Germany, and it is even more
democratic than the ruling C.D.U. If the Republic were in real
danger one might even imagine a coalition government of C.D.U.

---

[16] See Taylor Cole, "The West German Federal Constitutional Court:
An Evaluation after Six Years," *Journal of Politics*, XX (1958), 278-307.

[17] For the recent election statistics see *News from Germany*, August,
1958, and November, 1958, a publication of the Executive Committee of the
S.P.D.; *The Bulletin*, Nov. 25, 1958.

and S.P.D. leaders, similar to the coalition that has governed Austria in recent years.[18]

The regime in West Germany, in short, shows every promise of outlasting its master statesman, who in April, 1959, announced his plans to retire as Chancellor.

This does not mean that the people of West Germany have become overnight dedicated democrats. They have shown a marked degree of apathy toward politics and even the large votes for Adenauer may be interpreted as new evidence of the old habit of following a strong leader. But all in all the brief history of the Bonn Republic has shown a growing attachment to democracy and has been reasonably convincing that "National Socialism will not rise again." "No historical movement survives such a defeat as that of 1945," a West German voice assures us.[19] And James B. Conant, perceptive High Commissioner and United States Ambassador to the Bonn Republic has spoken similar words of reassurance "for those who, having studied the German past, look anxiously at the future": "In my judgment, it will not happen again; indeed, barring a world-wide economic disaster, a collapse of the NATO Alliance, or a global war, [West] Germany will continue to be one of the strongest fortresses of freedom." [20]

For almost ten years the Western Powers insisted that the Bonn

---

[18] See, e.g., Jess Byrd Hendricks, Jr., "The Foreign Policy of the German Social Democratic Party, 1945-1953," unpublished M.A. thesis, Tulane University, 1955; John L. Snell, "Schumacher's Successors," *Southwestern Social Science Quarterly*, XXXVI (1956), 333-342; S. L. Wahrhaftig, "Der Weg der Sozialdemokraten," reprinted from the *Frankfurter Hefte* of November, 1952, in Ossip K. Flechtheim ed., *Die deutschen Parteien seit 1945: Quellen und Auszüge* (Berlin etc., 1955), 103-115; Arno Scholz and Walther G. Oschilewski eds., *Turmwaechter der Demokratie: Ein Lebensbild von Kurt Schumacher,* 3 vols. (Berlin, 1952-1954), II, consisting almost entirely of post-1945 writings or speeches by Schumacher. On the Austrian situation see Herbert P. Secher, "Coalition Government: The Case of the Second Austrian Republic," *The American Political Science Review*, LII (1958), 791-808.

[19] Michael Freund, "Kann sich heute 1933 wiederholen?" *Die politische Meinung: Monatshefte für Fragen der Zeit,* III (June, 1958), 11-23. For comment in the same vein see Alexander, *Adenauer and the New Germany,* 11.

[20] James Bryant Conant, *Germany and Freedom: A Personal Appraisal* (Cambridge, Mass., 1958), last page. For a noted German historian's comments in a similar vein see Gerhard Ritter, *Lebendige Vergangenheit: Beitraege zur historisch-politischen Selbstbesinnung* (Munich, 1958), 3, 34 and *passim.* For a critical and realistic appraisal see Hiscocks, *Democracy in Western Germany,* 225-243, 294-298, and the briefer but important report in Hans Speier and W. Phillips Davison eds., *West German Leadership and Foreign Policy* (Evanston, Illinois etc., 1957), 294-304.

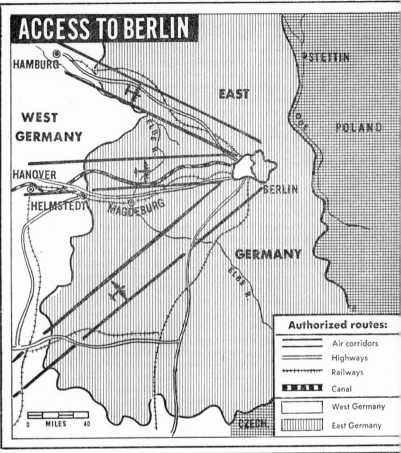

ACCESS TO BERLIN

HAMBURG

WEST GERMANY

EAST

°STETTIN

POLAND

HANOVER

HELMSTEDT

MAGDEBURG

ELBE R.

BERLIN

GERMANY

ELBE R.

CZECH.

Authorized routes:

	Air corridors
	Highways
+++++	Railways
▮▮▮▮	Canal
	West Germany
▥	East Germany

0 MILES 40

SECTORS OF BERLIN

EAST

GERMANY

FRENCH SECTOR

BRITISH SECTOR

SOVIET SECTOR

AMERICAN SECTOR

▥	East Germany
	West Berlin
▦	Soviet Berlin

0 MILES 10

Republic could never give way except to a government for a reunited Germany, elected by the free votes of Germans of East and West. The West German state has won greater respect and trust for Germany than the West has felt since before 1914. Between 1950 and 1954 plans were made to build a West German Army of 500,000 men as military partners in a European Defense Community, thus scrapping all the involved schemes for the permanent disarmament of Germany that the Allied experts of 1941-1945 evolved.[21]

The Bonn Republic has been as generously praised by the West for its virtues and rewarded for its reliability as Hitler's Germany was punished for its faults. It has won back the coal-rich Saar territory, while the East German regime continues to recognize the Oder-Neisse line as the "peace frontier" between East Germany and Poland.[22] It is a remarkable fact that public demands for the return of the areas beyond the Oder-Neisse line have been heard only in West Germany, where refugees from Silesia publish the cadences of Friedrich K. Kriebel, *"Doch weh dem, der das Land vergisst, das unser Erbe ist und eigen.—Kein Herz, kein Mund darf müde schweigen bis alles wieder unser ist."* [23] But even more remarkable than occasional outbursts of nationalism in West Germany is the extent to which the Bonn Republic has willingly subordinated its own sovereignty to supranational agencies such as the European Coal and Steel Community. But for the opposition of France, German rearmament might have been achieved in 1954 within the supranational European Defense Community. When this failed, the Federal Republic was admitted to the North Atlantic Treaty

---

[21] Lewis J. Edinger, *West German Rearmament* (Maxwell Field, Alabama, 1955); Calvocoressi and others, *Survey of International Affairs, 1949-50*, 61-81, 150-168; Calvocoressi and others, *Survey of International Affairs, 1951* (London etc., 1954), 60-70 and *passim;* Calvocoressi and others, *Survey of International Affairs, 1952* (London etc., 1955), 55-141; Coral Bell and others, *Survey of International Affairs, 1954* (London etc., 1957), 129-148; Raymond Aron and David Lerner eds., *France Defeats EDC* (New York, 1956).

[22] See Ludwig Dischler, *Das Saarland 1945-1956: Eine Darstellung der historischen Entwicklung mit den wichtigsten Dokumenten,* 2 vols. (Hamburg, 1956). Alexander, *Adenauer and the New Germany,* 179-202.

[23] Printed in full under the title "An der Oder und Neisse" in *Schlesische Rundschau, die Zeitung aller Schlesier: Offizielles Organ der Landsmannschaft Schlesien für die Bundesrepublik und Berlin,* Sept. 15, 1956. Loose translation: "Woe to them who forget the land that is our own inheritance.—No heart, no mouth can become silent in weariness until it is all ours once again."

Organization in 1955.[24]

In ten years the Bonn Republic has done much to atone for Germany's past. It has done much to win firm Western support in whatever the future may hold.

BERLIN: CENTER AND SYMBOL OF THE DILEMMA OVER GERMANY

In Berlin the two Germany's meet, but they meet on unequal terms. The city is an island—"an island in the Red Sea," say some West Berlin wits—more than one hundred miles to the east of West Germany. The only legal right the Western Powers have to stay in Berlin rests basically upon the wartime occupation agreements reached in September and November, 1944, by the European Advisory Commission, supplemented by agreements of 1945 and 1949. Thus, although the "occupation" of West Germany ended in 1955, the Anglo-French-American "occupation" of West Berlin continues. Only in this way have the western parts of the city, with a population of more than two million people, remained a part of the anti-Communist world.

The majority of West Berliners have proven themselves since 1945 as before 1933 to be staunch Social Democrats in their politics. They have prospered economically under a free political regime. Berlin has been a political haven for refugees from the East. In the period from September 1, 1949 to January 1, 1959, 54.7 per cent of East German refugees to West Germany came by way of West Berlin. Half of those who fled East Germany in 1958 came to the West by way of West Berlin, and the percentage climbed to 66 per cent in the autumn of 1958.[25] Partly because the S.E.D. has won no sympathy in West Berlin, partly because of its use as an escape hatch by East Germans, and most of all because it harbors the military, economic, and ideological power of the West in the very middle of Soviet Germany, West Berlin has been a great embarrassment to the unfree and unprosperous East German government and its Moscow patrons. Reacting to this serious challenge—a Western garrison city deep inside Soviet

---

24 See, e.g., Henry L. Mason, *The European Coal and Steel Community: Experiment in Supranationalism* (The Hague, 1955); David Wightman, *Economic Cooperation in Europe* (New York, 1956); Arnold J. Zurcher, *The Struggle to Unite Europe, 1940-1958* (New York, 1958).
25 *The Bulletin*, Jan. 27, 1959.

Germany—the East Germans and the Russians in 1948 first attempted to establish their full control over the former capital of Germany.

The 1948 attempt to dominate West Berlin was instigated by the Russians as a means of disrupting the movement in West Germany toward the creation of the Bonn Republic. All transit by ground from West Germany to Berlin through the Soviet zone was stopped in June. But the "Berlin blockade" boomeranged. The dramatic "Berlin airlift" of supplies from West Germany to West Berlin was expanded and sustained into 1949 notwithstanding the possibility—soberly acknowledged in both London and Washington—that it could lead at any moment to full scale war with the U.S.S.R.

The 1948 attempt to starve West Berlin into submission and the West out of the city also boomeranged in other ways. It provoked a counter-blockade which cut East Germany's fragile economy off from trade with the West. It revealed a magnificent determination of the West Berliners to hold out against Soviet force, and it intensified hostility to Communism throughout Western Europe. Worse yet, it provoked the greatest build-up of Western air power in Europe since World War II, and was instrumental in bringing the nations of Western Europe together in the North Atlantic Treaty Organization, formally signed on April 4, 1949. The Berlin blockade failed, meanwhile, to prevent the creation of the West German state. Since it had been worse than a failure, the Soviet Union in May, 1949, gave up the blockade. On June 20, 1949, the U.S.S.R. assumed "an obligation" to assure freedom of transportation and communication between West Germany and the western sectors of Berlin. The first great crisis over Berlin thus passed, and with it passed the closest approach to an East-West war in Europe since 1945. It showed that Soviet Russia was not then prepared to grab West Berlin if it would mean war against the West.[26]

---

[26] Frank L. Howley, *Berlin Command* (New York, 1950), 196-276; Calvocoressi and others, *Survey of International Affairs, 1947-1948*, 241-242; Clay, *Germany and the Fight for Freedom*, 57; C. H. Pegg, "Die Verhandlungen zwischen Ost und West über die Berliner Blockade von Mai bis September 1948," *Europa Archiv*, XII (Jan. 5, 1957), 9503-9512; Strang, *Home and Abroad*, 298; Zink, *The United States in Germany, 1944-1955*, 340-351; W. Phillips Davison, *The Berlin Blockade: A Study in Cold War Politics* (Princeton, 1958).

But the Red Army and the Pankow regime erected barriers against transit between the Western sectors of Berlin and their own area of the city. Two cities gradually developed in the former capital of the unified Reich. After the crisis of 1948-1949 Berliners found themselves trying to cope with two separate currencies, two police systems, two gas and electricity systems, two postal systems, and even two telephone systems. (To telephone a relative in East Berlin, a West Berliner in 1958-1959 had to place a long distance call by way of Frankfurt-am-Main and Leipzig.) But even these measures left some contact between East and West, enabling East Berliners to compare their lives with those of West Berliners in a way that left no doubt about which "had it better."

Stalin's death in March, 1953, brought a temporary and small relaxation of East German tyranny, but a second crisis over Berlin soon erupted. On June 16 a spontaneous strike was started by East Berlin workers against the provocative economic policies of the Pankow regime. The American radio in West Berlin immediately encouraged the strikers and helped spread news of their resistance to all parts of East Germany. In some areas men on bicycles carried the news from factory to factory. Next day, June 17, 1953, strikes began to turn into political rebellion in all the major industrial centers of Soviet Germany. Tens of thousands of workers struck against Communism in cities that had been before the Nazi era the "Red" centers of Germany. Ulbricht's own native Saxony was the scene of some of the largest and most radical outbreaks. The workers demanded not only economic improvements but also free elections.

What started in East Berlin thus threatened to overthrow the Soviet-sponsored government of East Germany. This the Russians could not allow. On June 17 Red Army tanks clattered their ominous way into the East German cities, reviving grim and hopeless memories of 1945. At Schwerin in the northwest and at Stralsund in the northeast; in Saalfeld, Jena, Chemnitz (now "Karl Marx Stadt"), Dresden, and Goerlitz across the south; and in Leipzig, Halle, Magdeburg and Berlin itself in the middle of the Soviet zone—in these and many other cities Red Army tanks broke the violence of the strike. Here and there men refused to go back to work until June 22. Then, cowed by gunfire, lacking organization and leadership, and needing wages, the workers went back to their jobs. Most crucial of all, the East German rebels were not aided by forceful intervention by the West. Thus, if the Berlin crisis of 1948 showed that Stalin shrank from grabbing West Berlin at the cost of an all out East-West war, the failure of the West to liberate East Germany—or even East Berlin—in 1953 proved that the West also shrank from unifying a free Germany at the cost of an East-West war. The stalemate over Germany that had shown in the debates at Yalta and had hardened into the two German states remained unbroken after two crises in which Berlin centered.[27]

The next year saw Berlin again the center of international attention, though in a contrasting atmosphere of deliberation instead of violence. For three weeks the foreign ministers of the U.S.S.R., France, Great Britain, and the United States discussed the major problems of East-West relations—including the problem of German reunification—in Germany's major metropolis. The Russians dropped propaganda hints to the West Germans that their obstruction of the North Atlantic Treaty Organization and refusal to rearm might be rewarded by some kind of German unity. The Soviet representatives continued as before to resist the Western proposal that free elections throughout Germany should be the first step toward unity. Instead, Molotov demanded that an equal number of representatives from the parliaments of East and West Germany should form a unified government for Germany. This was an obvious bid to win parity for the East German regime, in spite of the gross inequality of the populations of the two states. Since loyal Communists would undoubtedly be picked as Soviet zone representatives, they would have 50 per cent of the power in such an all-German government from the outset. The Berlin meetings of early 1954 thus brought Germany no closer to unity than it had been before the Big Four ministers arrived in Berlin.[28] West German rearmament was approved that fall, though the attempt for a European Defense Community failed. On May 5, 1955, the Bonn Republic won full sovereignty. On

---

[27] Stefan Brant, *The East German Rising: 17th June 1953* (New York, 1957); Castellan, *D.D.R.*, 194; Oppen, *Documents on Germany under Occupation*, 590; United States Department of State, *American Foreign Policy, 1950-1955: Basic Documents*, 2 vols. (1957), II, 1744-1746.

[28] Bell and others, *Survey of International Affairs, 1954*, 131-137.

May 9, 1955, it pledged its membership in N.A.T.O.

For a moment it appeared that confrontation with Western strength and the possibilities of internal unrest might cause the new masters of the Kremlin, Nikita Khrushchev and Nikolai Bulganin, to bend in the German question. After having resisted it for years, Molotov on May 15, 1955, cordially signed a state treaty with the Austrian Republic. Hopes of a German peace treaty— and thus of reunification—rose during the following months. On June 7, 1955, Molotov invited Adenauer to come to Moscow "in the nearest future." Meanwhile, in a spirit of cooperation not seen for ten years, the four Great Powers agreed to hold a "summit" conference at Geneva beginning July 18, 1955, to discuss the major issues in East-West tension. The problem of Germany's reunification was put by common approval at the head of the Geneva agenda. "Toward Germany," Eisenhower stated on the first day of the conference, "the four of us bear special responsibilities." But Bulganin insisted that German unification could be achieved only if N.A.T.O. were dissolved. As in Berlin, the U.S.S.R. proposed that Germany be neutralized and that a Europe-wide security pact should replace the Eastern and Western alliances before Germany could be united.

The Geneva meeting of July, 1955, ended with no agreement on Germany, but it seemed at the time that some progress had been made. The Soviet representatives agreed with those of the West at the end of the July conference that "the reunification of Germany *by means of free elections* [author's italics] shall be carried out in conformity with the national interests of the German people and the interests of European security." The four heads of government on July 23 agreed upon a directive to their foreign ministers to work toward this end, making "whatever arrangements they may consider desirable for the participation of, or for consultation with, other interested parties." But Bulganin had already indicated that a general European security pact must include the two German states, and had agreed to no specific measures to unite Germany.

John Foster Dulles caught the dilemma of the foreign ministers in their Geneva meeting of October 27-November 16 even before the July conference had ended: The U.S.S.R. feared that unification of Germany "would imply an indefinite postponement of European

240

security," while in Dulles' opinion steps toward European security "would involve an indefinite postponement of the unification of Germany." The impasse was hardened when, between the Geneva conference of July and that of October, the U.S.S.R. entered into a treaty which formalized its relations with the German Democratic Republic (East Germany) and estalished diplomatic relations with the German Federal Republic. This further solidified the partition of Germany, and Adenauer's trip to Moscow in September failed to break the deadlock. The foreign ministers could do no better. After three weeks at Geneva Secretary of State Dulles returned to report to the nation on November 18. "We tried hard, but in vain," said Dulles, "to get the Soviet Delegation to discuss seriously the problem of the reunification of Germany. When the Soviet Union came to face up to what was involved, it balked. Obviously, if Germany were reunified by free elections this would mean the end of the puppet regime which the Soviet Union has installed in East Germany. This in turn would almost surely have serious repercussions upon the other satellite countries of Eastern Europe." Thus Dulles could only report that "this Geneva meeting did not reach any agreements." [29]

The stalemate continued to develop in 1957 and 1958 as East and West entered the Sputnik era, an age of potential missile warfare. Polish Foreign Minister Adam Rapacki's proposal of a neutralized, nuclear-free area in Central Europe was much discussed but no one acted upon it. George F. Kennan, an early advocate of the policy of "containing" Soviet expansion which the United States adopted in 1945-1947, proposed in 1957 in his noted lectures over B.B.C. that troops be withdrawn from both East and West Germany, a realistic if premature acknowledgement that new, longer range weapons were diminishing the military significance of the German bases of both super-powers. Kennan's ideas found no favorable response in official Washington circles. The West talked instead of nuclear weapons for the defense forces of the Bonn Republic, and this brought forth strong protests from Moscow.

---

[29] Alexander, *Adenauer and the New Germany*, 215-238; United States Department of State, *The Geneva Conference of Heads of Government, July 18-23, 1955* (1955), especially 20, 35-43, 48-51, 67-68, 75; United States Department of State, *The Geneva Meeting of Foreign Ministers, October 27—November 16, 1955* (1955), especially 1-4, 297-304.

As early as April 27, 1957, Bulganin warned Adenauer's government that the arming of the *Bundeswehr* with nuclear weapons "must intensify the danger of war" and that, should war break out, Germany would be "the immediate target." Germany would be "reduced to a cemetery," said Bulganin.[30]   But threats failed to deter the Bonn government. On March 25, 1958, the *Bundestag* approved atomic armaments for the West German Army, and a desperate campaign by Social Democrats, church leaders, and others failed to mobilize public opinion against it by talk of *"Atomtod"* ("atomic death"). By the fall of 1958, nuclear armament of the *Bundeswehr* appeared assured, although agitation against it has continued into 1959. This threat of German nuclear power was the development in Germany that caused Moscow greatest concern in 1958. This, the flights of greatly increased numbers of East German professional people to the West in the autumn of 1958, talk in West Germany of making Berlin the capital of the Bonn Republic, and the pressures of Ulbricht's regime on Moscow for support, all these developments provided the necessary background for a new crisis—the current crisis, as this is written—over the troubled city of Berlin, over the divided German nation.[31]

The crisis of 1958-1959, marked by talk of world war on both sides, was touched off on November 10, 1958. More than by coincidence, Khrushchev chose a visit to Moscow by the Polish Communist leader Wladyslaw Gomulka as the occasion to open the new period of tension over Berlin's strange status. The Poles had watched with mounting anxiety the growth of West German power in 1957-1958. They could only view West German plans for nuclear rearmament with dread; demands for changes in the Oder-Neisse frontier aroused their undisguised hostility. They were driven by both into closer reliance upon Moscow. The Polish Communists as well as the Moscow Communists have hoped to see all Germany brought under Ulbricht's Soviet-controlled regime, if united at all.

---

[30] Alexander, *Adenauer and the New Germany*, 257-259; George F. Kennan, *Russia, the Atom and the West* (New York, 1957), especially 32-49.

[31] *Der Spiegel* (Hamburg), XIII (Jan. 14, 1959), 21, 24-25.

On November 10, at a Moscow meeting with Gomulka, Khrushchev, touched off the crisis over Berlin by asserting that he was ready to turn over control of East Berlin to East Germany and thus to end four-power occupation of the city. At Geneva in 1955 Bulganin had reaffirmed that the German problem would be settled "in accordance with decisions previously taken by the Four Powers." Now Khrushchev simply took unilateral action. He warned that any attack on East Germany as a result of the proposed cancellation of World War II agreements would be considered an attack against the U.S.S.R. He called Berlin the capital of the "German Democratic Republic." Two days later, warning that West Germany was "dreaming of a new crusade in the East" and was supported by the United States, Gomulka pledged Poland's support for Khrushchev's policy in Germany. On November 18 *Pravda* stated flatly that the question of Berlin would be solved "radically." Six days later, the East German puppet, Ulbricht, predicted that in a few days Khrushchev would announce Soviet plans to withdraw troops from Berlin. Ulbricht warned that the Western Powers must come to terms with his regime if they hoped to stay in Berlin. It was obvious that Ulbricht hoped to win not only Berlin but also diplomatic recognition for the "German Democratic Republic."

On November 27, as if on Ulbricht's schedule, the U.S.S.R. sent identical notes to the Western Powers and to Bonn which brought the 1958-1959 crisis over Berlin into full focus. Complaining that the Western Powers were "ruling the roost in West Berlin" and were using it as a base for "subversive activity" against the East German state and the U.S.S.R., Khrushchev proposed that West Berlin be made independent of both East and West Germany, that it be demilitarized, and that it be self-governing under international supervision as a free city. He explicitly denounced the agreements of World War II which provided for Anglo-French-American occupation. He warned that in six months—by May 27, 1959—the U.S.S.R. would turn over all of its functions in Berlin and East Germany to the Pankow regime unless Berlin were reorganized as a free city. Since Soviet functions include control over Western access to West Berlin, Khrushchev thus held out prospects of a new Berlin blockade; and he threatened war if the Western

Powers should try to break it by military action. Proving that Berlin was only the center and symbol of bigger plans, Khrushchev on November 27 called—as he had done for three years—for re-unification of Germany in the form of a confederation of East and West Germany, to be achieved by negotiations between the Pankow and Bonn regimes on an equal footing.

The United States answered Khrushchev's threat only after deliberations with its N.A.T.O. partners, among whom some differences had arisen. In its reply to the Khrushchev note of November 27 the United States on December 31, 1958, refused to accept the unilateral Soviet repudiation of the wartime and postwar agreements between East and West concerning Berlin. It rejected the proposal that West Berlin be made into "a so-called 'free city'."

In the days that followed, as elections in West Berlin approached, Ulbricht's propaganda machine urged West Berliners to show their approval of the new proposals by voting for the S.E.D. Ulbricht warned that a Western airlift into Berlin would be considered a military threat to East Germany. He repudiated again the Western idea of free, internationally supervised, elections in all of Germany as a prerequisite for the unity of Germany. Like Khrushchev, Ulbricht proposed instead a confederation created by East German and West German negotiations. He would have each parliament appoint an equal number of representatives to a 100-member "All-German Council," which would act—without free elections—as the first supreme governing body of a German confederation. Ulbricht's demand for "the comprehensive democratization of social and political life" in such a confederation showed that his ultimate aim was to remake West Germany in the image of the German "Democratic" Republic—Soviet Germany.

The vigorous West Berlin mayor, Willy Brandt, with his office and a potentially bright political future at stake, resolutely denounced Khrushchev's plan as "unbearable." He pointed out what was already obvious: removal of Western troops from West Berlin would leave the city—"the island in the Red Sea"—engulfed by Soviet German divisions. Thus, though Brandt is a Social Democrat, he has been as unwaveringly pro-Western as Adenauer. The new crisis only made him more so, and the West reciprocated with assurances of support. Both President Eisenhower and Prime Minister Harold Macmillan of Great Britain stated in November, 1958, that their forces would protect "the integrity of West Berlin." On November 30 the commander of the United States Army in Europe, General Henry I. Hodes, warned that the United States would not tolerate "any infringement" of United States communication with West Berlin.[32]

In this atmosphere of crisis West Berliners seemed confident of the future. Businessmen continued their plans of economic expansion: twice as many applications for governmental loans were made in December and in January, 1959, as in the same period a year earlier. Confidence was shown politically on December 7, 1958, when West Berliners voted once again for their city parliament. About 93 per cent of the eligible voters cast their ballots. Willy Brandt's S.P.D. won 52.6 per cent of all the votes. The C.D.U. won 30.4 per cent. Confirming the trend toward two parties among free Germans, no other party won as much as 5 per cent of the votes.[33] The Federal Republic summarized other election results in its acknowledgment of Khrushchev's utimatum. On January 5, 1959, Adenauer informed Moscow that the people of West Berlin, by giving only 1.9 per cent of their votes to the S.E.D., had thus "unequivocally rejected the proposal for the creation of an allegedly 'free' city." The Bonn note of January 5 repeated the Federal Republic's argument that "the present unnatural situation of Berlin can only be normalized by restoring to Berlin its natural and historic role: to be the capital of a reunited German State." [34]

Five days later the Soviet Union proposed that a twenty-eight nation peace conference be staged to approve a treaty of peace for Germany, and that the four-power foreign ministers soon meet to make arrangements for such a conference. Moscow sent along its own draft treaty for consideration by the proposed conferences.

---

[32] For excerpts from the Soviet note of November 27 and for the United States reply of December 31, 1958, see United States Department of State, *The Soviet Note on Berlin: An Analysis* (1959).

For the developing crisis in November and December, see *Der Spiegel*, XII (Nov. 19, 1958)—XIII (Jan. 7, 1959). On Brandt's position see *Der Spiegel*, XIII (Feb. 4, 1959), 18-23.

[33] *The Bulletin*, Dec. 9, 1958; *Deutsche Korrespondenz* (Bonn), Jan. 21, 1959.

[34] *News from the German Embassy* (Washington), Jan. 9, 1959, gives the complete Bonn note to Moscow in English translation.

In this note of January 10, 1959, the U.S.S.R. continued to insist upon neutralization of Germany and unification in a confederation.[35] The Western Powers dispatched their reply to Moscow in mid-February. They firmly reserved their right "to uphold by all appropriate means their communications with their sectors of Berlin." They rejected the notion of a large peace conference on Germany, saying that unification should first be achieved. But they agreed to participate in a meeting of foreign ministers in Geneva or Vienna, and there were new suggestions in Washington and London during the winter crisis that free, all-German elections might be made a second step in the unification of Germany rather than an indispensable prerequisite.[36]

The Soviet Union in the early spring of 1959 held out little hope for reunification of Germany. Moscow instead began negotiating a treaty with the East German regime. Though Khrushchev on March 2 agreed to an April meeting of the foreign ministers, he carefully circumscribed the potential effectiveness of such a meeting. In its note of March 2, 1959, the U.S.S.R. reminded the Western Powers—and indirectly the Germans—of some unpleasant truths: "Whereas, fourteen years ago Germany, though divided into zones, remained a country with a single social system, today there exist two German states that are developing in different directions." The note reiterated this theme: the "postwar development of Germany has introduced onto the agenda different problems from those that faced the four powers in the first years after the destruction of Hitlerite Germany. It is now impossible to take even one step forward in the German problem if it is approached from a former point of view [treatment as a unit?], without taking account of the existence of two different German states and the fundamental differences in the direction of their development. This situation will not be changed one iota by any number of notes or statements by the Western powers in order to refute facts created by life itself."

The U.S.S.R. in this message of March 2 again hinted that it would accept only a confederation of East and West Germany,

---

[35] *Der Spiegel*, XIII (Jan. 21, 1959), 13-15; XIII (Jan. 28, 1959), 13-14.
[36] New York *Times*, Feb. 14-16, 1959.

negotiated by the Germans themselves, as a step toward unity. But it did at least bring some relief in the high tension that had developed during British Prime Minister Harold Macmillan's troubled visit to the U.S.S.R. in late February and early March. The Soviet warning that the April meeting of foreign ministers should last "not more than two to three months" was a face-saving retreat from Khrushchev's six-month's ultimatum of November 27. The Soviet hint that a "summit" meeting could bargain better than a conference of foreign ministers was not lost upon the West. In a forceful radio and television address of March 16 President Eisenhower stated that the United States was willing to participate in a summer meeting of the heads of government if the foreign ministers should make suitable preliminary progress toward an honorable solution of the German problem. But he also assured the Russians and the people of free Berlin that the United States would not retreat an inch from its rights in Berlin.[37]

Tension remained intense in East-West relations after March 16, and it was likely to remain high at least for several months. The world could face the approach of May 27, 1959, with reasonable certainty that it would bring neither war nor a solution to the problems of Berlin and Germany as a whole. Nor was it likely to bring an end to what C. Wright Mills has called the "balance of fright," and C. L. Sulzberger has named "an equilibrium of terror." [38]

If this situation places crushing responsibilities upon the great protagonists in the Cold War it also places heavy responsibilities upon the German people. They cannot yet forget the large part they have played in creating the dilemma that claimed them as its most obvious victims at the end of World War II. They must acknowledge Germany's guilt while complaining of her fate. Both the Germans and their guardian-suitors can scarcely improve upon the guidelines Konrad Adenauer has so carefully established in the following analysis:

---

[37] The Soviet note of March 2 is given in English translation in the New York *Times*, March 3, 1959. *Ibid.*, March 17, 1959, offers a full report of Eisenhower's address to the nation on March 16.

[38] C. Wright Mills, *The Causes of World War III* (New York, 1958); C. L. Sulzberger, *What's Wrong with U.S. Foreign Policy* (New York, 1959).

We live in a time of transition and I think it began in 1910. There have been such ups and downs, such drastic changes in life, such shifts of economic and political power that one cannot expect things to stabilize in a short time. We must have great patience for many years until things have calmed down and another, firmer shape follows the transition. These ups and downs still continue. There is no tranquility, so we must have patience, sticking to the cause that seems right despite defeats and failures. I repeat again and again, "Patience."[35]

THE GREATER DILEMMA

"Ein Volk, ein Reich, ein Führer!" In the late 1930's this Nazi cry was a call to arms for World War II. Today, fourteen years after the end of that war, the Germans are no longer "one people." There is no German "Reich," save in the memories of one generation and the dreams of another. There is no single "leader" to mobilize the divided Germans. Ultimate decisions on the destinies of the German people must come, as they have since 1944, from Washington and Moscow. Economically recovered, Germany as a nation lives politically in the ruins of World War II. Germany remains the greatest dilemma in Europe, as it was in World War II and had been for a generation before.

How long will the dilemma last? There are few factors that could bring a quick solution to the problem of Berlin and the unification of East Germany with the Bonn Republic. The seemingly controlling factors might well cause the division of Germany to last as long as co-existence itself. It is quite possible that the only way to unification lies in the triumph of the Soviet Union over the West, or of the Western Powers over the Soviet Union, in a global war. That kind of unification would be only a greater curse for the Germans than the one they have borne since 1945. Aside from the destructiveness of such a war, Germans at best would find in it only unification and control by one set of outsiders or the other, not independence. And yet, short of war, the Soviet leaders are not likely to surrender their influence in Ulbricht's Germany. It would certainly violate one of the most fundamental

---

[39] Quoted by Flora Lewis, " 'Der Alte' at 83: Symbol of a New Germany," *New York Times Magazine*, Jan. 4, 1959.

principles of their system if they were to release to the non-Communist world a significant area that has once been Communist-controlled.[40] Comparisons with Tito's Yugoslavia are not helpful in estimating the future chances for a united and free Germany.

Whether unified or divided, Germany will continue to form the center of East-West controversy. The wartime policy of postponement must be seen along with the current crisis against the background of a formidable complex of historical developments of the last two centuries. The German dilemma combines in dangerous microcosm four broad sets of problems. It fuses the nineteenth century goal of nationalism with the twentieth century necessity of European unification. It also fuses the nineteenth century problem of Russian expansion—artificially checked between 1918 and 1941 by the turmoil of internal reorganization—and the twentieth century problem of expanding American influence, checked like Russia's by internal circumstances between the two world wars. As early as the 1830's Alexis de Tocqueville was able to foresee that Russia as well as the United States seemed "intended through some secret design of Providence to hold in its hands the destinies of half the world." Knowing de Tocqueville's prediction makes it all the more sensible to accept Walter Lippmann's 1958 reminder that we must "live on the same globe with the Communist powers," and that "the less we plunge ourselves into hysterics, the more likely we are to take good care of our affairs."[41]

This book has only touched upon Soviet-American relations during World War II, but it should be remembered that the first phase of the interaction is to be found in the history of the First World War. The first battle in the "Cold War" was fought out in 1918, not after 1945. The first spokesmen in the war of words were Lenin and Wilson. Germany's world gamble under Hitler probably would not have been possible if either Russia or the United States had sustained between the world wars what their ideological warriors of World War I began. With the appearance of Lenin and Wilson upon the scene, a third fusion of German

---

[40] Henry L. Roberts, *Russia and America: Dangers and Prospects* (New York, 1956), 181.

[41] Walter Lippmann, *The Communist World and Ours* (Boston etc., 1958), 55-56.

problems occurred: the international dilemma over Germany fused with a domestic dilemma within Germany, a dilemma posed by the conflict of nineteenth century Marxism and twentieth century capitalism.[42] The challenge of the former and the accomplishments of the latter have nowhere so strikingly met as in Germany since 1948. More recently the controversy over Germany has fused with a fourth set of problems, the mid-twentieth century challenge of nuclear power and ballistic missiles—in considerable part German technological contributions—with the Faustian hope of the nineteenth century that mankind can master science for the unlimited improvement of the human condition.[43]

Seen in this kind of historical perspective the dilemma over Germany reveals no quick solutions. The statesmen of 1941-1945 found none. For this they cannot escape criticism. But every word of retrospective recrimination against them is a reminder of our own more recent failures. Without a profound change of policies in Moscow, the price of world peace—or even the unhappy approximation of peace that we call the Cold War—is likely to be the indefinite prolongation of the dismemberment of the German nation and the continued absorption of the German people into Eastern and Western supranational associations. It is an interesting commentary on the limitations of human vision into the future that the first of these prospects for the future—permanent partition—was finally abandoned in principle after much serious discussion by the East-West allies of 1941-1945; that the latter prospect—the integration of the Germans in supranational associations as allies of their wartime enemies—was not considered a serious possibility by the leaders of the wartime coalition; that most of the schemes for Germany that were advanced during the Second World War were put aside by 1949; and that the practical measures that were taken in 1944-1945 to insure uniform policies among the East-West

---

42 See, e.g., the following articles by the author of this volume: "Wilson's Peace Program and German Socialism, January-March, 1918," *Mississippi Valley Historical Review*, XXXVIII (1951), 187-214; "Die Republik aus Versäumnissen," *Die Welt als Geschichte*, XV (1955), 196-219; and the article previously cited in this volume, "The Russian Revolution and the German Social Democratic Party in 1917," *loc. cit.*, 339-350.

43 See Roberts, *Russia and America*, 1-36 for suggestive comments.

allies—including four-power occupation of Berlin—have become elements of controversy which partly caused and have always aggravated the Cold War and which could precipitate Orwellian horrors upon East and West alike in a Third World War. Adolf Hitler may yet do the world a service if the world will only remember his grim boast: "We may be destroyed, but if we are, we shall drag a world with us—a world in flames."

The East-West negotiators cannot forget the grim alternatives which confronted the statesmen of 1941-1945, for they remain to limit human accomplishment and to confound human intelligence. Now as then, one must accept either a powerful Germany or Soviet power in Central Europe. The only other possibility, a great European supranational federation, seems beyond early realization. It stands as a goal at once more noble and more practical than any other solution to the German problem, and to the greater problem of nationalism in general, the "ism" that was created as man's servant, which has become his master, and which may yet become his total ruination.

BIBLIOGRAPHICAL COMMENTS

It is hoped that persons interested in Germany and diplomatic history may have found in this volume a challenge, a stimulus, or a pointer to undertake investigations of various facets of the subject. When many monographic studies have been made, perhaps twenty years hence, the time will be ripe for a near-definitive synthesis. Such a volume will need to explore fully the interaction of forces which shape diplomacy, and which are only suggested in these pages: wartime emotions; national traditions; leadership; economic strengths, weaknesses, and rivalries; concern for security; the changing relationships of the military power of the enemy of 1941-1945 and "the strange allies"; and the ideological tendencies which reinforced or moderated the other factors.

No book on wartime discussions concerning the future of Germany has as yet been published which approaches definitive scope and quality, nor can one be produced for many years to come. Only after the archives of the United States, Britain, and the U.S.S.R. have been completely opened for scholarly research will such a study become possible. A definitive study of American policy alone would need to reflect research activities in the personal papers of Franklin D. Roosevelt at Hyde Park; those of Henry Morgenthau, Jr. at Hyde Park; the Cordell Hull papers at the Library of Congress; the Harry Dexter White Papers at Princeton University; the minutes of the European Advisory Commission; minutes and other records of the Working Security Committee and other State Department agencies; the full records, including correspondence and minutes of meetings of the Civil Affairs Division of the War Department; and the private papers of many persons who participated in large or small ways in the planning of United States policy toward Germany in World War II.

But enough by way of apology. The basic research for this volume was done in 1955-1956, and a typescript draft of about two hundred pages was then prepared. This draft served as a basis for the thirty-seven page chapter on this subject in John L. Snell and others, *The Meaning of Yalta: Big Three Diplomacy and the New Balance of Power* (Baton Rouge, Louisiana, 1956). My research was brought up to date and the original draft was completely revised in January, 1959. This study is largely based upon sources of information which have been published to date. They are already numerous and rich in detail. Supplementing the published sources, I have used the galley proofs of the soon-to-be-published State Department papers of the Potsdam Conference and other unpublished materials in the Historical Division of the Department of State. I am indebted to the several participants, mentioned at the front of this volume, who have helpfully answered questions on points which might otherwise have remained obscure.

Readers of this book who wish to explore further the wartime diplomacy of the Big Three, especially the planning for peace with Germany, may wish to consult the studies that follow.

GENERAL WORKS: At the present writing the two most comprehensive historical syntheses of relations between the "strange allies" of 1941-1945 are Herbert Feis, *Churchill, Roosevelt, Stalin: The War They Waged and the Peace They Sought* (Princeton, 1957), and a Royal Institute of International Affairs publication: William Hardy McNeill, *America, Britain & Russia: Their Cooperation and Conflict, 1941-1946* (London, 1953). The specific problems of planning for peace are treated by Snell and others, *The Meaning of Yalta;* Redvers Opie and associates, *The Search for Peace Settlements* (Washington, 1951); and the briefer study by William L. Neumann, *Making the Peace, 1941-1945: The Diplomacy of the Wartime Conferences* (Washington, 1950).

The various memoir volumes by Winston S. Churchill on World War II are indispensable sources. The memoirs of Anthony Eden will be published serially in *The Times* (London), beginning, perhaps, in the fall of 1959. On the American side, the memoirs of Cordell Hull, William D. Leahy, and Robert E. Sherwood's volume, *Roosevelt and Hopkins: An Intimate History* (New York, 1948) are the most valuable general sources that have been published. A documentary source of considerable value is the wartime correspondence of "the Big Three": Ministry of Foreign Affairs of the U.S.S.R., *Correspondence between the Chairman of the Council of Ministers of the U.S.S.R. and the Presidents of the U.S.A. and the Prime Ministers of Great Britain during the Great Patriotic War of 1941-1945,* 2 vols. (Moscow, 1957). These faithfully published letters are a valuable record which does not bear out the propagandist purpose set forth in the Foreword (I, 5). See the review article by Herbert Feis, "The Three Who Led," *Foreign Affairs,* XXXVII (Jan., 1959), 282-292. Less intimate glimpses of Soviet policy are provided by Andrew Rothstein, trans., *Soviet Foreign Policy during the Patriotic War: Documents and Materials,* 2 vols. (London, n.d. [1946]).

The German problem in Allied wartime diplomacy is treated generally by a number of studies. Valuable works are: Ernst Deuerlein, *Die Einheit Deutschlands: Ihre Eröterung und Behandlung auf den Kriegs-und Nachkriegkonferenzen 1941-1949* (Frankfurt and Berlin, 1957) and Günter Moltmann, *Amerikas Deutschlandpolitik im zweiten Weltkrieg: Kriegs-und Friedensziele 1941-1945* (Heidelberg, 1958). Both include very comprehensive bibliographies. German readers may find a very sensible brief survey of the whole subject in the article by Hendrik van Gergh, "Der Rest, der übrigblied: Die Deutschlandpläne der Allierten 1945," *Politische Studien,* VIII (July, 1957), 1-19. French readers will find a useful and provocative survey in the following articles by Georges Castellan: "La Politique Allemande de l'U.S.S.R., 1941-1945," *Revue d'Histoire de la Deuxième Guerre Mondiale,* VI (Jan., 1956), 38-54; *ibid.* (April, 1956), 31-46. See also the earlier studies by Harold Strauss, *The Division and Dismemberment of Germany* (Ambilly, 1952), well written and based upon extensive research, but often unsophistocated in interpretation; Heinz Günther Sasse, "Die ostdeutsche Frage auf den Konferenzen von Teheran und Jalta," *Jahrbuch für die Geschichte Mittel-und Ostdeutschlands,* II (1953), 211-282; Wolfgang Wagner, *Die Entstehung der Oder-Neisse-Linie in den diplomatischen Verhandlungen während des zweiten Weltkrieges* (Stuttgart, 1953). An English language edition of the nationalistic Wagner study is available: *The Genesis of the Oder-Neisse Line* (Stuttgart, 1957). See also G. Rhode and W. Wagner, *Quellen zur Entstehung der Oder-Neisse-Linie in den diplomatischen Verhandlungen während des zweiten Weltkrieges* (Stuttgart, 1956). Additional information about the origin of the Oder-Neisse line is to be found in Edward J. Rozek, *Allied Wartime Diplomacy: A Pattern in Poland* (New York, 1958).

As this book goes to press, Professor Walter L. Dorn of Columbia University and Professor Lionel Kochan of the London School of Economics are preparing scholarly studies of wartime planning for postwar Germany. Both studies may be expected to make significant contributions to the literature on this problem.

THE EVOLUTION OF UNITED STATES POLICY: The most valuable brief contributions on the development of planning by civilian officials have been made by two participants: E. F. Penrose, *Economic Planning for the Peace* (Princeton, 1953); Philip E. Mosely, "Dismemberment of Germany: The Allied Negotiations from Yalta to Potsdam," *Foreign Affairs,* XXVIII (April, 1950), 487-498; and, also by Mosely, "The Occupation of Germany: New Light on How the Zones Were Drawn," *Foreign Affairs,* XXVIII (July, 1950), 580-604. German readers may wish to consult an article which reflects Mosely's revelations: Wolfgang Wagner, "Besatzungszonen und Spaltung Deutschlands," *Aussenpolitik,* V (August, 1954), 496-508. Some of the key documents, and a very critical discussion, are presented by James P. Warburg, *Germany— Bridge or Battleground* (New York, 1946). The mechanics of State Department policy formulation, and some of the substance of German policy, are described in United States Department of State

(Harley Notter, ed.), *Postwar Foreign Policy Preparation, 1939-1945* (Washington, 1949). Public statements, and some not published until after the war, concerning American wartime policy toward Germany are set forth in the United States Department of State, *The Axis in Defeat: A Collection of Documents on American Policy toward Germany and Japan* (Washington, n.d.). Additional information on the Morgenthau Plan will undoubtedly be available in John M. Blum's authorized biography of the Secretary of the Treasury, based upon the Morgenthau papers; the first volume will be published in 1959 and will carry the story of Morgenthau's life to 1938.

MILITARY PLANNING: Two excellent studies which contain some information on military planning for Germany are: Forrest C. Pogue, *The Supreme Command* (Washington, 1954); John Ehrman, *Grand Strategy,* vols. V and VI in the (British) *History of the Second World War* (London, 1956-1957). United States Army planning has been discussed by several scholars who were participants. The most recent and scholarly is Walter L. Dorn, "The Debate over American Occupation Policy in Germany in 1944-1945," *Political Science Quarterly,* LXXII (Dec., 1957), 481-501, an article which "represents the substance of several chapters" in the forthcoming volume by the same author. See also the studies by Merle Fainsod and Dale Clark in Carl J. Friedrich and associates, *American Experiences in Military Government in World War II* (New York, 1948); Hajo Holborn, *American Military Government: Its Organization and Policies* (Washington, 1947), and Harold Zink, *American Military Government in Germany* (New York, 1947). The following study is a very thorough examination of military planning, which shows the impact of high level inter-Allied policy upon United States Army plans: Paul Y. Hammond, "JCS 1067 Policy for Germany" (part of the Twentieth Century Fund's Study of Civil-Military Relations, Harold Stein, Research Director, Princeton University). Arthur Bryant, *The Turn of the Tide: A History of the War Years Based on the Diaries of Field-Marshal Lord Alanbrooke, Chief of the Imperial General Staff* (Garden City, 1957) is of limited help. The promised companion volume on the period 1943-1945, *The Triumph of the West,* will probably contain useful material on wartime planning for postwar Germany.

THE GERMAN PROBLEM AT THE YALTA CONFERENCE: The essential facts and a persuasive apology for the Yalta commitments are most readily available in Edward R. Stettinius, Jr. (Walter Johnson, ed.), *Roosevelt and the Russians: The Yalta Conference* (Garden City, 1949). An excellent but highly critical brief survey is presented in Chester Wilmot, *The Struggle for Europe* (New York, 1952), 628-659. For a critical review article see Eric C. Kollmann, "Die Jaltakonferenz im Kreuzfeuer von Politik und Geschichtsschreibung," *Geschichte in Wissenschaft und Unterricht*, VIII (May, 1957), 272-292. Significant new material has been published in the last few years. The minutes of key participants and the basic records of the conference at Yalta are provided by the United States Department of State, *The Conference at Malta and Yalta, 1945* (Washington, 1955). Though the leading newspaper of the Soviet Union, *Pravda*, has asserted that these documents sought to "falsify history," they constitute in reality an extremely useful source. (For a report of the *Pravda* criticism see the New York *Times*, Jan. 21, 1956.)

THE GERMAN PROBLEM AT THE POTSDAM CONFERENCE: The best published sources on the Potsdam discussions of the future of Germany are the memoirs of three key participants, each of which is fuller than the others on certain aspects of the German problem. The best overall account is Harry S. Truman, *Memoirs by Harry S. Truman*, Vol. I: *Year of Decisions* (Garden City, 1955), 343-411. This should be supplemented, especially on the question of the eastern frontier, by Winston S. Churchill, *Triumph and Tragedy* (Boston, 1953), 648-671, and, especially on the question of reparations and on the general work of the foreign secretaries during the conference, by James F. Byrnes, *Speaking Frankly* (New York and London, 1947), 79-87. William D. Leahy, *I Was There: The Personal Story of the Chief of Staff to Presidents Roosevelt and Truman . . .* (New York, London, and Toronto, 1950), verifies and occasionally supplements points made by the three major published sources, but must be used on some points with caution. The memoirs will continue to be indispensable even after the Potsdam papers of the Department of State are published, perhaps by the end of 1959.

THE GERMAN PROBLEM SINCE 1945: Many of the volumes mentioned above provide information and opinions about the German problem since World War II. A bibliographical article which provides a remarkably comprehensive list of the materials on postwar Germany is: John Brown Mason, "Government, Administration, and Politics in West Germany: A Selected Bibliography," *American Political Science Review*, LII (June, 1958), 513-530. The following studies have been especially useful in the preparation of the last chapter in this book: Edgar Alexander, *Adenauer and the New Germany: The Chancellor of the Vanquished* (New York, 1957); Fritz R. Allemann, *Bonn ist nicht Weimar* (Cologne, 1955); M. E. Bathurst and J. L. Simpson, *Germany and the North*

Atlantic Community (London, 1956); the volumes edited by Peter Calvocoressi *(1947-1948, 1949-1950, 1951, and 1952)* and Coral Bell *(1954)* in the *Survey of International Affairs* series of the Royal Institute of International Affairs (London, New York, Toronto, 1952-1957); Georges Castellan and others, *D.D.R.—Allemagne de l'Est* (Paris, 1955); Lucius D. Clay, *Germany and the Fight for Freedom* (Cambridge, Mass., 1950); James Bryant Conant, *Germany and Freedom: A Personal Appraisal* (Cambridge, Mass., 1958); Gordon A. Craig, *From Bismarck to Adenauer: Aspects of German Statecraft* (Baltimore, 1958); Melvin Croan and Carl J. Friedrich, "The East German Regime and Soviet Policy in Germany," *Journal of Politics,* XX (Feb., 1958), 44-63; Ossip K. Flechtheim, *Die deutschen Parteien seit 1945: Quellen und Auszüge* (Berlin and Cologne, 1955); W. Friedmann, *The Allied Military Government of Germany* (London, 1947); Alfred Grosser, *La Democratie de Bonn, 1949-1957* (Paris, 1958), early in 1959 the most up to date and valuable single volume on West Germany, offering a very full bibliography; Richard Hiscocks, *Democracy in Western Germany* (London, New York, Toronto, 1957); Alistair Horne, *Return to Power* (New York, 1956); Fritz Löwenthal, *News from Soviet Germany* (London, 1950); Klaus Mehnert and Heinrich Schulte eds., *Deutschland-Jahrbuch 1953* (Essen, 1953); J. P. Nettl, *The Eastern Zone and Soviet Policy in Germany, 1945-1950* (London, New York, Toronto, 1951); Beate Ruhm von Oppen, *Documents on Germany under Occupation, 1945-1954* (London, New York, Toronto, 1955); J. K. Pollock ed., *German Democracy at Work* (Ann Arbor, 1955); Henry L. Roberts, *Russia and America: Dangers and Prospects* (New York, 1956); David Rodnick, *Post-war Germans* (New Haven, 1948); Abraham Shuckman, *Codetermination: Labor's Middle Way in Germany* (Washington, 1957); Hans Speier and W. Phillips Davison eds., *West German Leadership and Foreign Policy* (Evanston, Illinois and White Plains, New York, 1957); H. C. Wallich, *Mainsprings of the German Revival* (New Haven, 1955); Paul Weymar, *Adenauer: His Authorized Biography* (New York, 1957); and Harold Zink, *The United States in Germany, 1944-1955* (Princeton, 1957).

This bibliographical discussion is, of course, highly selective. The footnotes in this volume provide a more extended bibliography for readers who care to familiarize themselves with the extensive literature which is already available on this significant problem in contemporary history. The developing literature, as it is published, is carefully listed in the excellent bibliographical sections of the *Vierteljahrshefte für Zeitgeschichte.*

258

INDEX

Aachen, 90
Aarons, L. C., 67
A-bomb, 197
Adenauer, Konrad, 6, 11, 231-251 *passim*
Agrarian reforms: discussed, 93
Aircraft industry of Germany: prohibition discussed, 101, 118, 121
Albania, 194
All-German Council, 244
Allied Control Council for Germany, 108, 139, 158, 161-164, 166, 167, 178, 180, 194, 198, 217, 225, 230. *See also* United States Group, Control Council for Germany
Allied Reparations Commission (1945): origins of, 146-154 *passim;* 187-190, 211
American Agriculturalist, 65
Americas: postwar affairs in, 31
Anderson, John, 69
Antwerp, 135
Ardennes Offensive, 124, 135-137 *passim*
Argentina, 188
Asia. *See* Pacific War
Atlantic Charter, 15, 16
Atomic bomb, 197
Atomtod: campaign about (1958), 242
Attlee, Clement, 22, 55, 196, 206-213 *passim*
Austria, 38, 42, 49, 50, 56, 102, 142, 174, 181, 200, 240
Austrian State Treaty (1955), 240

Baden, 31, 49, 76, 102, 184, 185, 200
Balance of power: changes in, mentioned, 17-18, 59 *and passim*
Balkans, 39, 56
Baltic Sea, 39, 55, 173, 202
Bard, Ralph A., 178
"Battle of the Bulge." *See* Ardennes Offensive
Bavaria, 49, 76, 102, 125, 200, 232
Bayreuth, 31
Beaverbrook, Lord, 38
Belgium, 147, 148

Benes, Eduard, 34
Bentley, Elizabeth, 78
Berlin: mentioned, 20, 22, 55, 90, 116, 130, 138, 170, 173, 174, 222-251 *passim;* plans for postwar occupation of, 54-59, 108, 184-185; elections in (1946), 227; elections in (1958), 245
Berlin airlift (1948-1949), 236-237
Berlin blockade (1948-1949), 236-237
Berlin Conference (1954), 239
Berlin crises: (1948-1949), 236-237; (1953), 238; (1958-1959), 222-248
Bernadotte, Folke, 174
Bernstein, Bernard, 67, 70, 115, 116
Bethesda Naval Medical Center, 101
Bevin, Ernest, 196, 206-223
Bidault, Georges, 109-111 *passim*
Biddle, Francis, 123
Bierut, Boleslaw, 203, 205, 206, 207
"Big Three": mentioned *passim;* first meeting of, 45-51. *See also* Churchill; Roosevelt; Stalin
Bismarck, Otto von, 23, 231
Boettiger, John, 26
Bohlen, Charles E., 117
Bonn, M. J., 77
Bonn Republic. *See* German Federal Republic
Book of the Month Club, 10n
Boston, 8
Brandt, Willy, 244, 245
Braun, Wernher von, 132
Brecht, Arnold, 11
Bremen, 87, 108, 159
Bremerhaven, 87, 108
Breslau, 120, 155
Brest-Litovsk Conference (1918), 34, 40,
Bretton Woods Conference, 64
Briefing Book Papers on Germany: for the Yalta Conference, 117-123, 140; for the Potsdam Conference, 202
British Commonwealth, 222. *See also* Great Britain
British Institute of Public Opinion, 4
Brookings Institution, 27

Index

Index

187; casualties in World War II, 175; *Gestapo*, 187, rearmament of (1950-), 235-236, 237, 239-240, 241-242. *Wartime discussion (1941-1945) of plans for Germany's future are treated passim.* See Agrarian reforms; Aircraft industry of Germany; Allied Control Council for Germany; Danubian Confederation; Decentralization; De-industrialization; Demilitarization; Democratization; De-Nazification; Disarmament; Dismemberment; East Prussia; Eastern German territory; Economic controls over; Education; European Advisory Commission; France; Labor as reparations; Neisse rivers; Nuremberg Trials; Occupation of Germany; Oder River; Oder-Neisse Line; Poland; Policy of postponement; Prussia; Reparations; Rhine River; Rhineland; Ruhr; Saar; War Criminals; Western German territory

Great Britain: declares war (1939), 1; wartime attitudes toward Germany, 1-5, 19-23 and *passim;* War Cabinet, 16, 20, 23, 28, 88, 152, 153, 186; Chiefs of Staff, 22, 37; Foreign Office, 47, 54; House of Commons, 97; Labour Party, 97; zone of occupation in Germany, 174 and *passim;* powers in postwar Germany, 224-251; sector of occupation in Berlin agreed upon, 108. *See also* Aircraft industry of Germany; Allied Control Council for Germany; Danubian Confederation; Decentralization; De-industrialization; Demilitarization; Democratization; De-Nazification; Disarmament; Dismemberment; East Prussia; Eastern German territory; Economic controls over; Education; France; Labor as reparations; Neisse rivers; Nuremberg Trials; Occupation of Germany; Oder River; Oder-Neisse Line; Poland; Policy of postponement; Prussia; Reparations; Rhine River; Rhineland; Ruhr; Saar; War criminals; Western German territory

Gallup Poll, 9
Geneva conferences (1955), 240-241, 243
George VI, King of England, 15, 222
Geyer, Curt, 5
Goebbels, Paul Joseph, 97, 132
Goerdeler, Carl, 36
Goerlitz, 238
Gomulka, Wladyslaw, 242, 243
Great Russians, 7
Grosser, Alfred, 200
Grotewohl, Otto, 227-251 *passim*
Gusev, Fedor Tarasovich, 54, 55, 58, 183

Halle, 238
Halsted, Anna Roosevelt, 31
Hamburg, 49
Handbook for Military Government in Germany, 63, 67, 73, 74, 114, 115
Hapsburg Empire, 49
Harriman, W. Averell, 38, 95, 113, 125, 163, 194
Harris, David, 27, 51, 53
Harvard University, 31
Hassett, William D., 177
Hesse, 232
Hesse-Cassel, 49, 184
Hesse-Darmstadt, 49
Hesse-Nassau, 184
Heuss, Theodor, 231
Hilldring, John, 25, 82, 178
Himmler, Heinrich, 174, 177
Hitler, Adolf, *passim;* revolt against, 17, 127 - 130; personality of (1944), 130; last days of, 175
Hodes, Henry I., 245
Holland, 147
Holstein, 76. *See also* Schleswig-Holstein
Hooten, Earnest A., 8
Hoover, Herbert, 24
Hopkins, Harry, 18, 31, 60, 74, 75, 82, 84, 117, 153, 161, 163, 183, 187, 188, 227
Hull, Cordell, 17, 23, 27, 31, 38, 39, 52, 65, 72, 74, 83, 84, 92, 95, 96, 97, 100, 101; at Moscow Conference (1943), 41-45 *passim*
Hungary, 49, 50, 95, 103, 131, 200, 220, 231
Hyde Park, 73, 82

Informal Policy Committee on Germany. *See* United States, In-

262

Index

263

Index

Morgenthau Plan: development of, 64-93 *passim;* retreat from, 97-107 *passim;* repercussions of, 114-122 *passim; and see* 30, 120, 135, 154, 177, 180, 194, 195, 216

Morris, William, 169, 190

Moscow, 7, 39, 93, 96 *and passim*

Moscow Conference (1943), 32, 41-45, 49, 52

Moscow Declaration (on war criminals), 43-44, 157

Moscow Reparations Commission. *See* Allied Reparations Commission

Mosely, Philip E., 27, 51, 53, 54, 70-71, 106

Moulton, Harold G., 11

Mouvement de Liberation Nationale. See France, *Mouvement de Liberation Nationale*

Munich Conference, 19, 129

Murphy, Robert D., 90

Murray, Gilbert, 2

Mussolini, Benito, 40

National Opinion Research Center, 9, 81

National Socialism. *See* Nazism

NATO. *See* North Atlantic Treaty Organization

Navy, German: disposition of discussed, 188, 198, 208-209

Navy Department. *See* United States, Navy Department

Nazism: *passim;* German opposition to, 1-9 *passim,* 17, 127-130

Nazi-Soviet Pact (1939), 40

Neisse rivers, 110, 112-114 *passim,* 155-157, 202-208 *passim,* 220, 228-251 *passim. See also* Oder-Neisse Line

Neumann, Sigmund, 11

Newfoundland, 15

New Statesman and Nation, 106

New York *Times,* 90, 97

Nicolson, Harold, 2-4 *passim*

Nikopol: mines of, 131

Nisa, 202. *See also* Neisse rivers

Nizer, Louis, 10

North Atlantic Treaty Organization, 235-236, 237, 239, 240, 244

North-Rhine-Westphalia, 232

North Sea: 76; ports of, 184

Norway, 118

NSDAP, 118

Nuremberg Trials: origins of, 43-44, 157-158, 217-219

Occupation of Germany: wartime planning for, 12, 20, 22, 32, 41-51 *passim,* 53, 55, 56, 62, 87, 104, 107-112, 116, 139, 158-161, 174, 184

Oder River, 47, 50-51, 112-114 *passim,* 121, 137, 139, 155-157, 202-208 *passim,* 220, 228-251 *passim. See also* Neisse rivers; Oder-Neisse Line

Oder-Neisse Line, 120, 155-157, 198, 202-208, 220, 226, 228-251 *passim*

Odra River, 202. *See also* Oder River

Office of Strategic Services. *See* United States, Office of Strategic Services

Office of War Mobilization. *See* United States, Office of War Mobilization

Ollenhauer, Erich, 5

Orwell, George: oblique references to novel by, 1, 251

Osóbka-Morawski, Edward B., 203

Pacific War, 31, 96, 149, 159, 191, 196

Palatinate, 184

Pankow, 230. *See also* German Democratic Republic

Paris, 12, 79

Pasvolsky, Leo, 27

Patton, George S., Jr., 51

Pauley, Edwin W., 188, 190, 211, 212

Paulus, Friedrich, 5-6, 36

Pearson, Drew, 97

Pehle, John, 73

Pennsylvania, 228

Penrose, E. F., 22n, 59, 60, 70

Pentagon, 92

Persia (Iran), 45

Petsamo, mines of, 131

Pieck, Wilhelm, 6, 176, 227

Pinson, Koppel S., 11

Ploesti, 131

Poland, 32, 41, 47, 51, 55, 76, 94, 110, 112-114 *passim,* 119, 120, 131, 140, 148, 149, 155-157, 167, 169, 176, 188, 193, 202, 220, 224, 226, 228-251 *passim;* Committee of National Liberation, 113

Index

Policy of postponement, 13-39 and *passim*

Polish government-in-exile. *See* Poland

Polish Home Army, 94

Pollock, James K., 11

Pomerania, 119, 120, 155-157, 202

Post-War Programs Committee. *See* United States, Department of State

Potomac River, 60 and *passim*

Potsdam Conference, 184, 185, 190, 192-221, 223

Prague, 174

Pravda, 243

Prussia: wartime discussion of reorganization of, 3, 10, 11, 32, 41-42, 49-51, 76, 103, 119. *See also* East Prussia; Eastern German territory; Rhineland; Ruhr; Saar; Western German territory

Peenemunde, 132

Quebec agreements (1944), 86-89, 97, 98, 99, 134, 144, 154, 159, 189, 193, 195; retreat from, 94-126 *passim*

Quebec Conference (1943), 23, 28, 42

Quebec Conference (1944), 79, 86-89, 94, 95, 96, 133, 134; repercussions of, 90-107 and *passim*

Queis River (also known as Kwisa River), 207

Rapacki, Adam, 241

Red Army, 35, 41, 53, 55, 79, 94, 95, 112, 113, 136, 137, 138, 155, 157, 174, 176, 196, 197, 210, 227, 238

Red Cross: American, 147; Swedish, 174

Reparations from Germany: discussions of, 4, 12, 21, 24, 32, 38, 43, 47, 52, 64-93 *passim*, 104, 105, 120, 122, 125, 140, 181, 193, 198, 207, 223, 224, 225, 229; at Yalta Conference, 144-154; at Potsdam Conference, 144-154

Resistance, German. *See* Nazism, German opposition to

Riddleberger, James W., 75, 82

Rhine River, 53, 55, 76, 109-111 *passim*, 122, 135, 137, 154, 159, 170, 183, 198, 220. *See also* Rhineland; Ruhr; Saar; Western German territory

Rhineland, 12-13, 38, 76, 103, 109-111 *passim*, 125, 184, 189, 201, 201n, 225, 226. *See also* Rhine River; Ruhr; Saar; Western German territory

Romania. *See* Rumania

Romer, Tadeusz, 112

Roosevelt, Eleanor, 65

Roosevelt, Elliott, 46

Roosevelt, Franklin Delano, *passim*, and unconditonal surrender policy, 15-16; attitudes toward Germany's past and future, 29-33, 72-107 *and passim*; at Yalta, 139-168 *passim*; death of, 171; appraisal of, 172-173

Rosenman, Samuel J., 123, 185, 186, 218

Ruhr, 3, 4, 38, 49, 50, 55, 68, 75, 76, 82, 84, 85, 86, 87, 89, 90, 93, 99, 102, 103, 109-111 *passim*, 121; 122, 125, 142, 154, 167, 183, 189, 198, 200, 201, 201n, 204, 215, 220, 225

Rumania, 95, 131, 132

Russia. *See* Soviet Union

Rzymowski, W., 206

Saalfeld, 238

Saar, 49, 55, 76, 84, 87, 89, 99, 103, 124, 142, 154, 167, 183, 184, 200, 201n, 226, 235

St. Petersburg. *See* Leningrad

San Francisco Conference (1945), 188

Saxony, 6, 49, 76, 174, 238

Scandinavia, 39

Schacht, Hjalmar, 29

Schleswig, 76. *See also* Schleswig-Holstein

Schleswig-Holstein, 55, 173, 232

Schwerin, 238

Scotland, 228

Secretary of the Treasury. *See* Morgenthau, Henry, Jr.; United States, Treasury Department

S.E.D. (Socialist Unity Party of Germany). *See* German Democratic Republic

Seven Years War, 196

Index

Seydlitz, Walter von, 5
SHAEF (Supreme Headquarters, Allied Expeditionary Forces), 67-70, 90, 116, and *passim*. *See also* Eisenhower, Dwight D.
Silesia, 47, 76, 110, 119, 137, 155-157, 176, 202, 215
Smith, Fred, 68, 69
Smolensk, 36
Smuts, Jan Christian, 20
Social Democratic Party of Germany (S.P.D.). *See* German Federal Republic, political parties; Germany, Social Democratic Party of
Socialist Unity Party of Germany (S.E.D.). *See* German Democratic Republic
Soviet Union: wartime attitudes toward Germany, 5-8; invaded by German forces (1941), 6; plans for occupation of postwar Germany, 20, 22, 53-59 *passim*, 174, and *passim*; Communist Party of, 36; seeks United States loan, 80, 144; occupation sector in Berlin approved, 108; German devastation of in World War II, 144-145; German policy of (1945-1959), 222-251. *See also* Aircraft industry of Germany; Allied Control Council for Germany; Danubian Confederation; Decentralization; De-industrialization; Demilitarization; Democratization; De-Nazification; Disarmament; Dismemberment; East Prussia; Eastern German territory; Economic controls over Germany; Education of Germany; France; Labor as reparations; Neisse rivers; Occupation of Germany; Oder River; Oder-Neisse Line; Poland; Policy of postponement; Prussia; Reparations; Rhine River; Rhineland; Saar; War criminals; Western German territory
Spain, 138
S.P.D. (Social Democratic Party of Germany). *See* German Federal Republic, political parties; Germany, Social Democratic Party of
Spectator: quoted, 97
Speer, Albert, 175

Sputnik, 241
Stalin, Joseph, *passim;* wartime views on Germany, 34-38; at Yalta Conference, 139-163; at Potsdam Conference, 192 - 221 *passim;* death of, 238
Stalingrad, 6, 35
Standley, William, 48
State Department. *See* United States, Department of State
State-War-Navy Coordinating Committee. *See* United States, State-War-Navy Coordinating Committee
Stauffenberg, Claus von, 130
Stettin, 112, 120, 155
Stettinius, Edward R., Jr., 27, 51, 57, 60, 61, 101, 103-107, 117, 119, 139-168 *passim*, 186, 195
Stimson, Henry, 24, 57, 63, 73, 74, 83, 84, 85, 96, 98, 99, 117, 123, 179
Stralsund, 238
Strang, William, 54, 164, 196
Stuttgart, 224
Sulzberger, C. L., 247
Supranational association: discussed as a solution for the German problem, 4, 232-237 *passim*, 239-240, 250, 251
Sweden, 138
Switzerland, 138

Teheran Conference, 34, 41, 45-51, 52, 56, 63, 72, 103, 117, 142, 186
Texas, 8
Thuringia, 76, 174
Tito, Josip Broz, 228, 249
Tocqueville, Alexis de, 249
Trieste, 194
Truman, Harry S., 173-223 *passim*
Truman Doctrine, 231

U.K. *See* Great Britain
Ukraine, 7, 131
Ulbricht, Walter, 6, 226-251 *passim*
Unconditional surrender, policy of, 9, 15-19, 42, 128, 129
United Kingdom. *See* Great Britain
United Nations, 49, 95, 96, 149, 188, 207
United Nations Monetary and Financial Conference (Bretton Woods, 1944), 64

266

Index

Index

Wilson, Woodrow, 16, 64, 82-83, 128, 138, 166, 249
Wiltshire, 70
Winant, John Gilbert, 22n, 38, 54, 55, 57, 58, 70-71, 106, 183
Wismar, 173
Wolff, Karl, 170
Working Security Committee, 56. *See also* United States, Department of State
World War I, 1, 45, 65, 133, 146, 249
World War II, *passim*

Württemberg, 49, 76, 102, 184, 185, 200

Yalta Conference, 17, 20, 33, 34, 80, 87, 106, 107, 109, 111, 116, 117, 120, 123, 124, 136, 137, 138, 139-168, 169, 171, 176, 177, 183, 187, 188, 193, 203, 205, 209, 239
Yugoslavia, 95, 148, 249

Zhukov, Georgi K., 137